WEDEMEYER
on War and Peace

For Ted Gagne —
with the cordial
good wishes of the Editor,

Keith E. Eiler

April 8, 1988

D1738104

A.C. Wedemeyer
12 April 59

WEDEMEYER
on War and Peace

Edited with an introduction by
KEITH E. EILER

Foreword by
JOHN KEEGAN

HOOVER INSTITUTION PRESS
Stanford University, Stanford, California

Frontispiece charcoal drawing by C. D. Batchelor
was presented to General Wedemeyer by the artist.

The foreword is copyright 1987 by John Keegan.

Hoover Press Publication 367

First printing, 1987
Manufactured in the United States of America
91   90   89   88   87   9   8   7   6   5   4   3   2   1

Library of Congress Cataloging in Publication Data

Wedemeyer, Albert C. (Albert Coady), 1896–
Wedemeyer on war and peace.

(Hoover archival documentaries) (Hoover Press publication; 367)
1. United States—Military policy.   2. Strategy—
History—20th century.   3. Peace.   4. Military history,
Modern—20th century. I. Eiler, Keith E., 1920–   .
II. Title. III. Series.
UA23.W36934   1987   355'.0335'73   87-3847
ISBN 0-8179-8671-5
ISBN 0-8179-8672-3 (pbk.)

Contents

Foreword

The influence of General Albert C. Wedemeyer in shaping and directing the strategy by which the United States conducted its part in the waging of the Second World War is only now beginning to be recognised. In the fulness of time, he will surely come to be seen as one of the most influential officers of the U.S. Army at the moment when it emerged as a world force.

Wedemeyer stands out from his contemporaries as a military intellectual, a man interested in the theoretical basis as well as the practical problems of warfighting. This interest never left him, and he returned to it throughout the years when his progressively recognised abilities brought him promotion from one post of high responsibility to another. The result is that his career generated an archive of records unusually large by conventional standards. Wedemeyer is a compulsive writer—one of the reasons for which the historian has reason to be grateful to him—and it is his written work that Keith Eiler has used to such good effect in editing and introducing Wedemeyer's thoughts.

Perhaps no period in Wedemeyer's life exceeds in interest that he spent as the American student at the German staff college (*Kriegsakademie*) at Berlin in 1936–1938. The *Kriegsakademie* is the mother house of all staff colleges. Founded in 1810 and directed between 1817 and 1829 by Karl von Clausewitz, it was the school that began the systematic study of war and developed the methods—which have now been adopted by business schools—of active rather than passive learning of operational technique. The *Kriegsakademie*'s reputation as a forcing house of strategic expertise was in the end to be its undoing. Its closure was one of the conditions laid upon defeated Germany by the Allies at the Versailles peace of 1919. Its reopening was an early act of the Hitler regime and, as it had existed in clandestine form during the Weimar years, Wedemeyer's experience of its traditions and methods was identical with that of the students who had passed through it in the heyday of German war planning before 1914.

The experience, understandably, was to be formative for Wedemeyer's outlook. He came from a small, isolated military community which, though it had fought the first large modern war and taken part in the second, was technically and professionally unsophisticated. The *Kriegsakademie* opened his eyes to the fact that there were professional soldiers whose philosophy of life was rooted in the assumption that war was a natural activity—indeed "the continuation of politics by other means"—and that it was the business of the military professional to wage war with all the efficiency that the American business community brought to commerce and industry.

Wedemeyer's German education was to prove of the keenest significance to the mobilisation and conduct of the Allied war effort. Where other officers in the U.S. War Department in the years before America's entry groped for a focus to their war planning duties, Wedemeyer understood from the outset that against a power of the technical proficiency he had seen at firsthand in Germany, nothing less than the wholesale mobilisation of the American economy to the purpose of victory would suffice. His extraordinary "Victory Plan" was the outcome, a document that in large measure determined how the United States, and therefore the whole Western alliance, conducted its part in the Second World War.

The coming of the war elevated Wedemeyer to high office and command in exotic places, notably as chief of staff in the Allied mission to Chiang Kai-shek in China. The bulk of this fascinating collection of papers is drawn from those years. In them he discloses his skill as a military diplomatist to a difficult ally and his capacity as an interpreter of Asian acts and thinking to the more prosaic and positive minds of the U.S. government in the war years. Wedemeyer's task was, in many ways, an impossible one, and the fact that he succeeded in maintaining good relations with the Chinese allies, the British, and the leaders of his own army is testimony to his high gifts of political as well as military insight.

The connoisseur of the military mind may well reckon the papers from the Berlin years as the most interesting, nonetheless, and derive a principal pleasure from detecting the influence of a *Kriegsakademie* training—mediated by all the dynamism and optimism that are so distinctively American—on his later reports and action papers from the Far East. The Wedemeyer papers are destined to become a key archive for every researcher not only of the war years but also of the makings and workings of a modern military intellect. Keith Eiler, who served his old chief so well on active duty, has put future scholars in his debt by the devotion with which he has edited the thoughts and papers of a remarkable soldier.

JOHN KEEGAN
London, England

Editor's Note

In 1983, General Albert C. Wedemeyer, United States Army, Retired, deposited his personal papers in the Archives of the Hoover Institution on War, Revolution and Peace, at Stanford University. This collection, which fills over 100 archival boxes, includes a wealth of materials of historical interest dating primarily from the era of World War II.

I have selected from these materials for inclusion in this documentary volume a number of Wedemeyer's writings, which, taken together, convey the general contours of his life and thought. Along with an introductory essay and background notes, the selections are intended to provide the contemporary reader not only with an interesting excursion into recent military history but also with a challenging treatment of issues that remain of vital public concern. Although most of the documents relate to the General's military career, I stress his advocacy of policies designed to promote peace and enhance the nation's long-range welfare as well as its immediate military security.

Some of the documents presented herein have necessarily been excerpted in the interest of brevity. In trimming and cutting, however, I have taken pains to preserve the author's intent and to avoid distortion.

I hope that this volume will find its way into the hands of individuals who have been associated with General Wedemeyer at one time or other during his eventful career, and that they will share with me their insights and memories of the man as I continue work on a more complete study of his life.

I am grateful to the Hoover Institution for the generous support that made this work possible. To the ever helpful and most congenial staff of the Archives, I extend special thanks.

KEITH E. EILER
Stanford, California
January 1987

Introduction

Keith E. Eiler

"Pug" Henry, U.S. Navy, the sturdy protagonist of Herman Wouk's World War II epics, *The Winds of War* and *War and Remembrance,* had a special talent for being near the action. Cruising as confidently through the seas of high politics and diplomatic intrigue as on blue water, he turns up in an unlikely variety of places: Navy Headquarters in Washington, the White House, the chancellery of the Third Reich in Berlin, the bowels of the Kremlin, Pearl Harbor after the debacle, the scenes of the great naval battles of Midway and Leyte Gulf, islands of the far Pacific, Soviet army headquarters on the Eastern front, and Teheran in the Middle East. He plans operations, commands warships, stars at strategic intelligence, and undertakes secret missions for commanders-in-chief. In the course of his eventful career, Pug meets, advises, or links arms with many of the war's leading actors, including Franklin Roosevelt, Winston Churchill, Josef Stalin, and Adolf Hitler.

Pug Henry is, of course, a fictional character. One real-life American officer, however, actually touched many of Pug's far-flung bases, hobnobbed with most of the same famous people, and played a considerably more significant role in planning and managing the Allied war effort. That officer was Albert Coady Wedemeyer of the U.S. Army.

Wedemeyer served in countless corners of the globe, including Washington, Berlin, London, Manila, New Delhi, and Chungking. He played important roles in both the Atlantic and Pacific areas, and he came into personal (and in several instances sustained) contact with war leaders on the highest levels. Those leaders included, on the American side, President Roosevelt, Harry Hopkins, cabinet officers, the Chiefs of Staff, and senior field commanders; in Britain, Prime Minister Churchill and top members of the government and military establishment; in

China, President Chiang Kai-shek, Chairman Mao Tse-tung, and Chou En-lai; in Korea, Syngman Rhee; in Germany, General Ludwig Beck (Army Chief of Staff), General Friedrich von Boetticher (long-time military attache in Washington), and Colonel Claus von Stauffenberg (leader in the 1944 anti-Hitler plot); and, from the Soviet Union, Andrei Gromyko.

The foundations of Wedemeyer's career were laid in the small-town atmosphere of Omaha, Nebraska, where he was born in 1896. His father, Albert Anthony Wedemeyer, was the son of a Union veteran of the Civil War and a sometime military man himself. His mother, Margaret Coady Wedemeyer, was a daughter of nineteenth-century immigrants from Ireland who, for her grace and dignity, was affectionately known in Omaha as "the Countess." Her father, too, had been a soldier of the Civil War, as well as of the Mexican and Indian wars. Albert Anthony and Margaret Wedemeyer provided a comfortable and, by all reports, congenial home for their two sons, and family life was infused with such solid Victorian concerns as "building character" and preparing for a self-reliant but socially useful future.

Albert Coady, the younger son, had early set his heart on a career in medicine. After attending local public schools, however, and later being prepped by the Jesuit Fathers at Creighton, he decided to follow the example of many of his contemporaries and try his hand at soldiering. In 1917, he went east to the U.S. Military Academy at West Point.

The First World War temporarily foreshortened the West Point curriculum, with the result that the Class of 1921 sped through the Academy in less than two years and was redesignated the Class of 1919. Wedemeyer, commissioned first in the Cavalry but soon switching to the Infantry (after a postwar tour of the battlefields of Europe convinced him that the day of the war-horse was gone), entered a long apprenticeship in the peacetime Army. Contrary to the experience of many officers of the period, he found his seventeen-year stint as a lieutenant (1919–1936) generally challenging and pleasant. Stateside duty at Forts Benning, Sill, Sam Houston, and elsewhere was interspersed with tours in the Philippines and China. The educational value of those years was greatly enhanced by assignments as aide-de-camp to several experienced general officers.

Lieutenant Wedemeyer met his future wife, Elizabeth Dade Embick, on his first voyage to the Philippines in 1923. She was traveling with her family to the island fortress of Corregidor, where her father, Colonel (later Lieutenant General) Stanley D. Embick, was to assume command. The couple were married on Corregidor in February 1925.

In 1934, the well-seasoned lieutenant returned from a second tour in the Far East, along with his wife and two sons, to attend the Army's Command and General Staff School at Fort Leavenworth, Kansas. This important assignment afforded Wedemeyer an opportunity to transcend his undistinguished academic record as a cadet, and he made the most of it. During the concluding exercises that marked the end of the two-year course, the school placed him in command of the friendly "blue army" (the enemy army was traditionally depicted in red symbols on the situation maps)—a sure indication that he stood academically at or near the top of his class.

The years at Leavenworth sharpened Wedemeyer's military skills, especially in the command and tactics of larger field organizations. He realized the full benefits of that work in 1936–1938 as an exchange student at the German War College in Berlin. The comparative insights afforded by this study abroad proved unusually stimulating, as did the instruction he received in military history and geopolitics.

On his return from Berlin in 1938, Captain Wedemeyer met, briefed, and favorably impressed Brigadier General George C. Marshall, then head of War Plans Division of the General Staff in Washington. This meeting proved propitious for Wedemeyer's future. Two years later, Marshall—as Chief of Staff—ordered the promising strategist and German specialist to duty in the War Department.

As a staff officer in War Plans Division in the summer of 1941, Major Wedemeyer drafted the famed Victory Plan—a broad blueprint for U.S. participation in a possible war against the Rome-Berlin-Tokyo Axis. (After Pearl Harbor, this plan served official Washington as the basic guide for mobilizing U.S. manpower and industry and for deploying the armed forces.) Rising quickly in rank, Wedemeyer next played a leading role in developing U.S. and Allied global strategy, including plans for the invasion of Europe. Beginning in 1941, he attended conferences with the top warlords in Washington, London, Casablanca, Quebec, and Cairo. After Casablanca, President Roosevelt and the U.S. Joint Chiefs of Staff sent him eastward around the world to report results of the conference to Allied leaders in the China-Burma-India region and to General MacArthur in Australia. General Marshall sent him to North Africa and the Mediterranean area in mid-1943 to observe and report on the Allied invasion of Sicily. Later in 1943, he went to India as senior planner on the staff of Admiral Mountbatten's Anglo-American Southeast Asia Command (SEAC). Promoted to three-star rank in 1944, he assumed command of U.S. armed forces in China and became Chief of Staff in the Allied command structure to Generalissimo Chiang Kai-shek. He occupied these two posts in China through V-J Day and into 1946. President Truman sent Wedemeyer back to the Far

East in 1947 on a fact-finding mission, the report of which figured prominently in the domestic U.S. foreign policy debates that followed the fall of China to the Communists in 1949.

Wedemeyer remains of interest today, however, less as a relic of this heroic past—a past, to be sure, that currently is enjoying considerable vogue—than as a complex and controversial prophet. His reading of the past had convinced him, even before World War II, that the United States had warred unwisely in 1917–1918. Before the smoke of battle cleared in 1945, he concluded that mistakes of profound historical significance were again being made. A continuation of these patterns, he repeatedly has warned, will eventually spell disaster.

By thus projecting himself into the stratosphere of high policy, this soldier appears to have strayed—some would say improperly—from appropriate military terrain. Wedemeyer neither denies nor apologizes for his straying: The country's good, he argues, is always a proper concern of patriots, in or out of uniform. As a professional soldier, he has remained wholeheartedly dedicated to soldierly values—including a willingness to submit to civil authority. At the same time, he has been obsessed with a sense of the terrible costs of war and a feeling that vacuous or ill-considered policy has needlessly exacerbated those costs for the United States. Haunted by these concerns, and by what he regards as evidence of continuing inadequacy in American policymaking, he has worked tirelessly for reform.

To understand Wedemeyer's position, it is necessary first to recall his reactions to World War I. Like many of his contemporaries, he became profoundly disenchanted during the interwar years with the U.S. experience of 1917–1918. President Wilson had led the nation into that conflagration on the high-minded assumption that the United States could "make the world safe for democracy" in an era of universal peace. Wilson's decision had been influenced, in Wedemeyer's opinion, more by the passions and propaganda of the time than by realistic analysis. There had been little systematic weighing of ends and means within the Wilson administration; indeed, the president had forbidden activities, however prudent, that might have been construed as "war planning." Having committed the nation to arms with no more than vague impressions of the ultimate costs and implications of involvement, he found himself powerless after the armistice to realize the liberal peace of which he dreamed. Ironically, Wilson's high-minded (and costly) crusade had made it possible for the self-serving powers of Europe with which the United States was associated to impose a vengeful "peace" that only compounded the world's ills.

On contemplating this strange history, Wedemeyer concluded that

American statesmen could and should do better. The primary lesson he drew from the experience was that the United States should not again drift mindlessly or plunge emotionally into war—and certainly should not permit itself again to be manipulated or dragged in by others. Americans simply *had* to become more sophisticated in defining their own interests and pursuing their own destiny.

This outlook underlay Wedemeyer's thinking when he arrived at the War Department in 1940. It is not surprising that his personal attitude toward the question of U.S. intervention in the European war in the months before Pearl Harbor was one of extreme caution. (This stance inevitably marked him, from the perspective of the hawks, as an "isolationist"—a label he consistently rejected. Only fools, he argued, believe that the United States could or should remain isolated in the twentieth century.)

Charged in mid-1941 with the task of drafting plans to meet the gathering storm, Wedemeyer discovered to his consternation what he had only surmised about World War I—namely that official Washington was largely adrift. As a staff officer planning military strategy (that is, planning "the employment of military means to achieve the goals of policy"), he set out first to identify relevant policy goals. His search proved baffling. Beyond the crucial—but ultimately merely instrumental—goal of defeating the Axis powers, he found only vague aspirations toward universal peace and freedom in a world free of aggressors. Nowhere could he find realistic concern for the postwar future; nowhere could he find concrete war aims calculated to insure that military victory would in fact bear desirable political fruit. The "Rainbow" plans that had been prepared earlier for war contingencies struck him as largely irrelevant exercises; they dealt mechanically with such data as currents and gradients off foreign invasion beaches, but reflected little concern at all for the currents of history. That no one in Washington was thinking seriously about these matters seemed strangely irresponsible; even more troubling, to this military Cassandra, was the fact that few thought it important to do so.

When war came on December 7, 1941, a shocked nation rallied to regain its balance and come back fighting. In the face of that awesome challenge, only the present seemed to matter. Politics, it was said, had failed when the shooting began, so it no longer mattered. Policy—in the Clausewitzian sense of the intelligent faculty that ought to guide states in war as in peace—took a holiday. In effect, war was accorded a sovereign logic of its own, and the United States embarked on another high-minded and exhilarating crusade.

As a member and later head of the War Department's Strategy and

Policy Group, Wedemeyer pressed the military effort with unstinting vigor. On one major issue, however, he found himself in early and worrisome disagreement with prevailing sentiment, including that of his political superiors. That issue was the Soviet Union. Since June 1941, the Soviet Union had been locked in mortal combat with Hitler's Germany. As the enemy of our enemy, it thus became our natural ally—and indeed, in view of the very formidable power of the Wehrmacht, an extremely welcome ally. But did it make sense also to assume that the Soviet Union was a *friend?* Was Stalin a democrat at heart who could eventually be counted upon to cooperate with the Western democracies in building a better world? Wedemeyer felt that the evidence pointed strongly to the contrary. "We Americans," he confided to his diary on New Year's Day, 1942, "are committing ourselves to the defeat of one 'ism' with the clear prospect of strengthening a similar 'ism' under another cloak. Our fine country . . . must be victorious in battle *and* at the peace table."

Soldiers had no business questioning "policy," however—a matter on which no less an authority than Marshall occasionally cautioned Wedemeyer—so the relatively junior staff officer held his peace. Solidarity with the Soviet Union, in hopes for the future as well as on the contemporary battlefield, became a virtually undebatable presupposition of U.S. foreign policy. Within that policy, however, Wedemeyer did what he could as military strategist to guide events into channels he thought constructive; he became, in particular, an unyielding advocate of Allied plans to cross the English Channel and invade the continent in force as soon as possible. A major motive—perhaps his primary motive in pressing this strategy after 1942—was to insure that Anglo-American forces reached Central Europe ahead of the Red Army.

As history records, the Western Allies lost that race. The cross-channel invasion and the opening of the Second Front in Europe came not in 1943, as the U.S. military staffs had urged, but in 1944. By the time the armies under Eisenhower crossed the Rhine, the Soviets were already well established in the Balkans, and their forces were positioned to seize Warsaw, Berlin, Vienna, and Prague. Ironically, the map of postwar Europe thus showed gains not for the forces of freedom (on whose behalf the Western democracies had resorted to arms in the first place), but for another "ism" at least as dangerous as the one that had been destroyed.

Long before this denouement in Europe, however, Wedemeyer left the corridors of the Pentagon for the wars in the Far East. In Southeast Asia and China he undertook important assignments in Allied and U.S. field commands. But alas, in this part of the world as in Europe, his hopes for the emergence of a more just and durable peace would again be shattered.

V-J Day in 1945 brought China not peace but a resumption of mortal civil strife. At the same time, Soviet moves in Manchuria and Korea, and the Red Army's support of insurgent Communists in China, signaled the end of Great Power unity in the war against Japan and reminded a somewhat confused world that the future of East Asia was yet to be settled.

Wedemeyer, on station in Shanghai, could not forget that a major U.S. purpose of the war just concluded had been to frustrate Japan's aggressive designs on China. The United States, he reasoned, thus had a right—indeed a solemn obligation—to follow through in the Far East and to make sure, at the least, that no new aggressor rushed into the vacuum created by Japan's defeat. Unfortunately, it soon became apparent to him that leftist forces in China and elsewhere were intent on achieving precisely that objective. Meanwhile, the United States—exultant in victory and confident that all the dangerous dragons had now been slain—rushed headlong to withdraw its military forces and dismantle its military power.

The U.S. policy on China during the next four years was marked, in Wedemeyer's opinion, by a fatal mixture of myopia and folly. Washington dallied irresolutely with vain hopes, false starts, half-measures, and rationalizations while the future of East Asia tottered in the balance. In 1949, Chiang Kai-shek and his Nationalist government—agents of progressive reform in China since 1911, foes of communism, bearers of the burdens of government through the years of resistance to Japanese aggression, and faithful allies of the United States in the Pacific War—were driven into exile by the Communists.

The postwar scorecard thus reflected a resounding defeat for U.S. war aims on the Asiatic mainland and a further dangerous tilting of the global power balance in favor of anti-democratic forces. Most tragic of all, with mainland China in the grip of Mao Tse-tung, a trap had been set for American involvement in another full generation of devastating wars in Asia: in Korea during the early 1950s, and in Vietnam during the 1960s and 1970s.

The history of the Second World War thus echoed the patterns of the first: a costly but complete victory on the field of battle, followed by a failure to secure the fruits of victory. Contrary to the weight of conventional opinion, Wedemeyer still insists that these calamities were by no means inevitable.

What went wrong? In Wedemeyer's analysis, Americans have been (and remain) lamentably inept in the arts of statecraft. Their strategic sense—the need they feel to formulate and pursue international goals intelligently—is dangerously weak. They have known war as the exercise of naked force but have understood little of the rational uses of power. Not their view of the world, nor their methods of policymaking, nor their doctrines of civil-military relations have served them well in the twentieth century.

Mindful that the shortcomings of U.S. foreign policy—shortsightedness, vacillation, and incoherence, for example—characterize in varying degrees the behavior of *all* democratic states, Wedemeyer has nonetheless insisted that greater rationality is possible within the American constitutional system. Indeed, he argues, at least the rationality of ordinary good sense must be achieved if the nation is to survive. In this spirit he long ago set himself the task of devising constructive proposals for reform, and perennially has urged his fellow citizens to join in the quest.

The war taught Wedemeyer one supreme lesson: Military strategy and foreign policy are ultimately inseparable. Neither in theory nor in practice can they usefully be treated in isolation from one another. It therefore made no sense to pretend (as Americans long have done) that "strategy" is an exclusively military business. Rejecting altogether this narrow use of the term, Wedemeyer began expounding an alternative. Strategy, he insisted, should be regarded as the province not solely, or even primarily, of soldiers, but of statesmen. It was "the art and science of employing *all* the nation's resources [not merely military means] in pursuit of national goals." He included among those resources the entire range of means and methods—political, economic, psychological, and cultural—that scholars normally encompass under the rubric "instruments of policy."

The surface plausibility of this formulation concealed some underlying difficulties. For example, the insistence that policy and strategy are inseparable clashed head-on with the traditional notion that war and peace are radically different modes of national existence presided over by men-at-arms and civilian policymakers, respectively. (A U.S. Army field manual of the 1930s stated official doctrine: "Politics and strategy are radically and fundamentally things apart . . . Strategy begins where politics end. All that soldiers ask is that once the policy is settled, strategy and command shall be regarded as being in a sphere apart from politics.") Wedemeyer's doctrine thus threatened the sacred walls that separate things military from things civil: From a civilian viewpoint, he was exposing the country to the dread dangers of militarism; from the military perspective, he was improperly urging soldiers into the distasteful (as well as forbidden) realm of politics.

In explicating his thought, Wedemeyer insists that policymaking is the function solely of responsible civil authorities. Although military men have an indispensable part to play in the process, their role should not be decisive. If civil authorities are to know and practice their true art, however, they are obliged to develop an active sense of strategy. They can no longer drift aimlessly, busying themselves primarily with reactions to unfolding crises. Nor can they pretend that force is the province and instrument solely of military experts.

Far from militarizing the state, Wedemeyer argues, a comprehensive strategic approach on the part of responsible civilian leaders can reduce the relative importance of military factors in both foreign and domestic spheres. If the nonmilitary instruments of policy are employed in a timely, coordinated, and imaginative manner, the nation's long-term security and economic well-being can be enhanced, and the frequency of the destructive wars in which we engage can be substantially reduced. Indeed, he continues, the failure to use nonmilitary means in a timely and purposeful manner leads again and again to situations in which naked force remains the only option. At the same time, intelligent forethought can increase the probability—when resort to arms does become necessary—that the aims of the conflict are in fact achieved, and at minimum cost in lives and treasure.

While it is reassuring to assume that good men produce good policy in any environment, it is equally important to appreciate the role that sound organizational arrangements can play. Accordingly, Wedemeyer has taken pains to explore the possibility of more effective institutions along with better doctrines. That goal has proved elusive. How can a system in which the responsible (and often inexperienced) officials of government come and go at frequent intervals accommodate the long-range imperatives of strategy? What organ of strategic consciousness can be devised which, if given the task of defining national goals beyond the crises of the hour, would not come into fundamental conflict with established constitutional agencies? And what mechanisms for pursuing those goals would not encounter the same difficulties?

Wedemeyer's first attempt at a resolution of this dilemma was made during the grand strategic debates that agitated U.S. and Allied councils in the early years of World War II. Concerned about the haphazard manner in which policy seemed to be evolving in Washington, he proposed the establishment of a board designed to give more thoughtful attention to the war's basic aims and strategies. Although various interdepartmental committees, ad hoc groups, and statutory agencies were constituted from time to time, both during and after the war, this matter of purposeful coordination never received the attention he thought it merited.

The decades since 1945 have found Wedemeyer active, in mufti as in uniform, on many fronts, and in an endless series of civic, educational, patriotic, and free-world causes. It is not surprising that his primary interests have continued to focus on national policy and policymaking, especially in foreign and defense fields. In addition, as before, he has frequently found himself out of harmony with prevailing thought. The successive doctrines of war and schools of strategy that have flourished in the age of atoms and missiles have all seemed to him partial and inadequate. The doctrine of limited war—much touted by officials of the Truman administration in the wake of the Korean conflict as a body of enlightened new insights—struck him as the rediscovery of the obvious (or, in the particular circumstances of Korea, a rationale for failed policy). The subtle analyses of the technologists and theoreticians that have dominated the field of strategic war since the 1950s seem to him to have torn military theory unwisely from its broader social and historical contexts and reduced it altogether to mechanics. Disappointing, too, was the vogue of counterinsurgency, which, during the long agony of Vietnam, caught a valid sense of the complex intimacy of war and politics, but unfortunately responded only at tactical levels and on the enemy's terms.

Wedemeyer's emphasis on a positive U.S. strategy has sometimes been interpreted as a manifestation of narrow nationalism. This view quite misses the mark. Ardent patriot though he is, and perennial foe of "fuzzy-minded one-worldism," Wedemeyer's human sympathies, like his strategic outlook, are global. While viewing international life as an inescapable struggle for space and resources—a struggle compounded by fundamental ideological conflicts and made incalculably more dangerous by the nature of modern weapons—he clings unshakably to the hope that all freedom-loving people can and will cooperate in building a better world.

Now in his ninetieth year, Wedemeyer refuses to fade away. Still interested in ideas, and ever solicitous of his country's—and the world's—well-being, he continues to pursue his vision of a strategic outlook and policies that aim intelligently at peace as well as victory.

I

The Kriegsakademie Experience

1936–1939

Wedemeyer was a 39-year-old captain when he graduated from the U.S. Army's Command and General Staff School at Fort Leavenworth, Kansas, in 1936. The War Department thereupon dispatched him on a second major academic assignment, this time to the German Kriegsakademie in Berlin.

The Kriegsakademie was an institution with a past. Having nurtured the German General Staff from the time of Napoleon, it had become, in the eyes of many, a symbol of dread militarism. Its professional standards had at the same time become a model of excellence for all the world's armies. Suppressed during the years of the Weimar Republic, the school had reopened its doors in 1933 and by 1936 had resumed its traditional role in the life of the German army.

The spirits of Scharnhorst, Clausewitz, Moltke, Schlieffen, and others still haunted the lecture halls. The mood of the resurrected Kriegsakademie was by no means retrospective, however, for Germany under the National Socialists was bent on rapid rearmament. Although the professional officer corps was ambivalent (when not hostile) to the Nazi party, the officers shared the bitterness of most of their countrymen over the *Diktat* of Versailles, and earnestly hoped for the dawn of better days. Obsessed, moreover, by memories of the bloody but indecisive trench warfare of 1914–1918, they placed their military hopes on the promise of technologi-

cal and doctrinal reform. If the proud German army were to exploit the opportunities presented by the age of flight and radio and
motor transport—opportunities that promised drastically to trans-
form the arts of war—it could reasonably expect success in any
future conflict.

This was the milieu into which the "Yankee Captain"
Wedemeyer moved in the autumn of 1936. For two years thereafter he attended lectures, participated in daily "troop leading"
exercises (simulated tactical situations in which students played
specific command or staff roles), accompanied units of the German
army on field maneuvers, and visited historic battlefields. He mingled cordially with his classmates and instructors on social as well
as professional levels. He liked most of his associates, and they in
turn found him congenial and open-minded. Talk centered almost
exclusively on professional topics. The German officers tactfully
avoided discussion of politics, and their visitor did likewise. Although Wedemeyer struggled throughout with the German language (his skills at the outset were elementary), he pursued his
studies diligently and took careful notes for future use.

These notes were eventually forwarded to the War Department
in the form of long reports. Beyond providing an account of the
school and its methods, they told U.S. planners almost everything
they might have wanted to know at the time about the new German army: its organization, equipment, tactics, doctrines, and principles of leadership. Much of this material influenced revisions of
U.S. field manuals, and all of it was available for use in the design
and training of the new American army that soon would take the
field to fight World War II.

The following passages are selected from these reports as they
were forwarded from Berlin in 1938.

G-2 REPORT

From: Military Attache, Berlin. Report 15,999.
    [Report by Albert C. Wedemeyer, Captain, Infantry]
Subject: German General Staff School
Date: July 11, 1938

General Tactical Observations

For political and economical reasons, Germany must plan for a war of movement which contemplates early decision. Throughout the instruction at the Kriegsakademie, and based upon my observations while serving with troops or on maneuvers, I have been impressed with the thoroughness with which the military force as a whole is being trained to seize and maintain the initiative. An aggressive spirit is being inculcated in the leaders of all grades. When a map problem, a combat exercise, or a maneuver involves a defensive situation, there is great emphasis placed upon the fact that the defense is assumed *temporarily* to permit the creation of more favorable conditions for the attack, which inevitably follows.

During the two years' course of instruction, my class was given only three situations which involved defensive tactics (active defense situations, in Leavenworth vernacular) and five which required delaying action. The remainder, perhaps sixty in all, were various types of attack or aggressive action. No situation involved stabilized warfare, and we had only one which resembled slightly a passive defense as taught at Ft. Leavenworth.

In many of the situations, particularly during the first year, I often received the impression that an attack was launched prematurely—that the main effort was directed against hostile positions whose defensive strength (based upon the terrain and modern defensive means) precluded success, or at least would take an unjustifiable toll. However, after serving with troops and attending maneuvers, observing the mobility and considering the tremendous fire power of the infantry heavy weapons (howitzers and mortars), the automatic weapons (machine guns), and the long-range, heavy-caliber artillery, my doubts relative to the effectiveness of their aggressive tactics were greatly reduced. Vigorous reconnaissance, both land and air, is particularly emphasized to preclude or at least minimize the hostile effort to surprise or deceive. Often the instructors pointed out that it was practically impossible today, with modern reconnaissance means, to deceive the enemy for any extended length of time, and the ever-essential *surprise* element could best be accomplished through *mobility* and *rapidity*.

When the Germans are confronted by an enemy in a prepared defensive position which cannot be turned or avoided, there is naturally more caution and time involved in the preparations for the attack. However, compared to French conceptions, or even our own, the preparation is greatly accelerated. In such case there is intensive reconnaissance to clarify the situation as much as possible, rapid concentration of means for the main effort—and then the attack is on the way. When they concentrate for the break-through, they take no half-way measures, but insure that they have sufficient power not only to break through, but against strong resistance to provide succeeding impulses in the attack and finally, subsequent to the penetration, to exploit their success.

In view of the wide envelopment maneuver, which was greatly stressed at Fort Leavenworth when I was a student (1934–1936), I was particularly interested in the German envelopments. Practically all were close-in, that is, the enveloping force would immediately clear the hostile flank.

Discussion with German tactical instructors indicates the following views relative to the wide envelopment: That the defender's reconnaissance means would permit the opposing force to secretly move [the bulk of] his force several miles at night to the most vulnerable part of the defensive position selected seemed highly improbable if not impossible. . . . They believe that such a maneuver would rarely be successful, pointing out that it would not be possible to move the bulk of a large force from eight to fifteen miles around the defender's flank without the latter's knowledge, and with the natural result, a change in disposition to counter or avoid the blow . . .

Methods of Instruction

The most important point under the subject "instruction," I believe to be the method of presenting map problems. I found them realistic and practical. Most problems are carried on over a period of several days, so that the students do not spend hours reading into the situation. The instructor develops the march, deployment, attack, defense, delaying action, or whatever the type of maneuver, by introducing events which would transpire in battle. Students make decisions, estimates of terrain, issue orders (oral and written), and conduct themselves exactly as they would in the field. The Germans emphasize that a commander must not only know *how* to arrive at a decision but also *when*. They contend that it is better to render a partly faulty decision at the right time than to ponder for hours over various changes in the situation and finally evolve a perfect decision, but too late for execution. They visualize rapidly changing situations on the modern battlefield and emphasize "seizing and maintaining" the initiative . . . In some problems and terrain exercises, it was readily apparent that only a few minutes were available for a decision; in others, hours. Students were taught to budget their time accordingly, taking into consideration not only the time required for the issuance of orders, but for the execution of the plan. Finally there were situations presented wherein no new decision was required, the initial plan continuing in operation until more essential information was received.

Emphasis is placed upon the development of the student's firmness of will, judgment, confidence, acceptance of responsibility and self-control. In the course of the school year, instructors note the presence or absence of these characteristics and record same for final evaluation reports.

Leadership Doctrine

An indomitable will and broad military knowledge, combined with a strong character, are attributes of the successful leader. He must have a clear conception of tactical principles and their application. Only by continual study of military history and of the conduct of war with careful attention to current developments can the officer acquire the above stated attributes of leadership. Two of the most important characteristics of a leader are initiative and willingness to accept responsibility. "Procrastination" and "evasion," or shifting of responsibility, must be at all times *avoided*. Better a faulty plan or decision permeated with boldness, daring, and decisiveness than a perfect plan enmeshed in uncertainty. The leader must strive to maintain the initiative with respect to the enemy. Continual personal contact with own troops is very important. The leader can thereby learn their needs and better determine their capacity to carry on. When the troops realize that he is concerned with their comforts and is taking a personal interest in their pleasures and sorrows, then will they cheerfully and willingly give their last ounce of strength to accomplish the most aggravating tasks.

The leader must personally lead his troops, carefully consider every situation, give his decision, and insure that the orders are properly distributed. His spirit and character must dominate his staff, and at no time should he permit himself to fall into a subsidiary role.

The first requirement of a General Staff Officer: *Anticipate and accomplish every possible task without appearing to do so.* Further, General Staff

Officers must thoroughly understand the technical and tactical employment of all weapons. To insure such understanding, these officers must serve frequently with troops and experience in the field the limitations and potentialities of the various weapons. They must avoid thought of personal achievements and glories and happily recognize the success of their labors through the accomplishments and rewards of their leader and the entire command.

A most important role of the General Staff Officer is continual consideration of the future situation—anticipating every contingency and *not awaiting developments of the situation*. Plans for various possibilities should at all times be formulated, available for prompt inauguration.

The Infantry Division Commander

The Division Commander has a command which is tactically and administratively self-contained. There are fourteen different types of weapons whose tactical and technical employment in a broad sense he must understand. He is responsible for the training, welfare, and conduct in battle of over fifteen thousand men.

He must impose his will upon and inculcate a feeling of confidence and respect in all members of his command. In his relations with the staff, he must be friendly, yet the dominant personality. He may delegate certain authorities to members of his staff, but the responsibility for every occurrence within the command remains upon his shoulders. Decisions, broad policies, and tactical employment of the command are determined by the commander.

Summing up the qualities required of a Division Commander: He must possess moral courage and broad knowledge of the tactical and technical employment of all arms; he must have a dominant yet pleasing personality; finally, [he must have] a sense of loyalty to his subordinates as well as to his seniors.

Commander's Estimate of the Situation and Decision

One must thoroughly work oneself into the situation. Place the location of your own troops, and put the information you have about the enemy, upon the situation map. This information is built up by reports from various sources, that is, inhabitants, spies, air and land reconnaissance, goniometric intercept, captured letters, newspapers, telegrams, captured airplanes, balloons, carrier pigeons, examination of prisoners, and papers taken from killed or wounded enemy. Information must be evaluated objectively. One must be extremely careful not to interpret the information received as one would like it to be or as one hoped it would be.

A large part of the information one receives in war is contradictory, a still greater part is false, and by far the greatest part is very uncertain.

In considering the situation, the following principles govern:

> 1. The first and most important principle is to utilize to the maximum the available means. Any moderation in this regard is a deterring factor in attaining the ultimate goal.
>
> 2. Concentrate as much of your force as possible where you plan or believe the principal blow (the main effort) will fall and expose yourself disadvantageously at other points, in order to be more certain of success at the point of the main effort. The success of the main effort more than compensates for the minor losses sustained.
>
> 3. Lose no time. Unless special advantages accrue by delay, it is very important that you execute your plans as quickly as possible. Through speedy action many measures of the enemy are nullified in their initial stages.

Each situation must be independently weighed. One must restrict oneself only to consideration of the essentials.

In general, when confronted by a vague situation and difficult circumstances, as is often the case in war: Be active. Seize and maintain the initiative. Do not expect or await hints or suggestions from the enemy relative to your next move.

The decision must indicate a clear objective to be attained by the coordinated and aggressive use of your available means. The strong will of the leader must dominate at all times. Often the stronger will compels victory.

Never let anxiety over personal security interfere or influence in any manner the real task, which is annihilation of the enemy.

Calmly weigh the situation, thinking quickly but overlooking nothing essential. Insure that all assistants clearly understand your plans. Nervousness on your part is quickly reflected by subordinates.

Never hold a Council of War. Complication and confusion are frequently introduced by such methods, and generally only an incomplete decision results. One can much better think through a situation and reach a definite decision by *independently* estimating the situation.

Once a decision is made, do not deviate, except for excellent reasons. In this connection, one can bring about disaster by obstinately clinging to the initial decision when justifiable grounds are present for a change. The true art of leadership is the ability to recognize WHEN a new decision is required by the developments or changes in the situation. The *commander should be RESOLUTE but not OBSTINATE.*

Important General Principles for a Commander

First weigh the chance of success. Then risk the chance for success.

Put as much power in the main effort and as little power in the minor or subsidiary effort as possible.

Be quick to recognize favorable situations or a turn of events, and promptly utilize [them] to your own advantage.

Speed and surprise can make up for a considerable numerical inferiority.

Always remember to use every opportunity to refresh your troops.

Organization of the German Army

The German army is organized throughout on the "Einheit" principle, that is, insofar as practicable the component parts are independent standard units capable of being attached or detached at will without loss of tactical integrity and without administrative or supply difficulties. Sufficient weapons and manpower coupled with necessary supply and administrative means are given to each battalion, regiment, and division, so that they can carry on their respective roles when detached. This accomplishes flexibility without impairing efficiency . . .

The present German Infantry Division is equipped with the following weapons:

351 Light Machine Guns

133 Heavy Machine Guns

 20 Light Infantry Howitzers (75 mm)

  6 Heavy Infantry Howitzers (150 mm)

 87 Light Mortars (50 mm)

 54 Heavy Mortars (81 mm)

 75 Anti-Tank Guns (37 mm)

 36 Light Field Howitzers (Artillery) (105 mm)

  8 Heavy Field Howitzers (Artillery) (150 mm)

  4 Guns (Art: Heavy) (105 mm)

 16 Anti-Aircraft Guns (20 mm)

These figures are interesting because they indicate the special emphasis placed upon close-supporting heavy weapons for the Infantry. [The officers] feel that they now have sufficient fire power to neutralize hostile automatic weapons without constantly calling upon the artillery for close-support missions—an unsatisfactory procedure at best, according to their experience in the World War—due to the limitations of communications. Further, they feel that the artillery is released to concentrate upon essentially artillery missions (counter-battery concentrations, interdictions, harassing, and preparations) without parcelling out units for close support of the Infantry.

2

The Victory Plan

1941

When Hitler invaded Poland on September 1, 1939, Wedemeyer was at Fort Benning, Georgia, helping organize the U.S. Army's first anti-tank battalion. From this perspective he observed the march of events in the fateful first year of war: the defeat and dismemberment of Poland at the hands of Hitler and Stalin, the winter of "phony" war, the dramatic German thrust into Denmark and Norway in the spring of 1940, the even more dramatic sweep of the *Wehrmacht* across the Low Countries into France, the British retreat from Dunkirk, the fall of France, and the Battle of Britain. Aroused by the shattering impact of these events, the United States embarked on its own ambitious programs of rearmament and mobilization.

In September 1940, Wedemeyer (now a major) was summoned to the War Department to draft a field manual on anti-tank doctrine. This task completed, he moved into the War Plans Division of the General Staff.

U.S. defense preparations accelerated throughout these months as the dangers of involvement grew. The armed services expanded rapidly with the aid of the nation's first peacetime draft. Congress appropriated unprecedented sums for a proliferating series of new purposes, including Lend-Lease. Munitions output soared as civilian industry converted to defense production. Indeed, the many separate parts of the defense program had sprung up and grown like vigorous competing plants in a tropical jungle. As a result, vexing issues of priority arose, and problems began to appear in the form of materials shortages, wage and price distortions, labor migration, industrial unrest, and inflation. By mid-summer 1941 even the pragmatic President Roosevelt felt the need for some conceptual framework by which to judge and guide the entire vast enterprise. He asked Henry L. Stimson, the secretary of war, to take the lead in sketching such a framework. He wrote,

> I wish that you . . . would join . . . in exploring at once the over-all production requirements required to defeat our potential enemies.
> I wish you would explore the munitions and mechanical equipment of all types which in your opinion would be required to exceed by an appropriate amount that available to our potential enemies. From your report we should be able to establish a munitions objective indicating the industrial capacity which this nation will require.

Bland though these economic musings sounded, it was clear that great undertakings were contemplated. Providing meaningful answers to the President's inquiries obviously required more than routine logistic calculations, more even than broad planning for some future contingency. In the first instance, an answer to the question of needed industrial capacity depended on answers to the prior questions of how much production was needed, and when. These latter questions in turn could be answered only on the basis of realistic assumptions concerning prospective enemies, modes of warfare, broad schemes of strategic maneuver, theaters of operations, and a particular time frame. What was needed, in effect, was a specific war scenario—an outline plan for mobilizing and employing the nation's resources in an all-out effort.

After Secretary Stimson, Chief of Staff General George C. Marshall, and others had reflected and consulted on the President's letter, they passed it to the War Plans Division for staff action. There the matter was assigned to the officer whom General Marshall referred to as "that long-legged Major": Wedemeyer.

Drawing on earlier staff estimates, joint contingency plans, understandings with the British, and other sources, Wedemeyer plunged wholeheartedly into his task of strategic synthesis. That Germany and Japan were the nation's major potential enemies had become by this time a generally accepted assumption. That the long-discussed policy of "Hitler first" would prevail also seemed likely—and appropriate. Beyond these points of departure, however, the road or roads that might lead to ultimate victory lay shrouded in uncertainty. What kind of war would we *have* to fight? What kind of war ought we *try* to fight? Where, when, and with what types and numbers of forces? Most important, and logically prior to all other questions, with what aims?

Tentative answers to some of these riddles were incorporated in a bulky report (key sections of which had been drafted by Wedemeyer) that went to the White House two months later—on September 11, 1941. This "Victory Plan" provided, *inter alia,* for the mobilization into the U.S. armed forces of over ten million men, the organization and equipping of vast modern expeditionary forces, and the "rapidly accelerated" development of industrial capacity to prepare these forces for action by July 1, 1943. To avoid "a long drawn-out war of attrition," the plan emphasized the necessity of engaging and defeating Hitler on the continent of Europe "before he can liquidate or recoup from his struggle with Russia."

The scope and magnitude of Wedemeyer's proposals were at first considered unrealistic by some of his military and civilian superiors. A few thought the plan "defeatist" because of its staggering estimates of what would be required to defeat Hitler. When war came to the United States three months later, however—on December 7, 1941—the Victory Plan became Washington's basic guide to mobilization of manpower and materiel and to global deployment of forces.

The Victory Plan figured dramatically (if perhaps less importantly) on yet another level in the history of the period. Three days before Pearl Harbor, accurate summaries of that extremely sensitive top-secret document, including verbatim quotations, appeared on the front page of the *Chicago Tribune*. A news leak and security violation of incalculable significance obviously had occurred. The revelation that President Roosevelt was secretly "plotting war" while publicly talking peace aroused storms of controversy. As the staff officer who had played a central role in drafting and securing the plan—and who was known to entertain private doubts about the drift of U.S. policy—Wedemeyer came under immediate suspicion and investigation. Although he was utterly innocent of any wrongdoing in the matter—a fact of which the Chief of Staff and the Secretary of War remained fully satisfied—the identity and motivation of the culprit or culprits were apparently not established. Aside from the fact that the isolationist Senator Burton K. Wheeler was involved in transmitting the document to the press, the affair remains a mystery to this day.

The following paragraphs are taken from the Victory Plan as it went to the White House on September 11—and as it was leaked to the press on or before December 4, 1941.

ULTIMATE REQUIREMENTS STUDY:
ESTIMATE OF ARMY GROUND FORCES

The specific operations necessary to accomplish the defeat of the Axis Powers cannot be predicted at this time. Irrespective of the nature and scope of these operations, we must prepare to fight Germany by actually coming to grips with and defeating her ground forces and definitely breaking her will to combat. Such requirement establishes the necessity for powerful ground elements, flexibly organized into task forces which are equipped and trained to do their respective jobs. The Germans and their associates, with between eleven and twelve million men under arms, now have approximately 300 divisions fully equipped and splendidly trained. It is estimated that they can have, by 1943, a total of 400 divisions available in the European Theater.

The important influence of the air arm in modern combat has been irrefutably established. The degree of success attained by sea and ground forces will be determined by the effective and timely employment of air supporting units and the successful conduct of strategical missions. No major military operation in any theater will succeed without air superiority, or at least air superiority disputed. The necessity for a strong sea force, consisting principally of fast cruisers, destroyers, aircraft carriers, torpedo boats, and submarines, continues in spite of the increased fighting potential of the air arm. Employment of enemy air units has not yet deprived naval vessels of their vital role on the high seas, but has greatly accelerated methods and changed the technique in their employment. It appears that the success of naval operations, assuming air support, will still be determined by sound strategic concepts and adroit leadership. A sea blockade will not accomplish an economic strangulation or military defeat of Germany. Nor will air operations alone bring victory. Air and sea forces will make important contributions, but effective and adequate ground forces must be available to close with and destroy the enemy within his citadel.

It is therefore imperative that we create the productive capacity to provide equipment for the following:

   a. Appropriate forces distributed for the defense of the United States, outlying possessions, and bases selected to facilitate the defense of the country and the Western Hemisphere.
   b. Task forces which can effectively conduct military operations, primarily in the European Theater, as well as in the Western Hemisphere and in other strategically important areas.

c. The military forces of associates and friendly Powers committed to the policy of opposing Nazi aggression. Quantities to be limited only by our own strategic requirements and the ability of the friendly Powers to use the equipment effectively.

A sound approach to the problem of determining appropriate military means requires careful consideration of where, how, and when they will be employed to defeat our potential enemies and to assist our associates:

Where. Accepting the premise that we must come to grips with the enemy ground forces, our principal theater of war is Central Europe. Possible subsidiary theaters include Africa, the Near East, the Iberian Peninsula, the Scandinavian Peninsula, and the Far East; however, the operations in those theaters must be so conducted as to facilitate the decisive employment of Allied forces in Central Europe.

How. The combined and carefully coordinated operations of our military forces, in collaboration with associated Powers, must accomplish the following:

[*a.*] The surface and subsurface vessels of the Axis and associated Powers must be swept from the seas, particularly in the Atlantic and water areas contiguous to Europe.

[*b.*] Overwhelming air superiority must be accomplished.

[*c.*] The economic and industrial life of Germany must be rendered ineffective through the continuous disruption and destruction of lines of communication, ports, and industrial facilities, and by the interception of raw materials.

[*d.*] The combat effectiveness of the German military forces must be greatly reduced by over-extension, dispersion, shortage of material, including fuel, and a deterioration of the home front. Popular support of the war effort by the peoples of the Axis powers must be weakened and their confidence shattered by subversive activities, propaganda, deprivation, the destruction wrought, and chaos created.

[*e.*] Existing military bases (the British Isles and the Near East) must be maintained. Additional bases, which encircle and close in on the Nazi citadel, must be established in order to facilitate air operations designed to shatter the German industrial and economic life. Such bases may also provide feasible points of departure for the combined operations of ground and air forces. In disposing of our forces, we must guard against dispersion of means in operations that do not make timely and effective contributions to the accomplishment of our main task, the defeat of Germany.

[f.] The commitment of our forces must conform to our accepted broad strategic concept of active (offensive) operations in one theater (European) and, concurrently, passive (defensive) operations in the other (Pacific).

When. The following factors with regard to the time element are important in determining the production capacity necessary to realize our national objectives:

[a.] The lag between plan and execution is considerable. Past experience indicates that from eighteen months to two years are required.

[b.] How many months will Germany require to defeat Russia, to reconstitute her forces subsequent to Russia's defeat, and to exploit to any perceptible degree the vast resources of Russia? It is believed that Germany will occupy Russian territory west of the general line: White Sea, Moscow, Volga River (all inclusive) by July 1, 1942, and that militarily, Russia will be substantially impotent subsequent to that date. Thereafter, Germany will "Coventry" all industrial areas, lines of communications, and sources of raw materials east of the line indicated, unless a drastic Nazi treaty is accepted by Russia. Germany will probably require a full year to bring order out of chaos in the conquered areas, so that it will be July 1, 1943, before she will largely profit economically by her "drive to the east." The maintenance of huge armies of occupation has become unnecessary. By totally disarming the conquered people, maintaining splendidly organized intelligence and communications nets, and employing strategically located, highly mobile forces (parachute, airborne, mechanized, and motorized), Germany may control the occupied areas with relatively small forces, thus releasing the bulk of the military for other tasks. Obviously, our war effort timetable, covering the production of munitions, the creation of trained military forces, and the increase of transportation facilities (air, ground, and sea), is strongly influenced by events transpiring in the Russian theater.

[c.] We are confronted by two possibilities: first, a rapidly accelerated, all-out effort with a view to conducting decisive offensive operations against the enemy before he can liquidate or recoup from his struggle with Russia; second, a long drawn-out war of attrition.

Under our present production schedule, we will soon have adequate military means to defend our outlying possessions and bases and to provide for the security of the Western Hemisphere, but we will not be able to provide sufficient appropriate forces for timely offensive action in the principal theater of operations. The urgency for positive action exists, particularly while the enemy is contained militarily in Russia. It would strongly contribute to the early and decisive defeat of the Axis powers, if the Allied forces could seize and firmly establish military bases from which immediate air and subsequent ground and air operations might be undertaken.

[*d.*] The United States is approaching its task in a logical manner, but the production of materiel must be greatly accelerated to permit its accomplishment. At present, the bulk of our production has to be devoted to the support of Great Britain and associates, rendering it impracticable for us to undertake offensive commitments. But time is of the essence and the longer we delay effective offensive operations against the Axis, the more difficult will become the attainment of victory. It is mandatory that we reach an early appreciation of our stupendous task and gain the wholehearted support of the entire country in the production of trained men, ships, munitions, and ample reserves. Otherwise, we will be confronted in the not-distant future by a Germany strongly entrenched economically, supported by newly acquired sources of vital supplies and industries, with her military forces operating on interior lines, and in a position of hegemony in Europe which will be comparatively easy to defend and maintain.

[*e.*] The time by which production can reach the levels defined by our national objectives is highly speculative. July 1, 1943, has been established as the earliest date on which the equipment necessary to initiate and sustain our projected operations can be provided. The ability of industry to meet this requirement is contingent upon many intangibles; however, the program can be definitely accomplished, in fact, greatly exceeded, if the industrial potential of the country is fully exploited. The urgency of speed and the desirability of employing our present great economic and industrial advantage over our potential enemies cannot be overemphasized.

Strategic Employment of Ground Forces

a. The future alignment of powers and their respective combat capacities cannot be accurately predicted. In order to arrive at a plausible basis from which to determine our future requirements, the following assumptions pertaining to the world situation as of July 1, 1943, are made:

(1) Russia is substantially impotent militarily in Europe. Resistance in Siberia, to include the Maritime Provinces, probably continuing.

(2) The Axis military strength is materially weakened through economic blockades, by losses in the Russian campaign, by British air and sea operations, by the inability to exploit quickly the extensively sabotaged Russian industries and raw materials, and by lowered morale of the people.

(3) The military forces of Japan are fully involved with or contained by campaigns against a somewhat strengthened China, by the Russian forces in the Far East Maritime Province, or by the threat of U.S.-British military and economic reprisals.

(4) Great Britain and associates have increased their fighting forces by creating and equipping additional combat units.

(5) The French will probably continue their passive collaboration with Germany.

(6) Control of the Mediterranean Theater, including North Africa and the Near East, remains disputed.

(7) The United States is an active belligerent and is collaborating in an all-out effort to defeat Germany.

b. If these assumptions are correct, or even reasonably sound, on July 1, 1943, there will be no military bases remaining in Allied hands, other than the United Kingdom, possibly the northern coast of Africa and the Near East. The establishment of additional bases, for example, in the Iberian Peninsula, the Scandinavian Peninsula and Northwest Africa will be bitterly contested by the Axis. However, to bring about the ultimate defeat of Germany, those bases and others even more difficult to establish must be available to the Allies. Obviously, carefully planned action involving appropriate sea, air, and ground units must be undertaken. Allied success is directly contingent upon the coordinated employment of *overwhelming forces, surprise,* and *mobility,* supported by sufficient reserve in materiel and manpower to insure a succession of effective impulses throughout the operations.

c. Latest information pertaining to the potential industrial capacities and military strengths of the opposing powers (excluding the United States) as of July 1, 1943, indicates that the Axis Powers will have about 400 divisions available in the European–Near East

Theater, and the Allied powers approximately 100 divisions. To accomplish the numerical superiority, about two to one, usually considered necessary before undertaking offensive operations, the Allies would have to raise about 700 divisions. A force of 700 divisions with appropriate supporting and service troops would approximate 22 million men. If Great Britain and the United States should induct so many men for military service, added to the tremendous numbers already under arms, the economic and industrial effort necessary to conduct the war would be definitely imperiled.

d. It is believed that the enemy can be defeated without creating the numerical superiority indicated. Effective employment of modern air and ground fighting machines and a tight economic blockade may create conditions that will make the realization of the Allied war aims perfectly feasible with numerically less fighting men. Another million men in Flanders would not have turned the tide of battle for France. If the French army had had sufficient tanks and planes, and quantities of anti-tank and anti-aircraft materiel, France might have remained a dominant power in Europe. In June, 1941, when the Germans launched their invasion of Russia, they knew that their adversary was numerically superior and could maintain that superiority in spite of tremendous losses. They probably also knew that Stalin was creating a military force of great power, consisting primarily of effective modern fighting machines, and that if they delayed their "drive to the east" another year, Russia would possess armadas of air and ground machines which would not only render an offensive campaign impossible, but would make large demands upon the German military to secure her eastern frontier. The Crete campaign also presents illuminating evidence in favor of modern fighting means when opposed by superior numbers that are equipped with inappropriate means and are operating under World War I static tactical concepts. Approximately 17,000 Germans attacked and conquered the island, which was defended by about 30,000 British.

e. Our broad concept of encircling and advancing step-by-step, with a view to closing in on Germany, will remain sound regardless of future developments in the European situation, for it envisages the only practical way in which military and economic pressure may be brought to bear effectively against Germany. The loss of potential bases of operation, presently available, would render the accomplishment of our strategic plans extremely difficult and costly. It is important, therefore, that the Allies take effective measures to hold the United Kingdom, the

Middle East, and North African areas. Also the islands off the northwestern coast of Africa should be denied to the enemy. Before undertaking operations in connection with the establishment of additional military bases, for example, in the Scandinavian Peninsula, the Iberian Peninsula, Africa and the Low Countries, a careful survey of the areas of projected operations and a thorough examination of the enemy capabilities are mandatory.

The unfortunate Norway campaign of 1940 is a glaring example of a total lack of appreciation of such realities on the part of those responsible for the British expedition. The Germans employed approximately 175,000 men, strongly supported by the Air Force, to conquer and secure their lodgement in Norway. Special Task Forces, including two mountain divisions and numerous parachute units, made effective contributions to the success of the operation. Having gained a foothold, the Germans quickly established themselves in order to hold their bases and to facilitate exploitation. The British forces dispatched against Norway totaled about 20,000 men, with no mountain troops and with inadequate air supporting units.

The failure of the British Expedition is directly attributable to insufficient and inappropriate means. If and when the situation indicates the feasibility of an Allied expedition, against Norway, for example, powerful and appropriate means, especially trained and equipped for the task, must be provided. Large and effective reserves must be readily available to preclude dislodgement of the initial forces and to facilitate subsequent exploitation. A careful study of Norway, including the terrain and communications net, and a survey of possible enemy capabilities, indicate the necessity for mountain, infantry foot and motorized divisions, and numerous parachute, tank, anti-tank, anti-aircraft and airborne units. The force required for the entire operation may total several hundred thousand men. The execution of the plan would be predicated on sea and local air superiority. The size of this force may appear large. However, even though our enemy may not be strong initially in the area of projected operations, the mobility of modern fighting means will enable him to concentrate destructive forces against us with unprecedented speed and surprise effect.

The foregoing considerations apply with equal emphasis to proposed forces for other theaters of operations. Careful studies concerning the Scandinavian Peninsula, the Iberian Peninsula, the Near East, and Africa have been made by the War Plans Division of the General Staff, and these studies made important contributions in the determination of the estimated ground forces (see Table A). The enemy capabilities in those theaters in 1943 would obviously be conjecture. Task forces consisting principally of armored and motorized divisions must be created for possible operations in North Africa, the Middle East, France, and the Low Countries. The exact strength and the composition of the Task forces necessary to seize and maintain military bases will be determined immediately prior to the operation. We can avoid the unfortunate disasters experienced by our potential allies in Norway, France, the Balkans, and Crete by planning now and creating quickly the production capacity necessary to equip the ground forces recommended (Table A). We must not suffer ignominious defeat and be expelled from the bases that we elect to establish. If the premises and assumptions made earlier in this study are appropriate and sound, additional strategically located bases are vital to the splendidly conceived plans of the Air Force, and finally may serve as areas of departure for the combined operations of air and ground forces. The *seizure, retention,* and *effective utilization* of these bases is predicated on the successful operations of adequate sea, air, and ground forces.

Shipping was a bottleneck in the last war, and again increased demands will be placed on all transportation facilities, particularly water, by constant troop movements and the expanded war industrial and economic effort. In order to transport and maintain effective forces in European areas, several million tons of shipping and adequate port facilities must be made available essentially for military service. To transport five million men with their modern air and mechanized equipment to European ports over a period of approximately one year would require about seven million tons of shipping or 1,000 ships. To maintain such a force in the theater of operations would require about ten million tons of shipping or 1,500 ships. But it is highly improbable that the situation in Europe will develop in such manner as to permit or to require operations involving the movement of so large a force across the Atlantic within the limited time of one year, even if the ship tonnage were available.

The progressive building up of large military forces in the theater will probably extend over a period of at least two years. This progressive movement would greatly reduce the demands upon maritime shipping for essentially military purposes, and further would extend the period of time for the augmentation of maritime shipping now available. The realization of our present national policies may require operations in distant theaters by military forces of unprecedented strength. It would be folly to create strong fighting forces without providing the transportation to move [them to] and maintain them in the contemplated theaters of operations. The maximum possible shipbuilding capacity of our country, coordinated of course with other essential demands upon industry and raw materials, must be exploited and continued in operation for the next several years.

The foregoing considerations clearly indicate the importance of creating a productive capacity in this country that will provide the most modern equipment designed to give mobility and destructive power to our striking forces. The forces that we now estimate as necessary to realize our national objectives, and for which production capacity must be provided, may not be adequate or appropriate. No one can predict the situation that will confront the United States in July 1943. We may require much larger forces than those indicated below and correspondingly greatly increased quantities of equipment. Emphasis has been placed on destructive power and mobility, with a view to offensive maneuvers in our principal theater of operations (Europe). The forces deemed necessary to accomplish the role of ground units in the supreme effort to defeat our potential enemies total five field armies, consisting of approximately 215 divisions (infantry, armored, motorized, airborne, mountain and cavalry) with appropriate supporting and service elements. The strategic concept outlined in this paper contemplates distribution of U.S. ground forces approximately as follows (more specific data will be found in Table A):

Iceland	29,000
Scotland	11,000
England	41,000
Ireland	25,000
Hawaii	61,000
Puerto Rico	34,000
Panama	42,000
Alaska	29,000
Philippine Islands	25,000
Smaller Outlying Bases	32,000
Potential Task Forces	
First Army	775,500
Third Army	590,000
Fourth Army	710,000
Brazil	86,000
Colombia-Ecuador-Peru	37,000
Total (approximate):	2,500,000

Strategic Reserves for which production
    capacity must be established but whose
    activation, location, and *training* will be
    determined by developments in the
    international situation: 3,000,000
Troops in the Zone of the Interior and
    Fixed Defense Units (Ground):   1,200,000

    TOTAL GROUND FORCES   6,700,000

Table A

The ground forces estimated as necessary to provide for the security of the U.S. outlying possessions, the Western Hemisphere and to make available appropriate forces for projected military operations follow.

1. Units organized, fully equipped, and trained as soon as practicable:

a. Military Bases and Outlying Possessions.

Newfoundland	5,690
Greenland	2,531
Caribbean Bases	40,199
Puerto Rico	34,757
Panama	42,614
Hawaii	61,337
Philippines	25,397
Alaska	28,823
Iceland	28,709
Bases in British Isles	70,160
Total:	346,217

b. Potential Task Forces

Brazil

1 Army Corps (1 Div. foot, 1 Div. Airborne)	42,392
2 Artillery Battalions Pack	1,804
1 Cavalry Regiment	1,591
5 Parachute Battalions	2,590
1 Anti-aircraft Regiment and 2 Medium Battalions	3,619
2 Aircraft Warning Regiments	2,600
2 Tank Battalions (Light)	1,086
3 Anti-Tank Battalions	2,100
Services	28,864
Total:	86,646

Colombia-Ecuador-Peru

1 Division	15,245
2 Artillery Battalions	1,400
3 Parachute Battalions	1,554
1 Anti-aircraft Regiment and 2 Medium Battalions	3,619
2 Tank Battalions (Light)	1,086
1 Aircraft Warning Regiment	1,300
Services	13,035
Total:	37,239

First Army

1 Army consisting of 3 Corps of 3 Divisions ea.	242,216
2 Armored Corps consisting of 2 Armd Div. ea.	53,556
8 Divisions (4 Mtzd, 2 Mountain, 2 Airborne)	108,516
5 Parachute Bns.	2,590
13 Artillery Bns. (4 heavy, 6 105 mm, 3 75 mm How Pk)	9,906
20 Anti-aircraft Regts and 10 extra Bns. 37 mm	46,970
11 Tank Battalions (3 Medium and 5 Light)	4,839
12 Aircraft Warning Regts	15,600
10 Tank Destroyer Bns. and 10 anti-tank Bns. (Gun)	14,000
Services (Ord., QM, Sig., Engr., Med.)	278,069
Total:	776,262

Third Army

1 Army (3 Corps, 9 Divisions)	242,216
1 Armored Corps (2 Divisions)	26,778
2 Divisions Motorized	32,258
6 Artillery Battalions (Medium and Heavy)	4,300
1 Cavalry Corps and 2 H-Mecz Regiments	26,867
2 Airborne Divisions	20,000
5 Parachute Battalions	2,590
5 Anti-aircraft Regiments and three Medium Bns.	12,166
3 Aircraft Warning Regiments	3,900
15 Tank Destroyers or Anti-Tank Battalions	10,500
Services	207,860
Total:	589,435

Fourth Army

1 Army (3 Corps, 9 Divisions)	242,216
1 Armored Corps (2 Divisions)	25,394
4 Divisions Motorized	64,516
8 Artillery Battalions (Medium or Heavy)	8,800
4 Divisions (2 Mountain, 2 Airborne)	44,000
2 Parachute Battalions	1,036
15 Anti-aircraft Regiments and 10 Medium Bns.	37,345

8 Tank Battalions (Medium or Light)	4,839
6 Aircraft Warning Regiments	7,800
25 Tank Destroyers or Anti-Tank Battalions	17,500
Services	256,413
Total:	709,859
Total Task Forces:	2,199,441

c. The troops considered necessary in the ground forces, i.e., organized, fully equipped, and trained for current and future employment as security forces in military bases and outlying possessions and as striking forces in any theater, follow:

Military Bases and Outlying Possessions	346,217
Potential Task Forces	2,199,441
Total:	2,545,658

2. Production capacity should be created to equip approximately 3 million for the reserve units indicated below. Activation, location, and training of these units will depend upon the international situation.

Strategic Reserves
2 Armies (10 Army Corps, 27 Divisions)
14 Armored Corps (53 Armored Divisions)
51 Divisions Motorized
115 Artillery Battalions (Pack Medium or Heavy)
9 Divisions (2 Cavalry, 6 Mountain, 3 Airborne)
22 Parachute Battalions
129 Anti-aircraft Regiments and 133 Medium Bns.
89 Tank Battalions (70 Medium, 6 Light, 10 Heavy)
29 Aircraft Warning Regiments
290 Tank Destroyer Battalions
262 Anti-Tank Battalions (Gun)

Total (Approximate):	3,000,000
3. Ground Troops required for the Zone of Interior and Fixed Defense Units	1,200,000

4. Recapitulation of Ground Forces

Military Bases and Outlying Possessions	346,217
Potential Task Forces	2,199,441
Zone of Interior and Fixed Defenses	1,200,000
Total:	3,745,658
Units in reserve to be activated when situation requires	3,000,000
Total Army Ground Forces:	6,745,658

5. Air Force requirements (details submitted in a separate study)

Air Force Combat	1,100,000
Zone of Interior Service Units	950,000
Total Air Force:	2,050,000
6. Army Ground Forces	6,745,658
Army Air Forces	2,050,000
Total Army Forces:	8,795,658

3

Building The New American Army

1942

For the U.S. Army, the doldrums of the interwar decades dissipated in the crises of 1940. Explosive growth thereafter became the norm, and the usual ordeals of growth were aggravated by the necessity of understanding and coping with unfolding revolutions in weapons and warfare.

The forces of tradition and change both laid valid claims on the Army, and almost everyone had ideas as to how the balance should be struck. Lieutenant Colonel Wedemeyer of Operations Division (OPD—the wartime successor to War Plans Division) was one of these. Although not himself responsible for detailed force planning, he held well-developed and strong views on the design of the new army. Not surprisingly, preference for tried and true arrangements in such areas as organization, weaponry, and tactical doctrine tended to prevail throughout the service. Believing that the forces of standpat traditionalism were too strong within the War Department in the spring of 1942, Wedemeyer proposed a shift in emphasis.

WAR DEPARTMENT
WAR DEPARTMENT GENERAL STAFF
OPERATIONS DIVISION
Washington

MEMORANDUM FOR GENERAL HANDY [Brigadier General
Thomas T. Handy, Deputy Chief of Operations Division (OPD)]
From: A. C. Wedemeyer
       Lt. Colonel, G.S.C.
Subject: Air-borne Divisions
Date: April 27, 1942

1. In determining appropriate combat forces last summer in connection with the Victory [Plan], I tried to emphasize mobility and destructive power. The importance of the gasoline motor in modern warfare both in the air and on the ground was definitely confirmed in 1939, 1940, and 1941 in Europe. Accordingly, it was obvious that we should exploit our great industrial capacity to produce quickly ample quantities of air equipment (airplanes, gliders, and parachutes) and motorized ground equipment (tanks, armored cars, trucks, tractors, and mobile artillery platforms).

2. I realize that we must retain combat balance in the development of our military forces, however, I do believe that such "balance" should be determined by the experience gained in the military campaigns of the past few years. There are still strong proponents of military forces that comprise as a nucleus the traditional infantry-artillery team with all other means playing a supporting role. The difficulty of overcoming the inertia of Army tradition and of securing recognition of new concepts of technique in battle has been apparent for the past several months when the Arms and Services were required to translate the forces suggested in the Victory [Plan] into actual combat units.

3. It is my conviction that sufficient data are available to justify the following premises for future U.S. military operations.

    a. We must be prepared to fight in order to land on and to hold lodgments in the European and Far East theaters of war. We must train several amphibious divisions so that the difficult operations connected with amphibious warfare will be smoothly and efficiently executed.

    b. We must employ air and armored units *not as supporting means* but in lieu of the old infantry-artillery team. We will have occasion to use infantry divisions, but it is desired to emphasize the necessity for a recognition and acceptance in our preparation for combat, of the definite trend toward the employment of armor and motor in battle. By so doing we avoid the experience of the French in 1940 and we introduce American ingenuity and enterprise into a struggle which so far has been dominated by the Germans.

   c. We must create a "corps elite" of airborne divisions (the Victory [Plan] contemplates ten such divisions), comprising selected men who will give an excellent account of themselves for physical toughness, initiative, and fighting qualities.

4. If the premises in [the above] paragraph are sound, we must place emphasis upon the immediate activation of armored (action is being initiated by OPD in regard to armored and motorized divisions . . .) and air units. There are many officers in the War Department who agree with this statement; however, the lethargic attitude of many others is retarding the realization of our program.

5. It would not be difficult to convert existing infantry foot divisions into armored and airborne divisions; as a matter of fact, it would be highly desirable to do so. On the other hand, it requires considerable time and effort to prepare armored and airborne divisions for effective combat, and I believe that it would be wrong to visualize the last-minute conversion of such units as is often suggested. In connection with the airborne divisions, I recommended to the Office of the Chief of Infantry and certain officers in G-3 of the General Staff last summer that it might be advisable to organize such divisions into three regiments as follows:

1 regiment of 3 battalions parachute troops
1 regiment of 3 battalions glider troops
1 regiment of 3 battalions airborne troops

I visualize this unit as being employed in battle as a spearhead of thrusts that would be followed up vigorously by armored units. The parachute units would be employed to seize and secure suitable areas for the landing of glider troops which would follow and would assist in creating conditions favorable for the landing of the airborne units. In certain situations, the glider troops would be employed first, followed by the parachutists and then the airborne. The men of the airborne divisions would be highly selected for military qualities including strong physique, enthusiasm, bravery, and initiative.

6. Recommend that the proper agencies in the War Department:

1. Prepare a T/O [Table of Organization] for air division.

2. Activate two air divisions as soon as equipment can be made available (to be taken from infantry foot divisions provided for in 1942 troop basis).

3. Activate two more air divisions prior to April 15, 1943.

4. Activate four air divisions prior to December 31, 1943 (contingent upon development of situation as viewed in Spring of 1943).

5. Integrate existing parachute battalions into air divisions. The Victory [Plan] contemplates 48 Parachute Battalions, 11 of which are provided for in 1942 troop basis.

6. Initiate immediate action in order that appropriate equipment will be available and field training undertaken as early as possible.

7. Avoid the faulty concept of all-purpose divisions in the creation of combat forces. Adopt the principle in organization, equipment, and training of providing appropriate means for the tasks that will undoubtedly confront our forces. Recognize the fact that expedients and last-minute conversions of the type infantry division will not provide effective mountain, air, armored, and amphibious units to engage successfully the German army.

4

Strategy in Europe:
The View from Washington

1942

Pearl Harbor had jolted American attention sharply toward the Pacific. The spectacle of rampant Japanese conquest, especially the agonies of Bataan and Corregidor, tended to sharpen that focus. Within the high command in Washington, however, the guiding principle of global strategy remained what it had been: Defeat Hitler first. As agreed with the British at the beginning of 1941—almost a year before the United States entered the war—a posture of strategic defense would be maintained in the Pacific while the Allies gathered strength to challenge the supposedly more formidable and threatening adversary in Europe.

American planners lost no time in elaborating their concept for that offensive in Europe. Wedemeyer assumed a leading role. Transferring his responsibilities for detailed force planning to others, he joined U.S. Army, Navy, Army Air Corps, and Marine officers in a newly established Joint Planning Committee. In this forum as well as in his home office, Operations Division (OPD), he continued to stress his original prescription for victory in Europe: rapid concentration of Allied power in Britain for a massive, early assault of the continent before Hitler could conquer and consolidate the entire Eurasian land mass.

The operational scheme embraced several phases: (1) the buildup of strength in the British Isles (with rigid economies in all other theaters); (2) a progressively intensified campaign of aerial attack and harassment to soften up *Festung Europa;* (3) a large-scale cross-channel invasion of the northwest coast of France in 1943; and (4) a drive eastward across the relatively open terrain of western and northwestern Europe into the industrial heartland of Germany. The Allies would thus force an early decision by challenging whatever forces Hitler could spare from his embattled fronts in Russia and elsewhere.

Observers might see in this plan—with its emphasis on decision by pitched battle—the lingering hold of Clausewitz on the American military mind. (A much misunderstood Clausewitz, it should be noted.) Or, it could be read as a typical manifestation of the American style in war—a style vigorous, impatient, and confident in the ability to organize and deploy overpowering material strength, yet inclined to rashness and untempered by long and varied experience in the uses of power. Whatever the validity of these readings, an unmistakable third element was at work: an increasingly sophisticated sense of strategic purpose.

The following memorandum, drafted by Wedemeyer in the early months of 1942, illustrates this impulse. In summarizing contemporary American thought on European strategy, it represents an early outline version of several later plans, including those for the buildup of strength in Britain (BOLERO), the proposed cross-channel invasion of the continent in 1943 (ROUNDUP), and the invasion as it eventually took place in June of 1944 (OVERLORD).

WAR DEPARTMENT
Washington

MEMORANDUM
Subject: Operations in Western Europe
[Date: c. April 1942]

Western Europe is favored as the theater in which to stage the first major offensive by the United States and Great Britain. By every applicable basis of comparison, it is definitely superior to any other. In point of time required to produce effective results, its selection will save many months. Through France passes our shortest route to the heart of Germany. In no other area can we attain the overwhelming air superiority vital to successful land attack; while here and here only can the bulk of the British air and ground forces be employed. In this area the United States can concentrate and maintain a larger force than it can in any other. A British-American attack through Western Europe provides the only feasible method for employing the bulk of the combat power of the United States, the United Kingdom, and Russia in a concerted effort against a single enemy.

Another, and most significant consideration is the unique opportunity to establish an active sector on this front this summer, through steadily increasing air operations and by raids or forays all along the coasts. This initial phase will be of some help to Russia and of immediate satisfaction to the public; but what is most important, it will make experienced veterans of the air and ground units, and it will offset the tendency toward deterioration in morale which threatens the latter due to prolonged inactivity.

Finally, successful attack through Western Europe will afford the maximum possible support to Russia, whose continued participation in the war is essential to the defeat of Germany.

Decision as to the main effort must be made now. This is true even if the invasion cannot be launched during this year. A major attack must be preceded by a long period of intensive preparation. Basic decision is necessary so that all production, special construction, training, troop movements, and allocations can be coordinated to a single end. Until this process of coordinated and intensified effort is initiated, it is difficult to calculate even the approximate date at which a major offensive can be undertaken. *Decision now will stop continued dispersion of means.*

The element of *time* is of the *utmost importance*. Physical limitations both as to the time and strength of the attack are the shortage of shipping and landing craft. But we must begin a sustained offensive before Russia can be defeated and before Vichy France, Spain, Sweden, Portugal, and Turkey are drawn into the ranks of the enemy.

Our proposal, more fully outlined later, provides for an attack by combined forces of approximately 5,800 combat airplanes and 48 divisions against Western Europe as soon as the necessary means can be accumulated in England—estimated at April 1, 1943, provided decision is made *now* and men, materiel and shipping are conserved for this purpose. (Included preparations for an "emergency" offensive by fall of 1942 will be explained later.)

The plan contemplates three main phases.

> *a.* Preparation, involving: (1) immediate coordination of procurement priorities, allocations of materiel and movements of troops and equipment; (2) establishment of a preliminary active front this coming summer—for training, demonstration, deception and destruction; and (3) development of preparations for possible launching of an "emergency" offensive this coming fall.
>
> *b.* Cross-channel movement and seizure of beachheads between Le Havre and Boulogne.
>
> *c.* Consolidation and expansion of beachheads and beginning of general advance.

A special significance of the preparatory phase is that it presents opportunity for the intensive and specialized training of troops, without which the plan would have meager prospects for success. This special training, beginning with fundamentals of technique in loading and unloading of boats, must advance progressively through logical steps until it comprises constant raiding by small task forces at selected points along the entire accessible coastline held by the enemy.

The beneficial results to be derived from continuous raiding fall into two main categories. On the one hand there will be obtained a variety of useful information, applying to details of geography, hostile dispositions, tactics, and intentions. Some measure of deception as to time and the place of the final attack should result. The continuation of such raids over a long period may lead the enemy to believe that no all-out offensive is to be attempted or, conversely and equally valuable, may induce him to withhold from the Russian front air and ground units because of constant fear that the raids may develop at any moment into a major attack. In this latter event the raiding process would, on a limited scale, serve the same purpose as the opening of a new front on the continent itself.

But by far the greatest benefits to be anticipated from constant raiding will be the resultant increase in the battle efficiency of the participating troops. After troops have completed normal phases of training and maneuver, it is essential that, to avoid deterioration, they begin gradual entry into actual battle, preferably under conditions that, so far as possible, will guarantee the small success that raids seek, while minimizing losses in personnel and materiel. These successes can be assured by careful preparation for each venture, somewhat in the pattern of the trench raid of the first World War. The characteristics of each action will be a sudden concentration of overwhelming air superiority supported by gun fire where practicable, with speed, surprise, and precision in execution. For air forces, technical methods will be different, but the purposes and principles the same. In this way, troops will acquire that morale and self-confidence that only participation in battle can impart. They will perfect technique, methods, and coordination not only as among individuals, but also as among commanders, staffs, and units. Communications between land, air, and sea forces will be developed to a high level of efficiency. Equipment will be tested under combat conditions. Troops will be kept on their toes, mentally alert, and, by these means, gain that feeling of moral ascendency over the opponent that always characterizes a victory-imbued army. Successfully conducted, these raids will permit our troops to enter upon the final venture with an ability to meet, on equal terms, the battle-trained veterans of the German army.

Losses in landing craft, though small in each individual raid, will be considerable in accumulated total. Production plans must foresee and provide for this inescapable requirement and insure that equipment so lost will not be reflected in a diminished scale of attack when the final offensive is undertaken.

An advantage of this plan is that, during the preparatory period, it provides means to act promptly under either of the following eventualities: (a) If the imminence of Russian collapse requires desperate action, a sacrifice attack could be made immediately; and (b) if German forces are almost completely absorbed on the Russian front, or a deterioration of the German military power is evident, a prompt movement to the continent could be undertaken.

Outline Plan for Invasion of Western Europe

Assumptions

    a. That so far as the United States is concerned the line, Alaska–Hawaii–Samoa–Australia, will be held and Pacific garrisons increased from present approximate strength of 175,000 to an approximate strength of 300,000.

b. That present U.S. commitments in troops and ships will be executed. These include dispatch of the 41st and one additional division to Australia, one division to New Zealand, the loan of sufficient shipping to the British to move 40,000 troops to the Middle East, and the building up of a small air force in China-India. Providing the British furnish the necessary planes from aircraft now allotted to them, two groups pursuit, one group medium bombardment, and two groups light bombardment have been promised for the Middle East as the additional U.S. commitment to theaters other than Western Europe. Transfer of these air units will have a corresponding effect in diminishing the early U.S. air effort in Europe.

c. That Russia is still effective in the war to the extent that the bulk of the German forces are required on the Russian front.

d. That Axis forces in Western Europe remain at approximately their present strength.

Combat Strength Required

From an examination of the present hostile situation, it is estimated that combat power and readiness as follows is necessary for a successful attack:

a. Adequate air superiority over the enemy, involving the use by the Allies of a minimum of 3,000 fighters and 2,850 combat planes other than fighters (combined British and U.S.).

b. Sufficient landing craft to land in the first wave the major combat elements of an infantry and armored force of at least six divisions. At the beginning of the actual invasion, U.S. land forces in England or en route should approximate 30 divisions. Total U.S. strength in England at that time will approximate 1,000,000 men.

c. An ability to land on the western coast of Europe behind the leading wave, a weekly increment initially of at least 100,000 troops, and, after the invasion forces have landed, a continuous flow of reinforcements from the United States at the maximum rate that shipping will permit.

d. Sufficient naval support to assure freedom from interference by hostile surface and sub-surface craft.

Execution

The plan provides for the movement to the British Isles of U.S. air and ground forces comprising approximately one million men to participate with the British in an invasion of France between Le Havre and Boulogne. Logistic factors fix the earliest possible date for an attack on this scale at about April 1, 1943. Bottlenecks, as to time, will be shipping and landing craft, which will not be available in sufficient quantity by the time that aircraft, ground equipment, and ammunition can be supplied.

As previously explained, the operation is planned in three phases, with actual combat beginning in the preparatory phase. Immediately after approval of the basic plan, all production and allocation plans must be reviewed and coordinated to this objective to meet obvious shortages, particularly in shipping, landing craft, and aircraft. U.S. air and ground units must begin moving to the United Kingdom by every available ship. Plans for execution of an "emergency" operation are to go forward constantly, based always upon the maximum force that could be transported across the channel at any given moment.

The second and third phases are the cross-channel movement and beginning of the general advance. The invasion itself will consist of the seizure of beachheads between Le Havre and Boulogne. The main landing is to be made on a six division front. Parachute and airborne troops will be employed in addition to combat aviation in assisting the ground forces to establish beachheads and to prevent rapid movement of German reinforcements toward the coast. As soon as a beachhead is established, strong armored forces are to be rushed in to break the German resistance along the coast and to seize the line of the Oise–St. Quentin. A movement towards Antwerp will then follow to widen the salient and permit the movement of additional forces across the channel between Boulogne and Antwerp. Short range aircraft will be based on land fields as quickly as these are captured.

U.S. and British forces as follows should be in Great Britain or en route when the land attack begins:

U.S. Forces

Will be available, as modified by any airplanes sent to Middle East.

1,450 Fighter planes

1,800 Combat planes other than fighters

British Forces

Numbers of British aircraft shown are minimum requirements. Information is not at hand as to how many the British can make available.

1,550 Fighter planes

400 Transport planes

18 Infantry Divisions

6 Armored Divisions

5 Motorized Divisions

1 Air-borne Division

11 Parachute Bns.

30 AA Regts.

1 Parachute Brig.

1,000 Combat planes other than fighters

200 Transport planes

The British must provide at least the following ground troops:

15 Infantry Divisions

3 Armored Divisions

3 AA Gps.

The success of the operation will depend upon the availability of adequate naval forces for its support.

General Comments

An attack in Western Europe will have a protective effect on the remainder of the Atlantic area. The garrisons in the Atlantic should not require material reinforcement. This does not apply to the Pacific, to India, and to the Middle East; consequently our protective measures in those regions must be adequate.

U.S. troops will be equipped and trained in time for the operation.

American shipping available for movement overseas of the U.S. troops will transport only about 40% of the number involved by April 1, 1943, leaving some 600,000 men to be transported by shipping from British or other sources. If this movement must depend entirely on available U.S. shipping, the date of initiating the mission of France must be postponed until late Summer 1943, by which time U.S. shipping can effect this overseas movement of the entire force.

The shipping situation is under continuous study. However, it is believed that when the movement of reinforcements to the Middle and Far East now projected for 1942 has been effected, and the situation in those areas stabilized, sufficient British and U.S. passenger transports can be made available for the movement of U.S. troops to England to meet the requirements of this plan. Additional cargo vessels will have to be diverted after January 1, 1943, to support this operation.

Landing craft necessary for the operation are not available at present in sufficient quantities for the cross-channel movement. Some 7,000 landing craft are essential for the crossing. More should be on hand to cover losses. Only through intensification of the construction program immediately after agreement in principle to this plan has been reached can a sufficient number be obtained.

It is mandatory that we continue to send to Russia sufficient materiel aid to keep that nation actively in the war.

Development and construction of air fields, bases, cantonments, etc., in the British Isles in preparation for invasion of Western Europe in 1943 must be substantially completed in 1942.

Modified Plan

THIS LIMITED OPERATION WOULD BE JUSTIFIED ONLY IN CASE: (1) THE SITUATION ON THE RUSSIAN FRONT BE-COMES DESPERATE, i.e., the success of German arms becomes so complete as to threaten the imminent collapse of Russian resistance un-less the pressure is relieved by an attack from the west by British and American troops. In this case the attack should be considered as a sacri-fice in the common good; (2) THE GERMAN SITUATION IN WEST-ERN EUROPE BECOMES CRITICALLY WEAKENED. Because of the emergency basis on which a modified plan would be undertaken, it is impossible to predict the time for its execution. It is likewise impossible to fix the minimum scale, as to troop numbers, on which the movement might have to be initiated. It must be clear that the maximum forces that can be transported across the channel must be employed and that local air superiority must be assured.

The following represents the scale of possible American participa-tion on the basis of shipping now in sight, for an invasion of France in September–October 1942:

a. U.S. troops that can be made available in England by Sep-tember 15. (Figures include all troops of the Magnet Force.)

Air Forces: 400 Fighters, 300 Combat other than fighters, and 200 Transport.

Ground Forces: 2 1/2 Infantry Divisions and 1 Armored Divi-sion; *or* 1 1/2 Infantry Divisions and 2 Armored Divisions; *or* 1 1/2 Infantry Divisions, 1 Armored Division, 4 Parachute Bns., and 10 Anti-aircraft Regiments.

b. Inclusive of the above, a total of 6 Infantry, 3 Armored, and 2 Motorized Divisions, 4 Parachute Battalions, and 10 Anti-aircraft Regiments will be equipped and trained in the United States in time to participate in this operation. If necessary shipping can be found, all the American ground forces just enumerated can be available for duty in England by early fall.

Since a large amount of troop lift shipping becomes available late in the summer, the buildup of strength would be much more rapid after September.

    c. British troops.

Air Forces. Execution of the "emergency" plan would throw an additional burden upon the British, particularly their air forces, which, with the American help indicated, would have to gain and maintain air superiority over the area involved in the limited-scale attack. The minimum considered desirable, exclusive of U.S. air forces, is 2,600 fighters, 2,400 other combat type, and all available transport aircraft. However, due to the unforeseen circumstances that may demand a limited attack, even smaller air forces may be able to gain and maintain the necessary air superiority.

Ground Forces. Owing to the scarcity of landing craft this fall, large land forces could not participate. Unless production programs are immediately intensified, it appears probable that we cannot plan on sustaining more than about five divisions, half British and half U.S.

5

Strategy in Europe:
Conflicting Allied Perspectives

1942–1943

By early 1942, U.S. views on European strategy had been elaborated and were ready for coordination with the Allies. In April, Presidential Assistant Harry Hopkins, General Marshall, and Lieutenant Colonel Wedemeyer flew to London to present those views to the British military staffs and government. The British fully recognized the importance of a return to the continent—when circumstances permitted—and were wholeheartedly dedicated to speeding that day's approach. Subsequent discussions, however, revealed differences of outlook and intention that, though generally presented as matters of degree, were in fact so divergent as to constitute quite different strategies.

The timing of the invasion proved the central issue. The Americans were anxious to launch the great crusade in the spring or early summer of 1943. The British, on the other hand, were unwilling to settle on so early a date. The merits of these respective positions, and the complexities of motive and insight underlying them, have long been debated.

The strategy so ably promoted by Prime Minister Churchill might fairly be described as one of indirection. In contrast with the American eagerness to get onto the continent as soon as possible—and thus invite pitched battle—Churchill's genius was fixed on what Wedemeyer often called "scatterization" or "periphery pecking." The Prime Minister was brilliantly imaginative in devising tactical coups and maneuvers: He would intensify the blockade; step up air attacks and raiding activity; encourage subversion in German-occupied areas; spread disorder within the Reich; and seize opportunities to strike in Scandinavia, the Mediterranean, the Middle East, or the supposedly soft "underbelly" of Europe, the Balkans. All of this was designed to weaken the enemy (with continuing Soviet help, it was hoped) for the day when the Western Allies could return to the continent at acceptable levels of risk to deliver a coup de grace.

That this strategy made considerable sense, at least in terms of Britain's economic condition, history, and imperial commitments, seems clear. Churchill was painfully aware of Britain's depleted resources, even as he sought to defend and sustain as best he could the far-flung empire. Haunted by memories of carnage on the continent in the Great War (memories doubtless reinforced by the debacle at Dunkirk in 1940), he was understandably reluctant to risk everything on a single massive, and perhaps premature, attempt to storm the continent.

The American outlook, like the British, had deep and various roots. The impulse to direct action doubtless stemmed in part from the cult of the offensive that so strongly animated the U.S. Army. Perhaps it also reflected the vigor and buoyant self-confidence that supposedly characterized the spirit of the New World in general. Strategic calculation certainly played a part. Wedemeyer, as we have noted, had urged speed in Europe to defeat Hitler while the embattled Soviets remained militarily effective; or, if the Red Army should collapse, to challenge the Nazi dictator before he could consolidate and exploit the entirety of Eurasia. Secret reports of German progress on mysterious and potentially decisive weapons (atomic and otherwise) reinforced the case for speed.

Keeping war programs focused on strategic priorities proved a constant challenge. Demand for resources of all kinds inevitably exceeded supply. Every ally clamored for stronger support, every service for higher priority, every campaign for more men and equipment, every program for more money. Most of these demands were plausible, even urgent, and the channels for pressing them were endless and tangled. To the constant concern of those mobilizers and strategists like Wedemeyer who sought a modicum of rationality in the war program, the mechanisms for harmonizing supply and demand were at best erratic.

From the perspective of the U.S. strategic planners, no distractions proved more insistent than those promoted by their British allies. The case for committing resources piecemeal by seizing an opportunity here, or by reinforcing a weak point there—and conversely, the case *against* "single-minded" concentration for a dubious invasion—was urged again and again on many levels and in various contexts. American staffs felt short-circuited in certain key instances when Churchill and other top British spokesmen took issues directly (and successfully) to President Roosevelt.

In the meantime, Wedemeyer continued to press his case for "keeping our eyes on the strategic ball." In the following typical comments on a British staff document dealing with Allied production planning, he warns against indecisive diversions from agreed objectives.

WAR DEPARTMENT
WAR DEPARTMENT GENERAL STAFF
OPERATIONS DIVISION
Washington

MEMORANDUM TO COLONEL KIBLER
[Colonel A. F. Kibler, OPD]
From: ACW
Date: May 6, 1942

I have studied the attached paper and submit herewith some notes including my personal ideas on the subject matter. Also, I am giving you a complete resume covering the proposed U.S. approach to the creation of military forces along with the basic strategic ideas upon which it is based.

Comments

Paragraph 1

[Paragraph 1 of subject document indicated concern with combined Anglo-American production requirements only.]

The production requirements of U.S. and British military forces must be carefully integrated, and the employment of maritime shipping carefully coordinated by *all* of the United Nations in moving and maintaining those forces . . .

Paragraph 6

[Paragraph 6 emphasized that British and American staffs should work on "same strategic hypothesis."]

Although little mention is made of informing the Soviets of our plans, it seems important that the maximum coordination should be sought between the U.S.-British efforts and the Russians. The immediate accepted strategical objective is the retention of Russia as an effective combat component of the United Nations. Our whole strategy is based on this premise, yet no effort is being made to coordinate the British-U.S. offensive with Russian operations.

Paragraph 7

[Paragraph 7 suggested that British Chiefs of Staff had not accepted U.S. plan for operations on continent of Europe in 1943.]

We will never implement our accepted strategy unless we (the U.S. and British) definitely state the objectives we hope to attain in various theaters and also state the means we deem necessary to attain those objectives in the respective theaters. We are only paying lip service to strategical principles if we adopt a plan of operations similar to *Bolero* [buildup for 1943 invasion] and then vitiate that plan by accepting changes in our agreed-upon commitments. We must adopt and adhere to plans that are based on sound strategic considerations, with always uppermost, one objective—the decisive defeat of the enemy. In the past, the British planning appears to have been predicated upon maintaining the integrity of the British *Empire* or, in other words, upon [British] political and economic considerations.

Paragraph 8

[Paragraph 8 asserted impossibility of forming useful production planning hypotheses for 1944 "until issue of German attack on Russia becomes clearer."]

Disagree. We should have definite understanding with the British *now* under various sets of conditions. In paragraph 7 the paper states [that the production planning] hypothesis should be based on agreed strategy of defeating Germany while holding Japan. We must plan now for every contingency, including the early and absolute removal of Russia as an effective fighting power, and an invasion or an effective blockade (air and sea) of the British Isles.

Paragraph 9

[Paragraph 9 suggested that, in the absence of clear strategic guidance, production planning staffs might assume, *inter alia,* "offensive operations against Japan . . . "]

We cannot [now] conduct successful offensive operations against Japan. We do not and will not have for some time adequate or appropriate means. Further, it is perfectly asinine to visualize heavy commitments in the Far East (to conduct offensive operations, our commitments both in military forces and shipping must be large), while preparing for and initiating offensive operations in the opposite side of the world (Europe).

Paragraphs 10–17

These paragraphs propose an approach similar to that recommended in my notes under Paragraph 2. [Paragraph 2 outlined procedure by which production requirements would be computed from strategical requirements expressed in terms of projected "Orders of Battle"—that is, phased lists of planned military forces.] The important considerations of any logical approach, in my opinion, is the determination by the United Nations of the objectives to be attained in various theaters, the means necessary to attain those objectives, the assigning of nations that are to provide and maintain those means, and united resistance to dispersion of means that will militate against the realization of our strategy.

Attached:
(Resume of U.S. Strategy and creation of Forces to implement plans.)
[Omitted]

6

HUSKY:
The Allied Invasion of Sicily

July 1943

U.S. staffs failed in their efforts to promote an all-out cross-channel invasion of Europe in 1943. In effect abandoning that goal, the Western Allies launched a major assault on the Atlantic and Mediterranean coasts of northwest Africa in November 1942. This operation—codenamed TORCH—had been decided upon at top levels during the previous summer. Although the American planners regarded TORCH as a regrettable diversion from BOLERO, President Roosevelt had approved the North African venture as a means of bringing U.S. forces into more timely action against the Germans and of relieving the threat to Suez posed by Rommel's *Afrikakorps*.

With the success of TORCH, the stage was set for further operations in the Mediterranean. At the Casablanca Conference in January 1943, this course again was chosen. Contravening the views of at least some members of his accompanying staff (including Wedemeyer), the president agreed to exploit the momentum gained in TORCH by launching a second major Mediterranean campaign—a thrust across the sea from North Africa into Sicily.

In June 1943—several weeks before the curtain was to rise on this operation—General Marshall decided to send Wedemeyer to the Mediterranean to observe preparations and experience "the actualities of a landing operation."

For Wedemeyer, this opportunity to serve in a combat zone—

if only briefly, and as the eyes and ears of the Chief of Staff—
brought a welcome sense of professional fulfillment. Indeed, an
unexpected turn of events during the early days of the invasion
opened an opportunity for him to command a distressed infantry
regiment *in the line.* He promptly sought permission from the task
force commander, Lieutenant General George S. Patton, Jr., to do
so, offering at the same time to surrender his general's star for a
colonel's eagle. Patton, "always happy to help a fighting man,"
told him to take charge of the regiment as a brigadier. Much of
Wedemeyer's time in the area necessarily was spent, however, at
the higher echelons of command—with Eisenhower in Algiers,
Alexander in La Mersa, Patton at Seventh Army in Mostaganem,
Mark Clark at Fifth Army in Oujda, Omar Bradley at II Corps,
and Division Commanders Terry Allen (1st Division), Lucian K.
Truscott (3rd Division), and Troy Middleton (45th Division) in
their respective areas.

Before the convoys sailed from North Africa for Sicily, Wedemeyer dispatched a long personal letter to his immediate superior
in OPD, Major General Thomas T. Handy. His letter reflected
some of his thoughts and anxieties on the eve of the invasion, as
well as his concerns for the future course of the war. It is followed
by sections of the longer official report Wedemeyer made to the
Chief of Staff on his return to Washington.

July 4, 1943

[Major General Thomas T. Handy
Operations Division
War Department General Staff]

Dear General:

The trip from the States to Africa was uneventful. I was impressed with the efficiency of the Air Transport Command in handling a tough job . . . General Styer [Major General Wilhelm D. Styer, Chief of Staff, Army Service Forces] joined at Prestwick and accompanied me to Casablanca where he remained to inspect ASF facilities. During my brief stopover there I saw John Ratay [Brigadier General John P. Ratay, U.S. Army Commander in Casablanca area]. He looked fit—his bosom gaily bedecked with rows of ribbons, mustachio neatly clipped, immaculate uniform, black eyes gleaming from under beetle brows. John intrigues me. He is one of the most unusual characters in our Army. No one questions his courage. Everyone admits that he is damn intelligent. Occasionally his judgment is faulty but he is thought-provoking and very sincere. I'll wager that he could be ruthless in dealing out his form of justice sprinkled with oriental cunning. One hears nothing but praise relative to the discipline and order that he has accomplished in the Casablanca set-up . . .

I observed amphibious [training] operations, from Tunis to Oran, involving all of the U.S. units that will participate in HUSKY . . . Force 343 [The I Armored Corps (Reinforced), which became Seventh U.S. Army on D-Day] approaches HUSKY fairly well trained—excellent morale—with mediocre to superior leadership; and unless the enemy has a joker in the pack that has not been foreseen, the goal should be won. However, we will unquestionably have a difficult time, especially during the landing phase. My two-gun mentor, George Patton [Major General George S. Patton, Jr., Commander Force 343], who is really the most contradictory character I have ever known, plans to join the melee early, so that I shall have the enviable opportunity of observing why "the lions tremble when Georgie appears,"* as well as carrying on the more serious duty of noting what our boys do *right* as well as *wrong* in a critical phase of combat. General Patton and his staff, in fact all the senior officers at Force 343 with whom I have been associated, have impressed me with their earnestness, enthusiasm for the job, and ability

---

*[The Sultan of Morocco struck a medal for Patton after the latter's victories in North Africa. The citation thereon read: "Les lions dans leurs tanieres tremblent en le voyant approcher" (The lions tremble in their dens at the sight of his approach).]

to get things done. The staffs that I have observed vary in their solutions to the problems presented. This is attributable as much to the personal equation of the top man as anything else. Troy Middleton, good old Troy [Major General Troy H. Middleton, Commander 45th Division], accomplishes as much as Georgie Patton but with far less fanfare. Omar [Lieutenant General Omar N. Bradley, Commander II Corps] calmly resolves his problems, seemingly effortlessly, while Terry Allen [Major General Terry de la Mesa Allen, Commander 1st Division] has ants in his pants. They all get their jobs done, however, and have a fine spirit of cooperation and determination which should contribute much to the success of the overall operation.

Herewith a few ideas, some so obvious that you probably assumed that they were being executed. In preparing for a specific operation involving air, ground, and sea forces, from the inception of the plan it is necessary that responsible representatives of the commander of each of these forces be physically associated together on the Force Commander's planning staff to work out all details and to insure absolute coordination. In the planning for HUSKY this was not the case in Force 343; at least it was only with varying degrees of difficulty that Patton's staff members could so contact authorized representatives of the Air and Naval Commanders to plan the multitudinous details incident to their role in HUSKY . . . The Force Commander should have complete control and responsibility for the training, concentration, movement, discipline, morale, and employment of all the forces in his command. All units within each combat team or combat command should be brought together well in advance of the operation. The medicos, airmen, navy, ordnance men, doughboys, chemical, artillerymen, communications people, will then become acquainted, win each other's respect, facilitate teamplay, cooperation, and coordination—all of which are so very essential to success. There is no excuse for confusion, lack of sympathetic understanding, and failure to cooperate . . .

Shortly after my arrival Patton asked me to analyze the entire operational plan for HUSKY. It was a most interesting assignment. I submitted two criticisms, one the lack of direct air support, and the other, the absence of a tangible or realistic diversion. It seemed incredible to me that the plan did not provide for direct air support of ground units, at least during the critical phase of the operation when landings were taking place, and again when the enemy began to rearrange his forces for countermeasures after he determined where the center of gravity of our attack was located. Airmen like Tedder [Air Chief Marshal Sir Arthur Tedder], Coningham [Air Vice Marshal Sir Arthur Coningham], and Spaatz [Lieutenant General Carl Spaatz] . . . all stated categorically that the *primary* mission of the air forces was to neutralize enemy air and, if and when that is completely accomplished, then units will be committed to direct support missions.

I accept the importance of operations against the enemy air, but let me assume that they *do* accomplish exactly that and eliminate air from both sides altogether. Our operation, a most difficult one at best, then resolves itself into one with fewer attacking troops attacking numerically stronger defenders, who have the support of carefully prepared defensive fortifications. It didn't make sense to me, and I recommended to Patton that he ask for definite assurance of direct air support at the time of the assault on the beaches, and again when the enemy began to shift his reserves to launch counterblows against our lodgments. Jeff Keyes [Major General Geoffrey Keyes, Deputy Commander, Force 343] stated he had previously asked for direct air support from Force 141 Headquarters [Headquarters, 15 Army Group, under General Sir Harold R.L.G. Alexander] but had received no satisfaction. Patton suggested that I write a memo to CG Force 141 covering the subject. Patton signed this memorandum and it went forward. A few days later a final conference of all commanders—air, ground, and sea—was held in Algiers. I saw Ralph Huebner [Major General Clarence R. Huebner] and Art Nevins [Colonel Arthur Nevins of Eisenhower's staff] there and I was glad to hear them both say that Alexander was concerned about the attitude of the Air Forces with reference to *direct support* in the operations. During the course of the conference it became apparent that the British surface officers, ground and sea, were very definitely not pleased with the air plan. The following day General Alexander directed the Air Force to take appropriate and positive steps to provide direct support as above described.

I relate all this because it is indicative, in my opinion (and I hope that I am wrong), of milkweed acquiescence on the part of our senior air people here to RAF concepts which in the past have caused bitter recriminations, not to mention rotten air-ground cooperation. Also, it emphasizes my earlier point that air representatives who can speak for the air commander must be with the Force Commander's Planning Staff constantly, working out the details of integration with ground and sea officers. Here we were, with 10 days off, a HUSKY job confronting us and no definite assurance of—or what is even more to the point—no carefully coordinated plans for *direct air support*. This all reminds me of Mark Twain when he so tritely stated in effect—"I am an old, old man and have had many troubles, but most of them never happened." I pray that Twain's humorous attitude will have ample justification after HUSKY.

I have covered hastily my thoughts about direct air support in HUSKY. Concerning the other criticism of the overall plan, namely, absence of a diversion or feint, nothing probably could be done about it even if the powers that be accepted the importance of same. Patton didn't seem particularly interested, and it may not be important. However, supplemented by the Navy's proposed sonic warfare, I believe that the overall operation would be greatly strengthened by a tangible diversionary effort. HUSKY has always impressed me as a difficult task—one requiring the greatest care in preparation and execution, lest we come a cropper. The original HUSKY plan was inherently a sounder operation than the present one. We may now be required to supply our forces over the beaches for a period of from 30 to 45 days. I share everyone's enthusiasm for the "duck" [a 2 1/2 ton amphibious truck] but the tonnage for a force as large as ours is formidable and places a great responsibility upon those responsible for supply—the duck notwithstanding. We are justified in taking bold chances tactically but we must be secure logistically.

Our G-2 people (War Department) predicted that the Germans would conduct an all-out offensive against the Russians this year. This seemed logical, for, unless the Axis is able to eliminate the Slav colossus on the east, decisive victory will never be possible for Herr Hitler. However, I was informed before I left the United States that the drying season throughout Russia had come unusually early this year, and I therefore expected an earlier offensive by the Germans. If I recall correctly, they initiated their drives on June 22 in 1941 and June 28 in 1942. Here we have July, and no indication of an offensive. Anything can happen in war, and I hesitate to predict too freely but, now that we have no evidence of German offensive action in Russia, we should carefully consider Axis capabilities in the Iberian Peninsula, the Levant, the Balkans, and the central Mediterranean—assuming in each instance strategic-defensive operations on the Russian front.

I believe that we can reasonably expect a bolstering of the Italian position by German units in the central Mediterranean. I have never accepted the British optimism about the imminent collapse of Italy. There has not been, to my knowledge, any real evidence of such collapse. Germany has better sources of information in Italy concerning conditions, political and military, than do we or our cousins. I believe that Germany can reinforce Italy without strongly militating against planned operations elsewhere. Also, I have never retreated entirely from the position that Germany might attempt a drive down through the Iberian Peninsula to cut our lines of communications, once we have irretrievably committed strong forces in the central Mediterranean. The propitious time for such a move by Germany was last April—to relieve the pressure against von Arnim's forces. But the decision to abandon the African effort had probably been made by the Wehrmacht High Command due to logistical difficulties in maintaining forces in Africa. But again, the danger is present. While not unduly alarmed, I believe that we must anticipate either of the following German moves, particularly if the Russian front remains quiescent: (1) Strong reinforcement of Axis positions in the central Mediterranean; or (2) operations in the Iberian Peninsula with a view to severing the Allied lifeline to the central Mediterranean.

We must ask ourselves what we would do under either contingency. Even though HUSKY is successful after a bitter struggle, we never could drive rampant up the boot, as the P.M. [Prime Minister] so dramatically depicts in his concept of our continued effort over here. However, if we do decide to continue operations directly against Italy, greatly increased resources [over] those now envisaged or available in the area would be mandatory—to insure our position in the western Mediterranean and concurrently to provide sufficient punch in our blow against Italy proper. ROUNDHAMMER [plan for a modified cross-channel operation] would be even more remote, in fact, may be crossed off the books for 1944. If we could only convince our cousins that this European theater struggle will never be won by dispersing our forces around the perimeter of the Axis citadel! I lay in bed the past several nights trying to evolve an overall concept of winning the war in Europe—one that would stir the imagination and win the support of the P.M., if not that of his recalcitrant planners and chiefs of staff. There are three general approaches to the problem, and of course there would be various combinations and permutations of those.

To clarify the atmosphere I would ask my cousins to accept the following, which to me is reasonable:

The United Nations cannot win a decisive victory in Europe if either or both of the following conditions occur:

(1) Germany evolves a means of successfully defending against or neutralizing the effect of the United Nations air offensive;
(2) Russia is weakened militarily to a degree that permits Germany to employ effectively approximately half of her total military resources in other theaters.

Under the above conditions, the United Nations would of necessity be compelled to assume an opportunist role, resort to encircling and blockade operations, and establish forces in selected areas prepared to penetrate the Axis citadel when internal disruption occurs, as it inevitably would in such a cauldron of conflicting views fanned by hatreds, deprivations, and sufferings. But no one could estimate how many years might pass before the opportunity could be created to penetrate the enemy stronghold. The serious implications, political and military, in the United States and United Kingdom of a long drawn-out struggle are well known. Certainly the P.M. emphasized his concern no later than at Algiers with our Chief.

My hopes all along have been that Germany would continue to bend every effort to crush Russia militarily, and in so doing would involve the bulk of her military resources on that front. As for Russia, I have confidence that she could deal with the situation, yielding only to prevent catastrophe but always presenting the potential threat of a strong counterblow. While this situation maintained on the Eastern front, I hoped that we could get on to the continent, obtain control of France and establish airdromes in dispersed selected areas so that our bombers could more effectively reach vital installations of the Axis. France would be a mess of airdromes. We would have ports and shorter lines of communications, a friendly populace, and the threat of invasion from the West would present a spectre to the German High Command that could not be denied. But no, we supinely follow the P.M. in peripheral pecking—so-called underbelly operations which will make available a few limited areas from which we can a little more effectively bomb Germany. I wonder how the P.M. plans to win the war if, as I now suspect, the Germans have decided to conduct strategic-defensive operations on the Eastern front. It is true, by so doing the Germans accept the fact that they cannot win a decisive victory, but they can make a damn strong bid for a stalemate, which certainly would not be a victory for us.

I have heard unconfirmed rumors that the British plan some operations in the eastern Mediterranean post-HUSKY, possibly against Rhodes and Scarpanto. This may be a cover plan for post-HUSKY operations; however, the timing does not indicate that they are seeking cover. It seems to me that the United States should suggest to the British that a Mediterranean theater now be formed to include all areas contiguous to the Mare Nostrum under one theater commander, Eisenhower. Tedder already commands all of the air in that area, and Cunningham all of the naval forces. Alexander could be given the ground forces with Eisenhower over all three. It is a logical arrangement and will facilitate coordination of all United Nations' resources in the area. Also, it would preclude independent British expeditions similar to Djibouti, Madagascar, and the above mentioned projected operations, all of which appear trivial and innocuous at the start, but which might easily develop into serious large-scale affairs requiring strong reinforcements to insure success. It might so happen, too, that the reinforcements which are sent could be employed elsewhere more profitably in the overall effort—for example, in ROUNDHAMMER. Anyway, I believe that the CC/S [Combined Chiefs of Staff] should pass judgment on the operations if there is any possibility of involving considerable resources . . .

Tomorrow, July 5th, we board the ship here in the harbor, and the next day we move out for HUSKYLAND. Patton states that we will debark early, but he's not yet decided with which wave. He is certainly a splendid division commander. Our best bets over here are Bradley, Middleton, and Truscott . . .

Sincerely,

A. C. WEDEMEYER
Brigadier General, G.S.C.

STRATEGY AND POLICY GROUP
OPERATIONS DIVISION, WDGS
Washington, D.C.

MEMORANDUM FOR THE CHIEF OF STAFF
From: A. C. Wedemeyer
       Brigadier General, G.S.C.
Subject: Observer's report
Date: August 24, 1943

Pursuant to instructions, the undersigned officially observed the preparation for and the execution of the operation HUSKY and visited the American and British Planning Staffs in London. An abbreviated report of the observations made on this trip is submitted in the form of concise recommendations. Data and a narrative supporting these recommendations can be found in appendices to this report.

Recommendations based upon observations during the final preparations for HUSKY and during the first sixteen days of the actual operation. (Period covered: June 14 to July 25, 1943):

Administration

The administrative red tape of peacetime should be reduced to a minimum for any operation. Army commanders should be given more latitude in making decisions under combat conditions, even though such decisions may not conform to existing regulations.

Air-Ground Liaison

Air Support for Ground Elements. Task Force Commanders should be furnished with Air Control Parties to provide direct operational control of supporting air units. The commander of Force 343 should have had available at least two groups of fighter bombers (A-36) to provide direct air support as the situation developed, and at least one or two squadrons of P-51's for reconnaissance missions. In the HUSKY operation, it required three hours to get approval of a request for air support, twenty minutes for the air people to get underway, and one hour for them to reach the target. Even after airdromes on Sicily were available and operating it required three hours to get results, provided requests for such support were approved. The Commanding General, 3rd Division, asked for reconnaissance missions on four successive days without obtaining same . . .

Identification of Aircraft. More positive identification of aircraft must be insisted upon. The crews of LST's and LCT's shot indiscriminately at planes, friendly and otherwise. Friendly planes were fired upon by our forces as they passed near Malta by crews of friendly naval vessels and by friendly ground units.

Identification of Ground Units. It is equally vital that all friendly air units be kept constantly informed of the developing situation. P-38's on two definite occasions seriously blasted a combat command in the 3rd Division sector, even though the latter displayed yellow smoke, which was the pre-arranged signal to indicate friendly troops.

Employment of Airborne Units. The employment of airborne units must be meticulously planned. The enemy obtained information in some manner (probably through radar) of the approach of our transport planes, and very cleverly interspersed bombing attacks with the arrival of our transports bearing parachutists. This resulted in the shooting down of many of our own planes . . .

Countersigns

The dissemination of the proper countersign must be positive. For the HUSKY operation, a countersign was announced to all forces and it is believed that everyone was familiar with the signal. On D + 1, however, divisions and other units adopted countersigns of their own, and when our parachute troops landed in the area, they were not familiar with the countersign. This resulted in confusion and many of our parachutists were killed.

Discipline

General.   In the immediate vicinity of the Fifth and Seventh Army Headquarters, where the commanders and their staffs could exercise direct influence, the discipline was splendid. Elsewhere, the discipline of the officers and men observed was extremely poor. Their appearance was unkempt, slovenly, and sloppy, and salutes, if given at all, were seldom returned. I believe the responsibility for this rests entirely with the officers and particularly with the company and battalion commanders. A drive to correct this condition should be made throughout the armed forces.

Combat Discipline.   Combat discipline on the beaches was noticeably lacking. Men were hastily digging in when they should have been pushing forward; others who were lost from their units failed to organize themselves under the senior present and push forward; in a number of instances, vehicles were bunched together, thereby forming an excellent target for enemy air and artillery . . .

Landing Beaches

Control of Activities.   Decisions must be made promptly relative to the unloading of personnel and supplies at the selected beaches and for the evacuation inland of both. Great confusion resulted at the landing beach of the 1st Division because the Navy officer in charge did not know what to do and the Army officer in control of troops could not be located. There should be a Beach Master for each beach, clearly identifiable and provided with a loudspeaker. He should be a person with sufficient rank to [command] respect and with a considerable amount of training for his task. He must be a tyrant and a task master who definitely understands how to keep personnel and supplies flowing at the beaches under very difficult conditions . . .

Military Police Company.   A military police company must be included in the invasion force for early debarkation. This company can quickly take over the responsibility for prisoners and direct traffic. Combat units should not be required to handle such matters when they have their hands full fighting.

Naval Problems

General.   The Navy participation in the HUSKY operation was highly commendable. Unusual weather conditions during the movement of ships to HUSKYLAND added to the difficulties and called for a high degree of seamanship. Naval gun fire support was superb.

Command Ships.   The command ship *Monrovia* was very poorly arranged for such a purpose. At least two command ships similar to Admiral Mountbatten's should have been available in the Force 343 convoy.

Landing the 3rd Division.   Admiral Conolly cooperated in a splendid manner with General Truscott in landing the forces of the 3rd Division in the JOSS area at the times and places planned, and also in providing continued support, both fire and logistic. The fact that all of the 3rd Division forces landed on the assigned beaches indicated the high state of training of his coxswains.

Training of Coxswains.   However, the coxswains in other instances were improperly trained. One regimental commander in the 45th Division was landed six miles from his proper beach and his heavy weapons were also deposited on the wrong beach, even after daylight, requiring three days for him to recover them . . .

Personnel

Officers in General.   In many cases officers appeared to have sufficient physical courage but to lack basic knowledge of their tasks. Physical courage alone is not sufficient. They must know what to do, how to give orders, and how to insure that these orders are followed under the most trying circumstances . . .

Planning

Lack of Joint Planning. A noticeable lack of joint planning existed among the Army and Navy and Air Force headquarters participating in HUSKY. We must insist on joint and full collaboration among participating services from the inception of planning.

Deficiencies in Planning. Plans for HUSKY were deficient in: (1) Provision for direct air support, and (2) A tangible and realistic diversion.

Psychological Warfare

Psychological warfare pamphlets had considerable effect, causing people to yield and influencing soldiers to surrender. It is believed that psychological warfare agents should have been put into Sicily at an earlier date to reduce further the resistance of the enemy . . .

Tactics

Own Tactics. Our fronts were entirely too wide in the HUSKY operation. If strong resistance had been met, a catastrophe might have resulted.

Reserves must be provided. Divisions and corps operated the first several days without reserves.

Commanders should be employed in front areas. Brigadier generals commanding both infantry and artillery units of a division should be farther toward the front. Once combat is joined, they can best assist the division commander by making frequent visits to the front so that they can make appropriate recommendations relative to the employment of supporting weapons and continued operations.

Enemy Tactics. There were approximately ten divisions on the island when we attacked, the equivalent of five being disposed around the coast defenses, and five held mobile. Two of these latter five were German. As we pushed forward, their tactics seemed to be those of effecting maximum delay and inflicting losses. A battery of artillery supported by machine guns and mortars would cover our approach.

Occasionally tanks would make counterattacks to cover the withdrawal of their forces, firing until outflanked and then withdrawing. The Germans resisted quite stubbornly whereas the Italians were quick to surrender. The Germans would generally launch a counterattack in the late afternoon and then withdraw during darkness.

Training

Physical Conditioning. Troops in this operation appeared to be road-bound. Improved discipline in mobility and the ability to advance without trucks must be stressed.

Development of Aggressive Spirit. The defensive spirit is all too prevalent in our armed services. Soldiers dig in at the slightest provocation. During rest periods they lay aside their helmets and equipment. Combat training on maneuvers must be more realistic. Our men must be trained offensively, and to drive aggressively forward through hostile fire to reach the objective. They must be made tough. The killer instinct must be developed.

Development of a Sense of Responsibility. A lack of individual responsibility was evident among young commissioned and noncommissioned officers. They must be taught to get their men off the beaches and to push forward to the objective. Small detachments became lost when cut off from their main body and failed to act as an aggressive group. They must be taught that when lost they should remain as a nucleus to fight vigorously with whatever men they have, rather than to grope about seeking replacements . . .

The actual HUSKY operation was accomplished in a most creditable manner, all of which might render the above constructive criticisms rather inappropriate. In spite of this, and without depreciating the valor and splendid efforts of all the men participating, I believe that the points noted above are important and would further improve our combat effectiveness, thus reducing casualties and insuring military success and honor for our armies . . .

.   .   .   .   .

Observations made as a result of a short visit with the American and British Staff Planners in London are covered in Appendix A.

Comments on Commanders with whom I came in contact are contained in Appendix B.

Appendix A
Observations on British–American Staff Planning
(Period July 26–29, 1943)

Subsequent to my tour of observation in the North African Theater I visited London for the purpose of obtaining, on an informal basis, the views of the British Staff Planners regarding future operations.

I arrived in London on July 26 and met with the British planners at noon, that date. We had a very comprehensive and friendly discussion concerning the turn of events in the Mediterranean and possible subjects which might appear on the agenda for QUADRANT [Quebec Conference, August 1943]. I also paid my respects to the C.I.G.S. [Chief of the Imperial General Staff, Field Marshal] Sir Alan Brooke, and to the Chief of the Air Staff, [Air Chief Marshal] Sir Charles Portal, and to [General] Sir Hastings L. Ismay [Chief of Staff to the Prime Minister].

The overall information that was obtained as a result of talking to these British officers and to General Devers [Lieutenant General Jacob L. Devers, Commander, European Theater of Operations, U.S. Army (ETOUSA)], General Morgan [Lieutenant General Frederick E. Morgan, Chief of Staff to the Supreme Allied Commander (COSSAC)], General Barker [Major General Ray Barker, Deputy Chief of Staff to COSSAC], General Edwards [Major General Idwall H. Edwards, Chief of Staff, ETOUSA], and others in London resulted in the following notes:

A. ANAKIM [Plan to retake Burma and open the line of communications to China through the port of Rangoon]

The British are not going to undertake the operations visualized in ANAKIM. They feel that the operation CULVERIN [plan to seize northern Sumatra] is more realistic. They take issue with the U.S. estimate of China's capabilities, feeling that we are overly optimistic about the contribution that China will make either in effective combat forces or materiel. By implication, but unmistakably, I learned that the British do not want Chinese forces operating in Burma.

Wavell [Commander-in-Chief, India], who has been designated to succeed Linlithgow as viceroy, will not report to that post prior to October. All British officials acquainted with the Burma picture have been assembled in London to discuss operations in that area, and there is unanimity of opinion among them that the operation which we term ANAKIM cannot be done.

General Auchinleck [successor to Wavell as Commander-in-Chief, India] has already stated that he cannot hope to move his forces more than a few miles farther into Burma due to logistic difficulties. Most confidentially, the British Directors of Plans told me that they suggested that he, Auchinleck, be ordered to push forward as far as possible. However, Auchinleck has refused and stated categorically that he will assign only limited objectives to his forces. When the Prime Minister was informed about Auchinleck's reaction, he, the Prime Minister, blew up, stating that he had always wanted someone named Leigh (or Lee) for C-in-C in India, and a man named Wingate for Supreme Commander. (Wingate was the commander of the approximately 5,000 commandos who made an independent large-scale raid on central Burma early last spring.) I am told by my British friends in London that Wingate is well equipped to conduct large-scale raids, but is not potential material for a Supreme Commander. The British all incline to operations involving the Singapore area and would avoid entirely the Burma region.

B. Overlord

I am convinced that General Morgan is a most fortunate choice for his position. I am also convinced that General Devers was a happy selection. He is rapidly winning the respect and confidence of the British, and all of the Americans are uniformly pleased with the manner in which they receive decisions and sound directions. I believe that General Barker is a splendid choice as deputy to the Chief of Staff. Excellent relations exist between him and General Morgan and this in turn is reflected down through the lower echelons of the OVERLORD staff.

It is highly important that the Combined Chiefs of Staff consider the command echelons for OVERLORD. There is a tremendous amount of work to be accomplished, and a short time remaining in which to accomplish it, if the OVERLORD operation is actually to be executed. The Supreme Commander must be designated, and he of course must have his staff. In connection with the appointment of a Supreme Commander, I was informed on all sides that General Marshall would be perhaps the only American acceptable to the British and that they would receive his selection enthusiastically. I was told that General Alexander is being considered, also General Montgomery, as well as General Brooke. If I were asked to recommend a British Supreme Commander, I would nominate Sir Charles Portal. However, in that the United States will have a preponderance of forces, both surface and air, as the OVER-LORD operation unfolds, it is my conviction that an American should be designated Supreme Commander. Also, immediate consideration must be given to the designation of Army Group Commanders, Army Commanders, and Corps Commanders, all with appropriate staffs.

Concerning the OVERLORD operation, the Prime Minister is seeking every honorable avenue by which to escape British commitment to such an operation. Some of the British planners are enthusiastically supporting OVERLORD; others are paying lip service to that concept but are advocating continuing operations in the Mediterranean; and there are others who would welcome operations in the Balkans. The Prime Minister has recalled the Norway operation for examination, and I would not be surprised if such an operation were not strongly presented by the British at QUADRANT. The British planners are now examining the OVERLORD plan which was recently completed by Morgan's staff. The recent diversion of the convoy to Eisenhower's theater, thus reducing troop movements to the U.K., has been seized upon by the opponents of OVERLORD as an excuse for a complete re-examination of that operation . . .

D. TIDALWAVE [Raid on Ploesti oil refineries]

Members of the British Air Force do not favor the execution of TIDALWAVE. They prefer that the bombers involved in that operation be employed to bomb Italy and southern Germany from the Mediterranean. They believe that the aircraft factories in the vicinity of Vienna present a much more renumerative target. They state that the TIDALWAVE operation would result in about 80 percent loss of materiel involved, while accomplishing only 20 percent destruction of the target.

E. The War Against Japan

The American planners who recently returned from London, after presenting U.S. views of the war against Japan, made a very favorable impression in London. The British, however, are not in full accord with the American approach to this problem. As mentioned earlier, they do not accept the Chinese assistance visualized in the American view as realistic. They oppose an island-by-island maneuver and advocate the most direct penetration of the enemy stronghold. The whole matter is in discussion stages, and the British have sent a team of planners to continue the deliberations on the subject here in Washington . . .

Appendix B
(for General Marshall's Eyes Only)
Commanders and Others Contacted

The remarks that follow are an expression of my personal reaction to the character, personality and personal attributes of the various combat commanders with whom I came in contact during the preparation for and execution of HUSKY.

General Eisenhower [Lieutenant General Dwight D. Eisenhower, Supreme Commander of Allied Forces in the Mediterranean]. Is enjoying excellent health, following strict regime. He is greatly improved since Casablanca, both spiritually and physically. Eisenhower is respected—in fact loved by rank and file, both American and British. Occasionally one hears the remark that he favors the British, and on certain occasions he probably does, only because he is leaning over backwards to insure that as an American he is fair to the British. He has an excellent grasp of the situation— evaluates personalities, British and American, with keen appreciation of their capabilities. He is absolutely loyal and is not becoming spoiled by attention he receives as C-in-C. His ambition expressed simply, with absolute sincerity, is to serve you loyally and efficiently.

General Smith [Major General Walter Bedell Smith, Chief of Staff to Eisenhower]. Complements Eisenhower. Loyal and efficient in his duties as Chief of Staff in AFHQ. He understands the British better than any American officer whom I know—handles them effectively in that he knows "how" and "when" to say emphatically *no* to them and still retain their respect and admiration. He will always be most useful in operations or under circumstances requiring dealings with the British for they like him both in London and Africa.

General Patton [Major General George S. Patton, Jr., Commander, Force 343]. A born leader. Tremendous capacity for work. Inspires confidence in those with whom he comes in contact. Greatest weakness is his occasional over-indulgence in histrionics. Intensely loyal to you and to *his subordinates.* Latter sometimes results in embarrassing situations, for he supports men who are not always worthy. As Patton now occupies position which focuses public attention, I believe he should be more decorous—particularly with regard to his language which is too frequently obscene and disgusting. If I knew him better, I would have suggested this—almost did, but decided I would be presuming on a brief friendship, whereas there are officers who have known him for years who might very well suggest that he temper his language. Patton will not fail his country and his apparent "strutting" unfortunately conceals a fine character—sympathetic, kind and lovable.

General Keyes [Major General Geoffrey Keyes, Deputy Commander, Force 343]. The opposite type from Patton—very abstemious, quiet, unassuming. Complements Patton. Strives to serve his chief loyally and efficiently. He has a great deal of ability—good tactical sense, analyzes situations and personalities unemotionally and soundly, thus helping Patton materially.

General Middleton [Major General Troy H. Middleton, Commander, 45th Division]. Excellent commander who inspires confidence. Has plenty of force supported by sound tactical judgment. His division provides ample evidence of his ability to train and lead men.

General Truscott [Major General Lucian K. Truscott, Jr., Commander, 3rd Division]. He has trained the 3rd Division perhaps to the most effective degree of any U.S. division in the Mediterranean. Truscott is a "doer"—is intolerant of weak and vacillating people. He knows what he wants and goes after it, overcoming what might appear to a less aggressive officer as insuperable. He believes that we must emphasize more strongly the conditioning of our men for combat, both mentally and physically. He advocates more marching in our training—even of motorized units.

General Allen [Major General Terry de la Mesa Allen, Commander, 1st Division]. He impressed me as the most colorful and courageous leader of the U.S. contingent. He is not unintelligent, but gives that impression on occasion because he is disinterested in details of planning. If provided with an effective assistant division commander and staff, Allen would, in my opinion, emerge as one of our most successful commanders. He has those attributes of a real leader—most important when the situation appears critical and requires calm, deliberate action.

General Roosevelt [Brigadier General Theodore Roosevelt, Assistant Commander, 1st Division]. A man of great physical courage . . . Of very limited ability in handling men in combat. Apparently lacking in basic military training and knowledge.

General Barker [Major General Ray Barker]. A splendid choice as deputy to the Chief of Staff for COSSAC.

General Clark [Lieutenant General Mark W. Clark, Commander, Fifth U.S. Army]. He possesses many fine ideas about training. He is self-seeking and ambitious. . . .

Admiral Conolly [Rear Admiral Richard L. Conolly, Commander, Naval Task Force 86]. Achieved a method of cooperation with General Truscott which is highly commendable.

General Devers [Lieutenant General Jacob L. Devers, Commander, European Theater of Operations, U.S. Army]. A most happy selection as CG, ETO. Perhaps a better field man than a negotiator.

General Gruenther [Major General Alfred M. Gruenther, Chief of Staff to Clark]. Highly efficient; possesses an incisive mind, well trained, quickly penetrates to the root of problems and logically evolves a fine solution.

7

The War on the Other Side of the World: Southeast Asia

1943–1944

The Pacific War had begun in 1941 as a long series of Allied disasters. As the tide of Japanese conquest swept over Asia and the Western Pacific, the Allies' hastily contrived defenses collapsed, and remnants of their sea, air, and ground forces straggled westward toward India or eastward toward Australia and Hawaii.

By mid-1942 the Japanese advance had reached its limit. The Allies had regained their balance and reorganized their positions. Admiral Chester A. Nimitz had assumed command in the Central Pacific, General Douglas MacArthur in the Southwest Pacific, General Sir Archibald P. Wavell in India and Southeast Asia, and Generalissimo Chiang Kai-shek in China.

In global perspective, the Western Allies viewed the entire Pacific effort as a strategic defensive or holding operation. The major commanders were nonetheless expected to employ their resources to utmost effect: to deny the enemy opportunities for undisputed further advance, to weaken him as much as possible, and to lay the foundations for an eventual turn of the tide.

An American command under Lieutenant General Joseph W. Stilwell had been established early in 1942 to conduct various U.S. military activities in China, Burma, and India. To achieve more effective coordination among the numerous Allied commands in these areas, Roosevelt and Churchill, meeting in Quebec in August 1943, decided to establish a new inter-Allied Southeast Asia Command (SEAC) with headquarters in New Delhi. Admiral Lord Louis Mountbatten was designated Supreme Allied Commander. Stilwell, the senior American military figure in the area, was given the additional title of Deputy Supreme Allied Commander.

Wedemeyer was promoted in October to the rank of Major General and designated Deputy Chief of Staff for Plans in the new organization. He was not especially pleased with this development, for he would have preferred service with a combat command—an armored or airborne division, perhaps—as General Marshall occasionally had suggested. Marshall cited President Roosevelt's view, however, that Wedemeyer could make a needed contribution to the cause of Allied harmony in Asia. So Wedemeyer cleared his desk in the Pentagon and packed his bags for India.

The unique difficulties of coalition warfare and combined command were generally recognized. In the case of SEAC, those difficulties would be compounded by other factors, including the stresses of operating thousands of miles from bases of supply, in a theater of relatively low strategic priority, in disease-ridden lands of often hostile natives, abominable climate, and near-impossible terrain. To the inevitable tensions arising from distinctive national styles were added those rooted (at levels customarily beneath the surface of military discourse) in divergent political goals. Service rivalries and personal antagonisms within and among the Allied camps presented further complications: ground, sea, and air officers differed in their strategic outlooks; deeply rooted suspicions marred relations between the British and Chinese; the American commander, General Stilwell, was at odds with almost everyone, including British commander-in-chief General Wavell and other British officers, Chiang Kai-shek in China, and the U.S. commander of the Flying Tigers, Major General Claire L. Chennault. Such was the setting in which SEAC was born in the autumn of 1943 and given the task of organizing more effective Allied resistance to a resourceful and aggressive enemy.

Wedemeyer resolved to contribute his best to the accomplishment of that mission. Part of that contribution, he knew, was to help make the combined British–American organization a truly effective enterprise. Given the Allies' basic disagreement as to "the best road to Tokyo" (U.S. efforts focused on support of China and on the use of China as a base in the war against Japan, whereas the British were more interested in movement toward Malaya and the Indies), the devising of combined plans that would receive whole-hearted and vigorous support from all parties proved a continuing challenge. Wedemeyer set himself the goal of serving as a completely loyal member of the combined team without sacrificing his national identity. During his year with SEAC, he developed cordial relations with most of his Allied associates and came especially to admire the qualities of the Supreme Allied Commander, Admiral Mountbatten.

In May 1944, Wedemeyer toured the command's vast domains in India and Burma, including the several battlefronts, and visited China. These travels confirmed certain negative impressions he already had formed about Allied field operations. Instead of the "can-do" attitude and the vigorous and imaginative campaigning he thought necessary, he found, especially at the level of the British commanders-in-chief (the senior ground, sea, and air commanders), lethargy and pessimism. He reported his findings straightforwardly to the Supreme Commander. Portions of his report follow, along with comments Wedemeyer made several weeks later in a planning memorandum for the SEAC Chief of Staff.

HEADQUARTERS
SUPREME ALLIED COMMANDER
SOUTHEAST ASIA

MEMORANDUM FOR THE SUPREME COMMANDER

From: A. C. Wedemeyer
       Major General, G.S.C.
       Deputy Chief of Staff

Subject: A. SEAC Objectives Established by the Combined Chiefs
         of Staff
         B. Development of Operational Plans Within Southeast Asia
         C. Emasculation of Plans and Directives
         D. Analyses of SEAC Operations
         E. Conclusions

Date: June 5, 1944

Section A
SEAC Objectives Established by the
Combined Chiefs of Staff

.   .   .   .   .

It is crystal clear that the U.S. Chiefs of Staff are determined that a land
route with pipelines should be established between India and China in
order to provide timely air support for operations against the Japanese
inner zone. It is also patent that the Americans are not interested in
operations in the Malay-NEI [Netherlands East Indies] Barrier, at least
during the present phase of global strategy. The British, on the other
hand, although agreed that SEAC proposals relating to operations in
Burma were militarily sound, apparently do not feel that the points at
issue are of sufficient importance to support on Combined Chiefs of
Staff or governmental levels.

Therefore, SEAC should take full cognizance of, and wholeheartedly implement the existing agreed Combined Chiefs of Staff directive . . . If interpreted in the spirit of QUADRANT, SEXTANT and
AXIOM [Allied conferences held respectively in Quebec (August 1943);
Cairo (December 1943); and Washington and London (February–April
1944)] discussions, this directive envisages that SEAC will, *in timely
support* of Pacific operations: (a) Create conditions that will facilitate the

expansion and protection of the air ferry service to China, and (b) gain control of Upper Burma, thus permitting early development of over-land communications to China.

Section B
Development of Operational Plans
Within Southeast Asia

At the time of the arrival of the SEAC Staff in Delhi (October 1943), there existed two plans for operations in Burma which had been pre-pared under the supervision of the Commanders-in-Chief (land, air, and naval). These plans were known as TARZAN and ABNORMAL. The SEAC staff immediately examined the proposed operations and con-cluded that neither operation would actually accomplish the assigned objectives. Therefore, a new operational plan was prepared by SEAC staff and termed TOREADOR. This plan was designed to gain control of Upper and Central Burma by employing pincer movements with forces operating from India and China, effectively gaining control of that part of BURMA generally north of the 22nd parallel.

TOREADOR was opposed by the three British Commanders-in-Chief, who stated vehemently that logistical difficulties and the lack of appropriate resources definitely precluded success. The fourth com-mander concerned (Commanding General, Chinese Ledo Forces) ap-proved the plan. After considerable discussion, the Supreme Com-mander, on the advice of the British Commanders-in-Chief, decided that the TOREADOR plan would not be undertaken.

To fulfill the requirement embodied in the original SEAC directive concerning an amphibious operation, the three Commanders-in-Chief had prepared a plan for operations against the Andamans, termed BUC-CANEER. It was estimated that 50,000 troops would be necessary to overcome the estimated 7,000 Japs reported defending the Islands. At SEXTANT, the BUCCANEER plan was rejected by the Combined Chiefs of Staff and was also viewed with strong disfavor by the Prime Minister. Further, to facilitate operations in the Mediterranean, the Com-bined Chiefs of Staff decided at SEXTANT to remove the bulk of SEAC amphibious resources.

The removal of resources precluded a realistic amphibious operation and abrogated Allied commitments to the Generalissimo for a major amphibious operation in the Bay of Bengal. SEAC could not, therefore, be certain that the Chinese would collaborate in Upper Burma operations. These developments injected more intangibles into an already complex military situation; however, SEAC produced plans that envisaged offensive operations designed to improve the Allied position in Upper Burma and thus increase the flow of air supplies into China.

Section C
Emasculation of Plans and Directives

In December 1943, the SEAC staff proposed operations to capture Akyab, Kalewa and Kalemyo, and Myitkyina [towns in central and northern Burma]. These operations were successively reduced in scope by reviewing staff divisions, particularly on the Commanders-in-Chief level. Objections to the operations appeared the more vigorous concern of reviewing officers and staffs than the effort to resort to expedients and ingenuity for the accomplishment of the proposed tasks.

Finally, on January 14, 1944, operations were ordered by SEAC in Operational Directive No. 7 as follows:

a. The capture of Akyab in the Arakan area before 1944 monsoon.

b. Complementary operations in the Imphal area toward the Kalewa-Kalemyo area, exploiting to the east of the Chindwin River and giving vigorous support to LRP [Long Range Penetration Group (Commando)] action.

c. The advance by the Chinese-American forces, Ledo sector, to capture the Mogaung-Myitkyina area to provide additional security for the air ferry route and to cover the construction of a road and pipeline. Advance by the [Chinese] Yunnan Force across the Salween was included, but the elimination of amphibious operations rendered the Generalissimo's collaboration uncertain.

d. LRPs airborne to the interior of Burma to operate against the enemy line of communications and installations in support of the above operations.

During the course of discussions between the Supreme Commander and the three British Commanders-in-Chief, the Army Commander-in-Chief emphasized the importance of publishing timely information relative to proposed operations, and he was therefore authorized to publish a warning order ostensibly embodying the Supreme Commander's agreed objectives.

Factually, the Army Commander-in-Chief's directive (warning order), authorized as above indicated, with the exception of the objective given to the Chinese Ledo Force, did not incorporate the Supreme Commander's views relative to objectives the SEAC forces should attain prior to the 1944 monsoon. The tasks assigned to the 15th, 33rd, and 4th Corps were definitely reduced in scope as follows: (a) The objective of the Arakan Force became the capture of the Buthidaung-Maungdaw area, and (b) the objective of the Imphal Force [became] to kill Japs and advance to the foothills in the Chin Hills.

These objectives, as announced in official orders by the Commander-in-Chief, 11th Army Group, with the exception of that assigned to the LEDO Force, were limited and ineffectual, and they undoubtedly, therefore, should and would have been accomplished *had it not been that the enemy seized the initiative and undertook timely and effective operations* which resulted in placing the Arakan and Imphal forces definitely on the defensive along the general line, Maungdaw-Buthidaung-Imphal-Kohima.

Based on the 11th Army Group directive, the 14th Army and Eastern Air Command published on February 4, 1944, Combined Operation Instruction No. 4, which portrays indecision, apathy, and vagueness relative to the assignment of realistic military objectives. An extract follows:

> 4th Corps will cooperate by containing the enemy 33rd Division by advances in the CHIN HILLS and KABAW VALLEY, and enemy 31st and 15th Divisions by demonstrations and enterprises as strong as possible in the TAMANTHI area and along river CHINDWIN. 4th Corps will be prepared to take advantage in the greatest possible strength of any favorable opportunity created east of River CHINDWIN by action of 3rd Indian Division.

In the above published instructions of the 14th Army and Eastern Air Command, definite military objectives are not assigned. The terminology implies strong doubt about the ability of the forces to accomplish assigned tasks.

In the foregoing, it should be noted that there has been definite resistance to plans and/or operations proposed by SEAC Staff. The British Commanders-in-Chief, either jointly or individually, rejected or strongly emasculated plans of operations which required bold, daring, and aggressive maneuver and the acceptance of calculated risks.

Section D
Analyses of SEAC Operations

Objective analyses of operations conducted in Burma *during the pre-monsoon period 1944* suggest that the overall tactical position of the Allies in Burma is not as favorable as it was when the South East Asia Command assumed responsibility for operations.

In the ARAKAN, our forces advanced a few miles down the Mayu Peninsula. It is true that we have killed large numbers of Japs; however, such killing should be considered incidental to the attainment of realistic military objectives. It is my conviction that we could have seized Akyab and thus would have acquired an excellent airdrome from which effective bombing could be conducted against vital enemy lines of communications. Also, possession of Akyab and the disposition of approximately a division in the Myaungbwe-Sanbale-Minbya area covering potential lines of enemy approach up the Kaladan Valley would have enabled us to deny those lines of communications to the enemy and to increase the security of our lines of communications in the Arakan coastal area. Further, we could, after occupying the positions indicated, contain the enemy with approximately two divisions, thus releasing additional units for offensive employment elsewhere. It is accepted that naval and air support would be required to effect the capture of Akyab; however, appropriate resources in those categories are available. The problem of crossing the many deltas and tributaries of the Mayu and Kaladan Rivers in the vicinity of Akyab could have been overcome by the employment of available landing and small craft and improvised rafts as well as the use of pontoon equipment.

Early in 1944 a force of approximately 7,000 Japanese encircled Allied positions in the Arakan and our troops immediately moved into so-called boxes or all-around defense positions. At that time we had approximately a three-to-one superiority numerically on the ground and air supremacy, but we accepted defensive measures. However, it would appear sound that as soon as the enemy encircling forces had been successfully defeated and the Japanese thwarted in their daring action, our troops should have vigorously and promptly pursued the enemy with annihilation as their battle cry.

During my recent tour of the fronts, the situation on the Arakan front was as follows:

   a. *Ground Forces:*
      (1) Allied: 25th, 26th, and 81st Divisions and Corps supporting troops.
      (2) Enemy: 55th Division.

b. Air Forces:
(1) Allied: Overwhelming air superiority.

c. Situation (May 1944):
The 25th Division was deployed in a defensive position near Maungdaw. The 26th Division was located on the left of the 25th along the general line Tunnel Area–Taung Bazar. The 81st Division was operating generally southeast of Taung Bazar. The weather did not preclude offensive operations, yet only occasional artillery exchanges and light patrolling were in progress. Intermittently a small concentration of enemy would be discovered and the air would be requested to make a strike. If we continue almost complete inactivity in this area, the Japanese, utilizing his interior lines of communications, can leave a small force (approximately a regiment) opposite our three divisions and move strong reinforcements to the Mogaung-Myitkyina area. The Supreme Commander emphasized that aggressive action would be continued on all fronts to the limit of practicability *even during the monsoon.*

In the Imphal-Kohima area, we are confronted by numerically inferior enemy forces which have effectively cut all ground lines of communication leading into the Imphal plain. Had it not been for the splendid logistical support provided by the Air Transport Command, our vastly superior forces might have suffered a most ignominious defeat.

a. Ground Forces:
(1) Allied: 2nd, 7th, 5th, 20th, 17th, 23rd Divisions, 50th Parachute Brigade, 25th Tank Brigade, 23rh LRP, and Corps supporting troops.
(2) Enemy: 31st, 15th, and 33rd Divisions, with a tank regiment and miscellaneous supporting troops.

b. Air Forces:
(1) Allied: Overwhelming air superiority.

c. Situation (May 1944):
The enemy practically encircled in Imphal plain and restricted mobility of the Allied forces, and had intercepted the ground line of communications. Allied operations were being conducted with aggressiveness and vigor from Kohima southwards with a view to clearing the road to Imphal. These operations were progressing slowly due to precipitous terrain and thick jungles. The advances being made were definitely a credit to the

inspiring and competent leadership of the corps and division commanders concerned. In the immediate Imphal area, aggressive spirit was lacking. Instead of containing the enemy in certain isolated areas and using the surplus forces available for offensive maneuver, the operations had appeared to resolve themselves into one of attrition—killing Japs.

In the Ledo-Shaduzup area, the progress of Allied forces had been comparatively slow during March and April. However, the sudden capture of Myitkyina airfield (May 17) spurred our troops to increased effort and continued advance. Kamaing was being threatened from all sides.

    a. *Ground Forces:*
    (1) Allied: 22nd, 30th, 38th Chinese Divisions American trained and equipped. 50th and 14th Chinese Divisions, understrength and poorly trained and equipped. American GALAHAD Force. 3rd Indian Division.
    (2) Enemy: 18th Division.

    b. Air Forces:
    (1) Allied: Overwhelming air superiority.

    c. *Situation (May 1944):*
    The 22nd, 30th, and 38th Chinese Divisions were closing in on Kamaing, although the terrain and thick jungles precluded rapid movement. After the capture of that village, however, the valley broadens out and wide encirclements will facilitate more rapid advance. There was everywhere present aggressive spirit and the hope that the rains would not preclude offensives with a view to securing the Mogaung-Myitkyina area. In Myitkyina, it is believed that the city might have been captured had a concentrated, heavy air attack been delivered coordinated with the ground assault.

With a superiority on the ground of 2 1/2 to 1 on the Arakan and Imphal fronts, and with complete mastery of the air, we remain on the defensive and the enemy retains the initiative. Apparently the 4th and 15th Corps have no concrete plans for aggressive and decisive operations. The battle in those areas may be described as being fought passively on a day-to-day basis, countering enemy blows and hoping to bag many Japs in the process.

We thus find ourselves, with the monsoon period upon us, on the defensive militarily and psychologically in the Arakan and Imphal areas.

In the Kohima area southwards and in the Shaduzup-Kamaing-Myitkyina areas, an offensive spirit prevails.

Generalizations:

a. Air-Ground Support.   Employment of air forces in ground-air support activities could be greatly improved. Many of the road blocks that delayed the progress of ground forces for interminable periods could definitely have been reduced earlier by coordinated and concentrated air attacks followed up by aggressive assaults on the part of the infantry. The enemy has been maneuvered into a compact area around Myitkyina offering a very lucrative opportunity for a large-scale smashing air attack, promptly and vigorously followed up by ground forces. With the effective air resources available in this theater, we can and must adopt tactics involving smashing concentrated attacks with bombers and fighter bombers in lieu of the penny packet "strikes" which are being employed against isolated and relatively unremunerative targets.

b. Intelligence.   The unit commanders operating against the enemy in Burma are woefully lacking in information of the enemy. It is accepted that a division commander cannot dissipate his forces in large-scale day and night patrolling, for he would have insufficient strength left to conduct effective combat. Supplementary means should be provided, to include light airplanes, and enemy areas should be saturated with intelligence agents. At present the enemy maneuvers almost at will without fear of detection. Often the first intimation of enemy movements and concentrations occurs when actual contact is made with our main forces. The difficult terrain and the thick jungles do present a problem, but we can devise ways and means of obtaining more timely and accurate enemy information for our field commanders.

c. Maneuver.   The enemy has greater facility in slithering and infiltrating through jungles and in coping with difficult terrain or limited communication facilities. Our troops are uniformly roadbound. Commanders appear reluctant to maneuver far distant from roads. Air dropping of supplies should insure supplies and commanders must maneuver widely and continually off roads. We will suffer prohibitive losses both in time and resources if we persist in pushing almost directly against strong enemy positions instead of resorting to effective envelopments.

d. Military Objectives.   Commanders must be required to assign realistic military objectives. Objectives must be clearly defined in understandable military terms. Terminology should not inject doubt relative to the feasibility of accomplishing assigned tasks. Directives issued by the 11th Army Group, 14th Army, and Eastern Air Command included the terms: "If the situation permits, advance"; "if possible"; "kill Japanese"; "demonstrations and enterprises as strong as possible." It is at once apparent that such terminology is indefinite, apathetic, and vague and could not possibly result in the attainment of real military objectives.

e. Monsoon Operations.   Offensive action in the air and on the ground can and must be continued throughout the monsoons. This requirement necessitates a high degree of determination and guts on the part of all ranks and will tax to the limit the respective commanders' finest qualities of leadership in order to maintain high morale and offensive spirit. But the stakes are high and the will to go on in spite of hell and high water will pay dividends.

Section E
Conclusions

In the foregoing notes I have tried to indicate clearly the important tasks upon which the Supreme Commander, his staff, and all ranks must focus their attention and unrelenting energies. The SEAC has made a definite although indirect contribution to the global aspects of the war. Last fall when the command was formed, there were but four Japanese divisions and approximately 150 planes disposed in the Burma area. Today there are in Burma nine-plus Japanese divisions and over 250 planes. These resources are sorely needed elsewhere. The Japanese fleet was drawn to Singapore in the spring of 1944 prepared to cope with a threat from Southeast Asia. Unquestionably, this naval concentration in and diversion to Southeast Asia waters facilitated the advance of U.S. forces in the Pacific. The morale of forces under the South East Asia Command is steadily improving. Increased coordination and cooperation between Allied forces are resulting in more effective employment of combined resources in the area. Air and surface communications throughout the theater are functioning smoothly with previous capacities in some instances trebled. Tonnages over the hump have been greatly increased and favorable conditions are being created to expand further this important source of supply to China.

We must employ our ingenuity and energies to circumvent the difficulties presented by terrain, climate, and a tenacious enemy. The staff members of SEAC must fully appreciate that their duties do not end with the issuance of a directive. It remains their serious responsibility to insure that subordinate commanders *correctly interpret and execute* directives. Every advantage that we gain over the enemy must be promptly and vigorously exploited.

Napoleon once stated substantially as follows: "I do not want a general who, after winning a great victory, beats his chest and proudly exclaims 'See what a good boy am I!' I want the general who, after winning a signal victory, becomes immediately immersed in plans, ways, and means of winning the next and additional victories."

HEADQUARTERS
SUPREME ALLIED COMMANDER
SOUTHEAST ASIA
OFFICE OF THE DEPUTY CHIEF OF STAFF

MEMORANDUM TO CHIEF OF STAFF

From: A. C. Wedemeyer
        Major General, G.S.C.
        Deputy Chief of Staff

Subject: Reorganization of Planning

Date: July 29, 1944

.   .   .   .   .

I do not agree that the planning team[s] should be led by deputy directors. I especially do not agree that there should be a leader of the so-called strategy and policy team. It has been my desire to divorce the planners from the chairman, or leader, idea. I have also tried to eliminate rank and nationality and to encourage the free exchange of untrammeled opinions. This is imperative, in my opinion, in planning work. The antithesis is true on the executive side. There must be a recognized leader, and everyone must loyally accept his dictums; but plans, on the other hand, should be done on an intellectual plane and as soon as rank, chairmen, and so forth are introduced there is a tendency, which is human, to defer to said chairman . . .

8

Over the Hump to China

1944

China's prospects in its long struggle against Japanese aggression brightened enormously after Pearl Harbor. With much of the strength of the Western world suddenly thrown into the balance on China's side, the threadbare hopes it had so long nourished gave way to confident expectation.

From the U.S. viewpoint, it was extremely important to "keep China in the war." This policy was dictated by immediate military considerations as well as the long-range goal of a strong, united, and independent China. Keeping China in the war meant denying Japan the benefits of security in its own backyard: Japan would be obliged to maintain large and costly forces on the Asian mainland that otherwise would be used elsewhere. At the same time, China would provide bases from which air attacks could be launched against Japanese commerce, and from which the home islands themselves might eventually be assaulted.

Keeping China afloat was by no means easy. That unhappy land had already been at war for four years (in the most recent round of an ongoing conflict), and at times seemed perilously close to collapse. Though often fighting valiantly, its ill-equipped, ill-supplied, and indifferently trained and led armies had proven no match for the modern forces of Japan. The Nationalist government of Chiang Kai-shek had been driven from its capital, Nanking, to the distant inland city of Chungking. All the major Chinese ports were in enemy hands, as were all major industrial and communications centers and much of the most productive agricultural land. China's only remaining surface link with the outside world was the tenuous Burma road that meandered some 680 miles through jungle, swamp, and mountain from Kunming in Yunnan Province to Lashio in Burma. With the Japanese conquest of Burma in 1942, even that route was cut, and an isolated China was obliged to survive on the trickle of supplies that could be flown across the Himalayan "hump" from India.

A volunteer group of fliers under a retired U.S. Army officer, Colonel Claire Lee Chennault, had provided crucial air support to China in the months before Pearl Harbor. A specialist in tactical air warfare and an intrepid combat leader, Chennault had been recalled to active Army duty in 1942 as a general officer. He continued thereafter to serve brilliantly in China as commander of the famous "Flying Tigers."

Lieutenant General Joseph W. Stilwell also had been sent to Asia in 1942 to help stem the Japanese advance in Burma and to defend the land and air lifelines to China. Stilwell wore a variety of hats in addition to the battered campaign model in which he usually was photographed. He commanded U.S. Forces in the China-Burma-India (CBI) theater, served as chief of staff to Generalissimo Chiang Kai-shek in China, and was deputy allied commander of the Southeast Asia Command (SEAC) under Admiral Mountbatten. He had also personally led various contingents of Allied combat forces in the field, and his rugged tenacity in the face of overwhelming odds had buoyed Allied spirits in the cheerless early months of the war.

Unfortunately, chronic conflict had developed between "Vinegar Joe" Stilwell and Chiang Kai-shek, as well as between him and the British in India and Burma. When the Stilwell-Chiang relationship become so embittered in late 1944 that the Generalissimo insisted on his recall, President Roosevelt acceded. The CBI was thereupon divided into two independent theaters: China and India-Burma. Wedemeyer was ordered to leave his post in SEAC and succeed Stilwell as commander of U.S. forces and chief of staff to the Generalissimo in China.

Apart from two brief wartime visits, Wedemeyer had had little opportunity to familiarize himself with the situation in China. On his arrival in Chungking at the end of October 1944, a cloud of despair hung over the capital. Stilwell had already left. The economy was moribund; munitions and supplies of all kinds were in extremely short supply; inflation was rampant; the government and armed services were notoriously inefficient; and civilian and military morale was dangerously low. The Japanese, sensing opportunity in this dark hour, had resumed offensives that threatened not only the Allied airfields but the indispensable base at Kunming and the capital city of Chungking as well.

Before Wedemeyer left Washington in 1943, General Marshall had asked him to report to him confidentially from time to time. The first of these letters to Marshall from China was dispatched six weeks after Wedemeyer arrived in Chungking.

HEADQUARTERS
UNITED STATES FORCES
CHINA THEATER
Office of the Commanding General

Chungking, China
December 10, 1944

General George C. Marshall
Chief of Staff
War Department
Washington, D.C.

Dear General:

Six weeks have gone by since I arrived in China—the most hectic, contradictory, and yet interesting six weeks of my life. Frankly, I do not know how we will emerge from this situation. At times there are indications that the Chinese are striving to cooperate, and then the most unexpected and distressing things happen, contravening every promise and plan.

Initial survey of the situation and the relation of the Americans to the war effort here, in consonance with the China Theater directive, emphasized almost immediately after my arrival the following broad points:

   a. We must retain the Kunming area as our terminal of supply.

   b. Chungking should receive second priority, for its loss unquestionably would have disastrous political, economic, as well as psychological effect.

   c. The Chinese have no conception of organization, logistics, or modern warfare.

   d. The Generalissimo is striving to conduct the war from Chungking. The management of affairs of State in itself would require a Disraeli, Churchill, and Machiavelli all combined in one. The Gissimo will not decentralize power to subordinates.

Subject (a).   In early conferences with the Generalissimo, I pointed out that we should make disposition of forces and allocation of equipment as early as possible to insure the defense of the Kunming area. I presented a plan for this purpose and he approved that plan. This was about four weeks ago. Now I find that he is vacillating—in fact, he has ordered movements of divisions from the Kunming area without my knowledge. There are increasing indications that he no longer fully accepts the premise that Kunming should receive first priority. Apparently his advisers in the interim have emphasized the necessity for holding Chungking which, as stated above, we agree as necessary, but only after we have made appropriate preparations for the defense of Kunming.

Recently, in discussing the defense of Chungking with the Generalissimo, I mentioned that we should make plans now for evacuation should the enemy advance continue on the capital and require our withdrawal. The Generalissimo categorically stated that he intended to remain in the capital and die here, if necessary. He has stated this on two other occasions, General, once in Nanking and again in Hankow, but was prevailed upon by his advisers to get out at the last minute. My purpose in making plans is to preclude chaos and confusion under the circumstances and to insure that we could set up a seat of government in some other appropriate location, preferably Kunming. There are so many political implications in everything we do here that this may not materialize. For example, the governor of Yunnan Province and the Generalissimo are very unfriendly. Further, the Generalissimo wants to remain near Szechuan Province, which I am told is one of the most thickly populated (65,000,000) and one of the most productive. If he goes to the Kunming area, the governor of Yunnan may kidnap him or at least place him under protective custody. Also, he would be cut off from provinces to the north, Szechuen, for example.

In connection with the Americans, I have plans for their evacuation—in fact, I am gradually moving officers and men to the Kunming area. I will remain here with the Generalissimo as long as possible, but not long enough to be captured by the Japs, I hope. I understand that the Generalissimo has considered moving his capital to Laochow in Sinkiang Province. We would be out of touch with the military situation there. Politically he could still carry on, but militarily he would be impotent from that area.

The above may suggest that I am beginning to accept as inevitable a successful Japanese advance on Chungking and Kunming. I want to assure you that we are not defeatists. In fact, we are going to give everything we have to hold Kunming and Chungking and to insure that it can never be said that Americans abandoned China in the final and decisive stages of the Sino-Jap War. In this connection, I wish you could witness the spirit our American officers and men have. Everyone is working hard. If we can but get Chinese collaboration, stop this business of last minute changes in plans, and inspire the men to fight, we have confidence that everything will come out all right. Most of us are resilient and can accept frustrations and disappointments and still come back for more.

My approach to the Generalissimo has been friendly, direct, and firm. I believe that he likes and respects me now. It is the influence and chicanery of his advisers, who have selfish, mercurial motives and who persuade him when I am not present to take action that conflicts with agreed plans. I have been uniformly careful to massage his ego and to place myself in an advisory position so that he will not lose face or feel that I am trying to coerce him in action not in consonance with sound military plans.

Subject (b). We have recommended dispositions which, if the Chinese will fight with determination and elan, should insure the security of the capital. Also, we are moving an ample supply of munitions centrally located for the troops. We could make a continued Japanese advance costly, in fact prohibitive, in time and effort. It is difficult to imagine the pressure that is being brought to bear from various facets and high officials to concentrate for the defense of Chungking in lieu of Kunming. In this connection, it is amusing and also tragic to note that many high ranking Chinese officials are asking me to facilitate their evacuation to America by air. One very high-ranking Chinese general stated that he wanted to take forty outstanding Chinese army and naval officers to Europe very soon to study the European battlefields. Tactfully but firmly I told him that if he had that many Chinese officers who were highly trained, we needed them right now during this critical hour in China, and that we could employ them in key posts in connection with plans for the defense of their country. Another Chinese general asked me for permission to send ten Chinese officers to America to study strategy, particularly the employment of armored units. My answer to him was along the same lines. This is indicative of the psychological approach of Chinese who should know better. . . .

Subject (c). We have taken steps to improve the diet of Chinese soldiers. The Chinese soldiers are starving by the hundreds. This due to graft and inefficiency. I have told the Generalissimo that until we insure that we have food—rice, pork, and some vegetables—for our soldiers, we cannot expect them to fight effectively. I have emphasized this point over and over again and have explained to him that if we feed our troops well I am sure that the desertions will drop down materially—in fact, we will have men eager to join the army. We have evolved a good plan for feeding the men, and I hope to supplement their diet with vitamins and dehydrated foods from America. A wire has been sent to Somervell [Commanding General, U.S. Army Service Forces] in this connection. I am instituting plans that will be executed under American supervision to eliminate graft and insure better and ample food for the army.

In connection with troop movements, the Chinese march an outfit from A to B and make no provision for bivouacs, food, and so forth along the route. This is being taken care of. If only the Chinese will cooperate! American officers have been designated to supervise such movements and we are well on the way to exercising constructive influence with regard to this very important factor. The Generalissimo often asks me to move by air 50,000 men from A to B, and after carefully studying such movement we make appropriate arrangements. Suddenly he will order a change and there are all kinds of ramifications involved which render it impossible or at least impracticable to comply with his wishes. Neither he nor his advisers really understand supply and movement problems. But they ask for the most astounding troop movements to implement their strategy, which is really piecemeal, uncoordinated employment of forces.

The Chinese S.O.S. [Services of Supply] is terrifyingly inefficient. I have placed my S.O.S. Major General Cheves, who is fine and able, in charge of supply and movements in the area between Kweiyang and Kunming. The Chinese S.O.S. is responsible for supply and movement in the Chungking area. I have given the Chinese S.O.S. four of my officers to assist. If they would but listen to the American officers and heed the advice given them, many of our difficulties would be alleviated. I have established a policy in the Theater that no Chinese soldier will be moved by air or truck if he is physically unfit. I now have American medical officers present at points of departure (air or truck) to examine the men. The Generalissimo approved this, but old China hands tell me I am going to decimate the army, for so few are really fit. To get around this, our standards cannot be so high and later, if we do succeed in building up the men physically, we will raise our physical standards for combat.

Subject (d). I have already indicated to the Generalissimo that here in Chungking we must issue broad policies and directives to responsible commanders in the field, and that we definitely must not tell them how to carry them out. If we find that these commanders are not complying, then relieve them. I emphasized that it is wrong to direct operations from Chungking. Although he has agreed to the soundness of this approach, he violates his agreement almost daily, and this adds to our difficulties . . . .

·   ·   ·   ·   ·

I was most reluctant to make recommendations to the Chiefs of Staff with reference to the removal of divisions from the Burma Theater. Perhaps no one is more familiar with the implications, and I recall vividly the disappointment of British and Americans alike in SEAC when, at the Cairo Conference a year ago, amphibious resources were taken away for operations elsewhere. Today I am making recommendations that will stultify Admiral Mountbatten in the midst of a successful effort in Burma. In so doing I recognize that I may be jeopardizing the operations that would create a land route to the China Theater. I was careful not to recommend prematurely that this be done and weighed every possibility and resorted to every expedient to minimize our requirements. There have been indications that Mountbatten feels very keenly about this; however, I want you to know that I made these decisions only after careful deliberation. If I hurt him I am sorry, but the war is bigger than individuals, either in his case or my own. I did exactly what I think you would have done under similar circumstances.

If we are successful in riding through this crisis until June 1, 1945, we can, I believe, create conditions that will make an effective contribution to continued effort against the Japanese on the continent. Tonnages over the hump, by air, pipeline, and road will increase to approximately 100,000 tons per month by that time, and that quantity of materiel should certainly support a sizable striking force, particularly in the air. We will plan amphibious operations against the coast with a view to securing a lodgment with sea communications. Having firmly secured an area on the coast with suitable airfields, we might advance up the coast in scallops so that we could establish air and sea striking bases closer to the heart of the Japanese inner zone. But all of that is fantasy at this time, when realistically we are confronted with a precarious situation in our front yard!

With reference to Chennault, I still feel that Hap Arnold should send an able air officer to this theater as his deputy commander of the 14th U.S.A.A.F. . . . Chennault himself has been very pronounced in his intentions to carry out directives from China Theater. I indicated that I expected him to comply with the broad directives issued by Theater headquarters and that I definitely would not permit any member of my staff to interfere with the execution. Further, I wanted him to know that I would support him to the hilt . . .

Chennault . . . informed me that he had never received any directive from Theater Headquarters and consequently felt very much alone. As a result, he did many things on his own initiative. This caused hard feelings between China Theater Headquarters and the 14th Air Force Headquarters. I believe that I have eliminated the cause for that feeling, but there are still members of both staffs who are suspicious and unco-operative. They must and will go . . .

•   •   •   •   •

I am increasingly certain that it would be sound to employ the XX Bomber Command against the Hankow area with maximum bomb loads. This area is a focal point for communications and also has vital air and industrial installations which contribute to the Jap effort. I do not accept the premise that such an attack would not pay commensurate dividends. If 100 B-29s with ten tons of explosives each were to be employed against Hankow, the Jap effort would be materially weak-ened. On two or more occasions these ships have been employed against Bangkok and Rangoon. Such strikes were not in my opinion as vital to our overall war effort as strikes would be against Hankow and/or Can-ton. I do agree that the XX Bomber Command should be employed to facilitate the projected Pacific operations, . . .

When I was home last August, both you and Alec Surles [Major General Alexander D. Surles, Director, War Department Bureau of Pub-lic Relations] spoke to me about my relations with the newspaper corre-spondents in SEAC. Apparently the newspaper correspondents return-ing to the States reported that I was aloof. You suggested that I see them occasionally and once in a while entertain them. Upon my return to Kandy [SEAC Headquarters had removed from New Delhi to Kandy, Ceylon, during Wedemeyer's tour], I gave a cocktail party for them. However, I was in a difficult position in Kandy with reference to newspa-per men. As a pick and shovel man on Admiral Mountbatten's staff, I felt reluctant to make any statements to the press. He is not one iota bashful about such matters and not only held a weekly press conference but saw many of the correspondents in between. Obviously there wasn't much that I could say of additional interest. However, Surles provided us with an excellent press relations officer and he had the situation well in hand in Kandy.

Upon my arrival in Chungking, the Generalissimo asked me to see the press not less than once a week, and I am complying. There are about fifty newspaper representatives who come to my office every Thursday. They ask questions, many of which are borderline or in absolute violation of military security. I am able to cope with such questions, but they also introduce subjects which, while not violating military security, would, if answered, tend to increase concern of the Chinese people or shake their confidence in their leaders. At the first meeting of the press, I asked them never to quote me, and stipulated that all communiques going out from Chungking were to be sent out over headline from China Theater Headquarters and not from General Wedemeyer's Headquarters. I received information from friends at home stating that the press there is presenting me in the light of a publicity seeker, and I felt badly about it. General Embick [Lieutenant General Stanley D. Embick, Wedemeyer's father-in-law] even radioed me concerning this matter. I have been so busy with other pressing matters that I have not checked personally the dispatches emanating from these headquarters. My press relations officer is inexperienced and I asked General Surles to send me a capable man. Also, my press censor does not appear particularly capable. With the arrival of an able press relations officer, the present unsatisfactory situation will be alleviated.

Perhaps in no theater is the problem of handling the press more acute and dangerous. I appreciate this fact and will strive to avoid pitfalls. I abhor personal publicity and am encouraging correspondents to stress human interest stories about subordinates in the field. I do hope that my relations with the press and the information published will not cause you or the United States Government embarrassment.

Congressman [Mike] Mansfield of Montana reported here a few weeks ago as a special representative of the President. I had a few conferences with him and he impressed me very favorably. I placed every facility at his disposal to get around in the Theater and see conditions for himself. I hope that upon his return you will be able to have a heart-to-heart with him. He, of course, would give you political views that do affect our military effort. Nelson [Donald M. Nelson, long-time chairman of the U.S. War Production Board, and presidential representative in China for war production matters] should be able to provide an economic picture, and Hurley [U.S. ambassador to China, Patrick J. Hurley] the diplomatic. I will send an officer with Hurley to give you military information, and also explain our requirements in personnel. I do hope that we will overcome what now appears to be almost insuperable obstacles and that I can give you more optimistic reports about the future of China Theater.

* * * * *

With Sincere good wishes for a Merry Christmas and continued success throughout the New Year.

Faithfully yours,

A. C. WEDEMEYER
Major General, U.S.A.

9

Working with the Generalissimo

1944–1945

The basic missions of the U.S. command in China had not changed: keep China in the war, and help it carry on that fight as effectively as possible.

From the time of his arrival in Chungking, Wedemeyer interpreted these missions as requiring attention to a broad range of matters—economic and administrative factors in particular—that transcend the normal concerns of military command. As a prerequisite of success, he emphasized the development of mutually respectful relationships between the American command and its Chinese allies and hosts. In frequent, almost daily conferences with Chiang, he discussed in tactful but straightforward fashion all the pressing problems of the war and the factors bearing on its effective prosecution. He organized—with Chiang's hearty approval—a combined staff of Americans and Chinese to plan and coordinate the joint effort. Noting that many of the inefficiencies that plagued the army and government of China were rooted in age-old practices of a traditional culture, he dispatched a steady barrage of memoranda to the Generalissimo giving advice on all sorts of matters and offering proposals for all sorts of reform.

A representative selection of these memoranda are presented herewith.

HEADQUARTERS
UNITED STATES FORCES
CHINA THEATER

No. 256
MEMORANDUM TO HIS EXCELLENCY,
THE GENERALISSIMO

From: A. C. Wedemeyer
Major General, U.S.A.
Commanding

Date: December 1, 1944 (Chungking, China)

In order to slow down, and eventually stop, the enemy advance towards Kweiyang, it is considered essential that all available Chinese troops be organized immediately to attack to cut Japanese lines of communication in the Changsha area and to the south and southwest . . .

To achieve the most effective results, operations should be conducted at night wherever possible. This will minimize casualties and insure the element of surprise.

The U.S. Army is prepared to send a total of one hundred officers and one hundred enlisted men to troops indicated . . . They will be prepared to assist in reorganization, demolitions, supply, radio communication, and any other function which may be required of them.

In order to achieve results, definite orders to Chinese commanders concerned should be sent by the Generalissimo to strain every effort for the immediate organization of troop units.

It is recommended that troops for this mission be organized as guerrilla units, each group to contain between 1,000 and 2,000 men . . . The minimum indicated is 25 guerrilla units or groups. If authorities on the ground find it practicable to organize additional similar units, they should have authority to do so . . .

Where practicable, the U.S. Army will undertake to air-drop supplies and ammunition. This means of supply cannot be depended upon due to uncertainty of weather and the nature of the terrain. Arrangements will be made, if weather permits, to air-attack objectives in coordination with ground attacks.

Having cut the lines of communication, every effort must be made to hold the roads and railways for as long as possible. If temporary guerrilla units are compelled to withdraw, they must attack immediately at other points in order to insure that enemy-held installations are permanently destroyed.

HEADQUARTERS
UNITED STATES FORCES
CHINA THEATER

No. 272
MEMORANDUM TO HIS EXCELLENCY,
THE GENERALISSIMO
From: A. C. Wedemeyer
       Major General, U.S.A.
       U.S. Chief of Staff to the Generalissimo
Subject: Alpha Plan
Date: December 2, 1944 (Chungking, China)

The Alpha Plan was made mandatory due to the advance of the
Japanese army in considerable strength on Kweiyang, and was necessary
to effect immediate disposition of all available Chinese and American
forces for the security *first* of the Kunming area, *second* the Chungking
area.

It was accepted by the Generalissimo that the loss of the Kunming
area would affect China's war effort politically, economically, and militarily, and would definitely [cripple] the United States' ability to further
support the Chinese war effort in that no supplies could be brought into
China either over the hump or by the Ledo road. The loss of the
Kunming area would mean the termination of American assistance to all
Chinese ground forces. It was also understood that the defense of the
Kunming area was to be given *first priority* in the disposition of Chinese
ground forces, equipment, and supplies.

It was definitely and jointly agreed that there should be a strong
defense set up for the defense of the Chungking area, but it was considered that the loss of the Chungking area would affect China only along
political, economical, and psychological lines, and would not be a death
blow militarily. It was further understood that the Chungking area
would receive *second priority* in the disposition of forces, supplies and
equipment; this was one of the basic tenets of the Alpha Plan which was
approved by the Generalissimo.

All movements planned for, and the transport of supplies to certain
areas were made on the basis of, the approved Alpha Plan.

Present movements now in course of completion have been greatly
interfered with by changes in the Alpha Plan. It was definitely understood, and orders were issued, to move the 57th Army from Sian to the

Chanyi area. This movement began on December 1st and was made possible by unusual efforts and at a large sacrifice in planes and hump tonnage by the Air Transport Command. In the Alpha Plan, the 57th Army was definitely designated for the Kunming area, and [this] was approved by the Generalissimo. It is now proposed to move the 57th Army into the general Chungking area. Such a decision, arrived at without considering the logistical problems involved, is impossible, and certainly cannot be made effective without great loss of time and effort.

The 45th Division of the 57th Army which had already arrived, in part, in the Chanyi area, and which was definitely committed to the Kunming defense area, was given sudden orders to march to Pi-chieh, which is in the Chungking area. I have not yet been informed of this change from Chinese Headquarters.

The 53rd Army was tentatively set up for movement by air from the Salween to the Kunming area, and it was believed that the Generalissimo had approved this move, but sudden orders were issued which countermanded movement orders, with resultant loss of time and effort on the part of all air and ground forces and S.O.S. personnel.

It was further desired under the Alpha Plan to move the 5th Army eastward to facilitate the defense of the Kunming area, and when definite plans were made for the movement of this army, I was informed that they could not be moved for political reasons.

As your Chief of Staff, I coordinated with all Chinese and American agencies concerned in the execution of the various parts of the Alpha Plan, and they all are now very much upset by sudden changes which make all previous planning efforts and movements of supplies and stores of gasoline and so forth wasted. I recommended the Alpha Plan to you, and it was my understanding that you had accepted it fully and completely.

As Commanding General of U.S. Army forces in the China Theater, it is my direct responsibility, by a directive from the President of the United States and the Combined Chiefs of Staff, that I employ all U.S. resources in the China Theater to insure continued effective employment against the common enemy. Obviously, if I lose the vital Kunming area, which is my only base of supply, I could not comply with my directive nor could I furnish maximum support to the Chinese forces. I urgently request that the Alpha Plan as modified herein be executed as a matter of necessity, and that all commanders, Chinese and American, be given clear, concise, and correct orders to preclude any future mistakes or misunderstandings to insure full cooperation and compliance in the execution of the Alpha Plan . . .

It [also] is urgently recommended that you come to a definite decision in regard to the employment of Chinese communist forces on the northern and eastern flanks of the Japanese lines of communication. As I have previously indicated to you, I will send U.S. Army personnel into the communist area and report definitely on their use and disposition of all weapons, supplies, and equipment furnished them. The supply of this force will be by air. I feel that it is absolutely necessary for me, as your Chief of Staff, and in my dual capacity as Commanding General of U.S. Army forces in China, that we come to an early and irrevocable decision on the above matters.

HEADQUARTERS
UNITED STATES FORCES
CHINA THEATER

No. 536
MEMORANDUM TO HIS EXCELLENCY,
THE GENERALISSIMO
From: A. C. Wedemeyer
       Lieutenant General, U.S. Army
       U.S. Chief of Staff to the Generalissimo
Date: April 26, 1945 (Chungking, China)

Confirming conference concerning the organization of the Chinese army, I wish to invite your attention again to the recommendations I submitted orally. I indicated to you that I have made a very careful analysis of all the operations conducted in the China Theater [over] the past four years. Also, I have reviewed the present and potential capabilities of available air, road, railroad, and water communications. I have compiled data covering the military organization of the Chinese, both on the ground and in the air. The object of my studies and analysis was to determine appropriate recommendations to you in order that we may derive the maximum benefit from American support as well as the contribution that China itself can make.

My analysis of the military operations reveals that there was no broad concept of operations which would permit appropriate coordination, not only in the employment of Chinese armies, but also their movement, equipment, and training. When the enemy advanced, countermeasures were taken to block such advance. Quickly discovering this fact, the Japanese advanced at many points simultaneously, causing complete dispersion and thus weakening the Chinese effort. There was no orderly, well-conceived distribution of supplies and equipment to Chinese units. In other words, our military effort was piecemeal and did not permit strength at any point for effective action. Today, the Japanese are making limited objective offensives towards Sian and Chih-kiang. We may reasonably expect them to make a similar advance from the Ho-chih area. Their object is, of course, to cause us to disperse our effort and to gain airfields or areas from which we [otherwise] might conduct air and ground operations effectively against them.

Recommendations

You and I and our combined General Staffs, as well as key commanders in the field, must resist to the utmost the continued dispersion of our effort. We should continue to place American personnel and material with the 36-divisions selected in Beta Plan, and should concentrate our training and preparations for combat in those divisions. We should accept losses in certain areas and concurrently use nonsponsored divisions to make the enemy pay dearly for his advances against such areas.

There are at present approximately 300 Chinese divisions, at least numerically recognized. This number of divisions is a tremendous strain on your impoverished resources. The Americans are striving [to] move appropriate equipment into China with a view to creating effective Chinese forces. However, it is crystal clear that the resources that the Americans can move in over the limited lines of communications definitely preclude equipping adequately such a tremendous number of divisions. Recognizing this fact, we decided to concentrate on 36 divisions immediately, and if feasible to build up to a total of 50 divisions. With 50 well trained and equipped divisions we could, supported by our splendid air force, impose our will upon the enemy when and where we desired in China.

[Further] Recommendations

That the Chinese-American Combined General Staffs be directed to make a study, in close collaboration with the National Military Council, to determine feasible plans for the early reduction of the existing number of divisions in China. In this connection, as units are deactivated, the older and less efficient officers, to assuage their feelings, could be sent to a war college for a course in strategy. The younger and more fit officers and men could be used as replacements in the sponsored 36–50 divisions. The remaining surplus of personnel made available by the deactivation programs could be organized into effective labor battalions to work on road maintenance and in the fields. The reduction in the number of divisions would enable me to concentrate American assistance so that we could promptly create a fine modern Chinese army similar to the five CAI [Chinese Army in India] divisions which were trained and equipped in India–Burma and which fought so valiantly and effectively in that area.

The above ideas are somewhat critical of past performances in this area on the part of the Americans and the Chinese. Conditions existing previously may have justified the actions and decisions reached during that time. I am certain that you want me to express my views frankly, and that you will accept the fact that my sole purpose in this theater is to help China in her war effort, and when victory is achieved, to leave China with the respect of the Chinese and other nationals with whom we Americans have come in contact.

HEADQUARTERS
UNITED STATES FORCES
CHINA THEATER

No. 609
MEMORANDUM TO HIS EXCELLENCY,
THE GENERALISSIMO

From: A. C. Wedemeyer
           Lieutenant General, U.S. Army
           U.S. Chief of Staff to the Generalissimo

Subject: Chinese War Production

Date: June 11, 1945 (Chungking, China)

The attached study [not included herewith] is an analysis of the Chinese war production, why it can and must be increased, and the necessary action to be taken in order to accomplish this increase . . .

Conclusions

By proper utilization of existing Chinese facilities, Chinese war production can be substantially increased.

In order to increase Chinese war production, the following steps must be taken:

a. Firm requirements must be established within the limits of Chinese production capabilities and Chinese budgetary capacity, and firm orders placed with the War Production Board to proceed with procurement to meet these requirements.

b. The money necessary for the procurement of munitions and supplies called for by these approved requirements must be appropriated to the War Production Board, and the War Production Board must be authorized to spend this money for this purpose. Such appropriations must be separate and apart from the present revolving funds already made available to the War Production Board.

c. Anti-inflationary controls must not be confused with necessary expenditures for war materials.

d. The power to fix price increases or decreases of basic materials essential to war production, including coal, should be delegated to the War Production Board, and it should be instructed to use its pricing powers to obtain maximum production of approved military requirements with the least possible loss of time.

e. The War Production Board is now empowered and should be instructed to prepare a list of items essential to war production, including coal, and to require, on pain of confiscation, all holders of such materials to register the quantity and location of their holdings with the War Production Board.

f. In addition to the U.S.-sponsored divisions, armies, and field armies, the Chinese government should designate approximately 80 divisions, with minimum required auxiliary troops, as Ministry of War troops. Serviceable stocks of munitions on hand, and current production, should be used to equip these Ministry of War troops in accordance with Tables of Equipment similar to those Tables of Equipment used by the U.S.-sponsored divisions. Application under Lend-Lease should be made to secure those relatively few items such as pack howitzers and motor vehicles which cannot be produced in China. The objective should be to have these approximately 80 divisions completely equipped by the end of 1945.

g. The money saved by the reductions in the size of the Chinese armies should be used first to procure the necessary equipment for the 80 divisions, and the balance should revert to the treasury of the government of China.

The Ministry of War should be charged with the responsibility of controlling the issue of initial equipment and replacement and maintenance supplies to all units of the Chinese army other than those which are U.S.-sponsored. First priority of issue should be given to the 80 divisions and necessary auxiliary troops herein designated as Ministry of War troops. After these troops have been completely equipped, remaining equipment, if any, should be distributed in accordance with the directives of the Chinese General Staff . . .

HEADQUARTERS
UNITED STATES FORCES
CHINA THEATER

No. 617
MEMORANDUM TO HIS EXCELLENCY,
THE GENERALISSIMO
From: A. C. Wedemeyer
       Lieutenant General, U.S. Army
       U.S. Chief of Staff to the Generalissimo
Date: June 18, 1945 (Chungking, China)

Just prior to my departure on a trip [a tour of inspection to northwest China], I desire to emphasize a few points that need your earnest consideration and support:

a. We must as early as possible adopt [a] uniform ration for all members of the Chinese military forces, including officers and enlisted men. Regardless of the area in which our men are located, and regardless of their mission, they should be provided a uniform ration—that is, a certain number of pounds of rice, a certain number of pounds of vegetables, and a stipulated amount of meat and condiments as well as a beverage.

b. The deactivation of units that you and I know are—according to both military and political requirements—surplus and a tremendous drain upon the limited resources of your impoverished country.

c. Reorganization of the Ministry of Conscription to insure proper treatment of young men conscripted, and also to preclude induction of men who are mentally defective or physically unfit for military service . . .

I urgently recommend that you insure positive action in connection with the above matters. They are all related one to the other. If we feed our men properly, the problems of your Ministry of Conscription will be quickly alleviated. If we deactivate unnecessary units, your financial problems in supporting the remaining necessary forces will be solved. The morale and the spirit of your entire army will be improved. Also, the civilians in China, particularly the peasants who are properly remunerated for the services rendered to their government—for example, in supplying food for the army—will feel that their support to the government and the military forces is an obligation, and no longer a duty to be avoided.

HEADQUARTERS
UNITED STATES FORCES
CHINA THEATER

No. 619
MEMORANDUM TO HIS EXCELLENCY,
THE GENERALISSIMO
From: A. C. Wedemeyer
        Lieutenant General, U.S. Army
        U.S. Chief of Staff to the Generalissimo
Date: June 18, 1945 (Chungking, China)

During the recent air movement of the New 6th Army from Chanyi to Chih-kiang, I was aware through progress reports that the movement was progressing smoothly and on schedule. I felt that close team play was being effected between the Americans and Chinese units and personnel involved. Otherwise, the movement could not have occurred, with troops, food, supplies and ammunition arriving at destination in a well-timed and coordinated movement.

The movement of an entire army and its animals was accomplished in the remarkably short period between April 21 and May 11, 1945. This movement contributed greatly to the successful action of the Chinese in turning back the Japanese thrust towards Chih-kiang airfield. These events together may well prove to be . . . a decisive turning point in the prosecution of the war in China . . .

I wish to express to you my appreciation of the full and enthusiastic cooperation of General Ho Ying-chin and his staff in making general arrangements and providing Chinese Services of Supply support . . .

It is appropriate that I should emphasize my conviction that the success of this truly "all out" effort was due in no small measure to the splendid spirit of cooperation which was manifested by all personnel involved in this mission—Americans and Chinese. It augurs well for our future operations in this theater, and it is my steadfast belief that the high devotion to duty exemplified throughout this movement will be an inspiration for all to follow in the increasingly important role this theater will be called upon to play in effecting the unconditional surrender of Japan . . .

10

Pacific Strategy

1945

Although additional territory and airfields were lost, the Japanese winter offensives of 1944–1945 in China were contained, thanks in part to extraordinary measures that included the repatriation of two U.S.-trained Chinese divisions serving with SEAC in Burma.

The Pacific War had gone well for the Allies on other fronts as well. MacArthur had returned to the Philippines at the end of 1944; Nimitz had seized bases in the Central Pacific as far westward as Saipan, Guam, and Palau. American planning was based on the assumption that victory would come only after an invasion of the Japanese home islands. As the war moved into its final phases, the choice of a strategy leading to that ultimate assault became a topic of lively debate.

In the early spring of 1945, Wedemeyer and U.S. ambassador Patrick J. Hurley were recalled from Chungking for consultation in Washington. On his return to China, Wedemeyer dispatched another of his personal letters to General Marshall. In this wide-ranging report, the perennial advocate of a direct approach in Europe applied similar logic to the closing phases of the war with Japan. He also provided the Chief of Staff with further background on current problems, plans, and personalities in China.

A.P.O. 879
April 13, 1945

[General George C. Marshall
Chief of Staff
War Department
Washington, D.C.]

Dear General:

I am deeply grateful for the assistance rendered by you and the officers of the War Department in connection with problems presented in China Theater. I was aware of an intelligent and sympathetic understanding of Far Eastern complexities in all of my contacts. I also noted a tendency to give me undue credit for accomplishments in China. Actually we have not scratched the surface. Intelligent and energetic employment of Americans and earnest cooperation of the Chinese may result in realistic contribution to the war effort. We are trying to bring this about.

I have given considerable thought to continued operations in the Pacific. My views as outlined in the informal memo I submitted to you and the Joint Chiefs of Staff while in Washington have been reaffirmed. The Okinawa operation [launched March 26, 1945] is indicative of strongly deteriorating enemy air and naval power. In talking to Nimitz and MacArthur upon my return trip I noted a tendency to diverge from the effort to concentrate and deploy for a decisive thrust at the heart of the Japanese war effort. *Nimitz* outlined many subsidiary operations that would encircle the Jap homeland. Some of these may be requisite preliminary operations to create appropriate conditions for the final thrust. However, in assessing enemy capabilities and our own, I earnestly hope that we will not permit ourselves to be drawn into resource- and time-consuming operations, unless they are absolutely proven essential to the accomplishment of the main task. *MacArthur* discussed further an operation against Borneo. Such operation is eccentric to sound strategic advance against the enemy. Herewith my views which may be refuted by your planners but might be worthy of consideration:

a. The Allies would obtain rubber from Borneo approximating 4,000 tons a month. I am not in position to assess urgency of the procurement of raw rubber, however, I recall that Ceylon produces approximately 110,000 tons. (Incidentally, this production is capable of 50 percent increase with proper management and increased labor. A plan to import Tamils from India was being considered when I was located at Kandy. The Indian and Ceylon governments could not agree on the scheme for repatriation of the Tamil laborers postwar, hence the plan did not materialize.) The 110,000 tons from Ceylon, supplemented by that from other sources including Africa, South and Central America as well as synthetics produced, may tide us over until more lucrative sources in Malay and Netherland East Indies can again be exploited. My comment: A Borneo operation may be necessary to obtain raw rubber; however, I am not convinced that this is so.

b. When the British Fleet (under Admiral [Sir Bruce] Fraser) was permitted to operate in the Pacific, our Navy made available the base facilities in Manus Island. MacArthur suggested that the British Fleet utilize Australian bases. Our own Navy now may regret that Manus Island Base was opened to the British because of postwar implications. That base may prove very significant in future U.S. Navy strategic plans. Therefore, it would be advisable now to acquire another water or port area that could provide base for the British. Brunei at northwest tip of Borneo offers good possibilities for such base. The British could be based there, leaving Manus in the Admiralty Islands exclusively for U.S. Naval use. Further, our Navy envisages continued operations under Nimitz in the Pacific. If MacArthur's resources are employed to the south, he will be involved and committed, thus eliminating, at least for the time being, competition between MacArthur and Nimitz advances. Comments: Two possible reasons that King [First Admiral Ernest J. King, Chief of Naval Operations] may support Borneo operations—U.S. Navy would remove British from Manus, and MacArthur would be involved to south.

c. Another possible justification for Borneo operation might be procurement of oil. Some time back I reviewed possibilities of oil development in Southeast Asia, and if my memory serves me rightly, the oil *is* in Borneo area; however, the time required to develop remunerative quantities would be unacceptable and out of phase with Pacific strategy. Comment: Procurement of oil does not justify Borneo operation in background of overall strategy.

d. There is also the possibility that pressure will be brought to bear for continued advance southward on Java, thus further committing resources and making more remote concentration and appropriate preliminary operations for decisive blow against Jap homeland. Comment: The historic example of being drawn along by the cliche "we must not lose our momentum," "we must exploit our initiative," you will remember, is the advance from Sicily on up the Italian boot.

While in Washington I discussed Far Eastern strategy with General Embick [Lieutenant General Stanley D. Embick, prewar Deputy Chief of Staff who headed several War Department boards during WWII. Father-in-law of Wedemeyer]. You know I admire him and respect his strategic judgment. The past several years we have generally agreed on strategy, which is all to my credit, for he does think soundly. However, we differed in regard to premises regarding present and projected basic Far Eastern strategy. In my memo [mentioned above], "continued and early large scale operations against Japanese homeland" are urged. General Embick cautions that Russia may retard her contribution against Japan if [she] is led to believe "that the U.S. regards the time factor as of overriding importance, regardless of cost to America, and, without awaiting Russian participation, is preparing to invade the home citadel of Japan." In the first place, no one, certainly my memo does not advocate rushing in "regardless of cost to America". . . . The strategy I recommended is designed to preclude a long drawn-out war with inherent great cost in lives and resources. The plans I suggested definitely envisage appropriate "softening up" operations as requisite preliminaries to final assault on Japan proper.

Upon my return to the Theater I was particularly concerned with the degree of cooperation that I received in absentia, and the fulfillment of directives, both oral and written, that I left with key members of the command. It is most gratifying to me, and I know it will be to you, to learn that General Chennault loyally and effectively carried on the Theater policies which I had initiated. I can not in fairness fail to register my complete satisfaction with his fine work. Inasmuch as War Department plans envisage the movement of all American air and ground personnel to the China Theater (excepting those forces and resources required within India-Burma Theater for communications zone functions), I felt that I should frankly and completely inform General Chennault of the contemplated movement of General [Major General George E.] Stratemeyer's Headquarters and the Tenth Air Force Headquarters to China. Upon my return, therefore, I explained that the Fourteenth Air Force would ultimately constitute the strategic air force and the Tenth Air Force the tactical of this Theater. This arrangement was obviously a disappointment to Chennault, for he will be under the command of General Stratemeyer and will no longer be the senior airman in the area, where he enjoyed prestige and complete control from an air viewpoint the past several years. He accepted these decisions like a soldier and stated categorically that he was prepared to carry on and do his utmost in any assigned role so long as his health would permit. He told me further that he had no postwar ambitions, and that after the war he visualized returning to his home in Louisiana where he could fish, hunt, and rest. He discussed very frankly his relations with prior officers with whom he served, including Stilwell, Hearn [Major General Thomas G. Hearn, Chief of Staff to Stilwell], Dorn [Brigadier General Frank Dorn, Aide and Field Commander under Stilwell], and Bissell [Brigadier General Clayton L. Bissell, Stilwell's Senior Air Officer]. I sensed no bitterness; however the difficulties that he had with them, he described as resulting from his sincere efforts to get on with the war and their probable lack of appreciation of the complex problems presented in China.

He also mentioned his direct correspondence with the President. When he was home at Trident conference [May 1943], the President voluntarily urged that he write occasionally. This General Chennault did, presenting the situation as he saw it. He stated that he at no time had the intention of circumventing General Stilwell or the War Department, and that it never occurred to him that he was being disloyal in the premises. I told him that, if I had been a member of his staff at that time and, if he had asked my advice, I would have suggested that such information that he might wish to reach the President should be processed through normal War Department channels, certainly through you. I believe that he now agrees that he should not have communicated directly with the President . . .

When I arrived in the Theater last fall I learned that there was a feeling of suspicion—almost hostility—between the Headquarters of the Theater and the Fourteenth Air Force. I believe that has been alleviated, and there now appears to be full cooperation and coordination. General Chennault has resisted openly some of my proposals, for example, when I wanted to introduce ATC [Air Transport Command] into the Theater, he advised strongly against such action. However, when I made the decision, there was no more about it. As I told you when I was home, I expressed the opinion that General Chennault and Captain Alsop [Captain Joseph Alsop, sometime journalist and Aide to Chennault] were not indulging in intrigue against me with the Chinese. I had been particularly alerted to such possibilities inasmuch as you explained about two years ago that they were doing so against Stilwell.

We have been trying to evolve a spirit of cooperation between our Headquarters and all activities in the Theater, and to create an atmosphere of mutual trust. This area was so rife with dissension and disorganization when I arrived it was, and continues to be, difficult to know exactly what brought about the regrettable conditions I found here last October. I have not had time to investigate fully, but did remove . . . most of the Theater staff who seemed imbued with a defeatist attitude, noncooperative spirit, and ideas of suspicion in their relations with other Headquarters. We now have a modicum of organization, and with the continued arrival of officers who are capable and straightforward, I believe we can get on with our more important task of assisting the Chinese against the Japs. Chennault repeatedly and emphatically stated that he would loyally and effectively support me to the hilt. I was very much impressed with his candor and pledge of wholehearted support to me and to the American effort in China . . .

Brigadier General George Olmsted [Civil Affairs Officer on China Theater Staff] will arrive shortly—in fact I visualize sending this letter by him. He has a fund of knowledge concerning lend lease matters, and has been very helpful in correlating War Production Board activities in China. Mr. T. V. Soong [Finance Minister] asked that he be present in Washington during his discussions concerning China economic matters, and the Generalissimo urged me to make this possible. I have the utmost confidence in General Olmsted's judgment, and I believe it would be helpful if you could give him a few minutes of your time.

The Generalissimo was very sad about the sudden and untimely passing of our Commander-in-Chief, the President, and expressed his heartfelt sympathy. He asked me to assure you that the Chinese would redouble their efforts to carry out the ideals as espoused by the President and would justify Mr. Roosevelt's continued loyal support to China.

Again I want to express my deep appreciation of your many personal kindnesses while I was home, and in making it possible to see my dear Mother and my two boys prior to my return.

Sincerely,

A. C. WEDEMEYER
Lieutenant General, U.S. Army
Commanding

II

Plans and Operations in China

1945

The war in Europe ended on May 8, 1945. At that time, victory in the Pacific still seemed a distant goal in an uncertain and bloody future.

In China, Wedemeyer continued to build strength for a major offensive in the fall. His objective was to seize a port on China's southeast coast, thus finally opening channels of sea communication to that long-starved theater. The Japanese hold on the Asian mainland could then be challenged, and China could serve as an ample base from which to launch the final Allied assault on the home islands.

In letters to three of his senior subordinate commanders, Wedemeyer explained his policies and discussed the future. His first letter was addressed to the famed commander of the Flying Tigers, Major General Claire Lee Chennault; the second to Major General George E. Stratemeyer, commander of U.S. Army Air Forces in India-Burma Theater (soon to become senior U.S. air officer in China); and the third to Major General Robert B. Mc-Clure, senior U.S. adviser to General Ho Ying-chin, commander of Chinese ground forces.

Wedemeyer also kept his former War Department associates informed of his plans and needs. Reprinted here are letters to Major General John E. Hull, Chief of OPD, and Brigadier General George A. Lincoln, Chief of Strategy and Policy in OPD.

A.P.O. 879
April 28, 1945

Major General Claire L. Chennault
Headquarters, Fourteenth U.S. Air Force
APO 627

Dear Claire:

In reply to your letter dated April 19, 1945, I wish first to state that the situation in the Hsian and Chih-kiang areas is also causing me concern. In each case I have attempted to counter the Japanese advances with minimum interference to the RASHNESS plan [plan for an Allied offensive in the fall aimed eventually at seizing a coastal port in southeast China]. Reaffirming my policy, I desire that the *minimum* air and ground effort be employed against the Japanese in order to deny complete liberty of action to the enemy while we concentrate on the preparation for RASHNESS. I accept that we must retain [a] flexible outlook in implementing RASHNESS. Conditions such as enemy action, acts of God, and local political as well as economic factors may require changes, but certainly not drastic revamping of our plans.

A detachment of Americans and some equipment have been sent to Hsian to assist the Chinese units there. The New 22nd Division is enroute to the Chih-kiang area and, as you know, I have decided to send the remainder of the New Sixth Army to the same area to try to stabilize the situation in that area. These countermoves on our part will, I trust, stop the Japanese thrusts and concurrently provide us with time and resources to train and equip RASHNESS forces and to bring these forces, together with air cooperation, to bear on the enemy in decisive action.

A fundamental difference of opinion on the relative effectiveness of ground versus air forces in the defense of an area has existed between us from the time I assumed command of this Theater. Your view—that air forces, assisted by weak, nondescript ground forces, can protect an area—has not been borne out during this war, certainly not in Europe or in this Theater. I feel that, by strengthening the ground forces, both combat and service elements, as I have done, in the areas under attack, and by utilizing ground demolition teams against the Japanese lines of communications, thus freeing the additional air for use in direct support of the ground, I will more surely stop the Japanese advance than I will if I increase the air effort at the expense of the ground forces.

I realize that my efforts to build up ground combat and service forces must temporarily reduce in some measure our overall air effort. However, I do not understand your statement that your 1945 operating rate is some 20 percent less than your 1944 rate, since you are receiving more than twice the tonnage you received last year without a corresponding material increase in the size of the Fourteenth Air Force.

I do not agree, nor do other competent air officers with whom I have talked, that the efficiency of an air force will be seriously reduced if it is forced to operate at 55 percent of some theoretical standard rate. I must accept the slight loss of fighting edge that may result from the enforced slowing down of your operations. ·

I do not agree that my failure to support the air force operations at the expense of the ground forces will place me on the defensive during the remainder of this year. On the contrary, I am determined to create an effective air-ground team that can and will strike offensively in 1945. The course of action I am following I believe will accomplish this. Further, the half-starved and ill-equipped ground forces with which I must work today are the result of the very policy you are advocating and which was implemented the past few years. These forces cannot conduct a realistic active defense. An objective analysis of operations in China the past four years confirms this statement.

While it may be that some of the people who are alleged to be familiar with logistics in China will not agree with my decision to build a balanced air-ground offensive team this year, I feel that I am as familiar with the overall logistical situation as they. Prior to my arrival there had been no true analysis of the logistics problems of this Theater. I have been continually examining and analyzing the logistical and strategic conditions affecting this area, and have made my decisions and evolved my announced policy accordingly. I have instituted measures [that], if properly implemented, will result in an increased utilization of air, rail, road, and water facilities to support our contemplated operations.

My policy has been stated and restated. I intend to carry it out. I am determined to create conditions favorable to building up a balanced ground-air striking force capable of offensive operations against the Japanese. This must be done as soon as possible; it can not wait until 1946. My experience in this Theater, together with my study of the situation which existed before my arrival, convince me that this balanced force must be created *now*. In the past, this Theater has followed the course which you now propose, only to find that the impotent ground forces could not protect the airfields which are so sorely needed today. A continuation of that policy can only lead to more advances by the Japanese and the loss of more airfields, if not the battle for China itself. Certainly I would be unable to carry out my mission which is to contain, divert, and destroy maximum enemy forces.

I am prepared to accept the risk of a reduced rate of operations for the air forces in order to build up a balanced ground-air striking force. I am prepared to trade "real estate" for the time and resources necessary to create such a force.

Joe Alsop and Howard Means [Colonel, 14th Air Force] handed me your latest letter and a copy of a plan for an air counteroffensive in the Chih-kiang area. In consonance with all of the above, I feel that you and Bob McClure [Major General Robert B. McClure, Senior U.S. adviser to Chinese ground forces] should maintain constant contact in following developments in order that air strikes against remunerative targets be made that will directly assist the ground forces now opposing the enemy advances in the Yellow River and Chih-kiang areas.

I always welcome my commanders' views honestly expressed. I am glad to have yours, especially since I know that you, as a real soldier, will loyally support the decision I have made. A separate letter covers subject embodied in the last paragraph of your letter.

Sincerely,

A. C. WEDEMEYER
Lieutenant General, U.S. Army
Commanding

A.P.O. 879
May 1, 1945

Major General George E. Stratemeyer
Headquarters, Army Air Forces
India-Burma Theater
APO 671

Dear Strat:

. . . . .

The tactical situation in China is not favorable. The enemy is pushing westward from the Yellow River area and also from Paoching. Unquestionably he intends to widen his corridor and deny airfields from which we have been operating effectively against his LOC [line of communications] and other installations. I have been trying to allocate inflowing tonnages broadly in two ways: (1) to create ground forces, both combat and S.O.S. [Services of Supply]; and (2) to [supply] air forces and units actually in contact with the enemy. My position is that of swapping time and space with the enemy while trying to prepare an air-ground team that can and will fight offensively in the fall.

We recently captured Japanese plans that indicate their intentions to conduct operations against Kweiyang, Sian, Chungking and Kunming. It may be their plan envisages an all-out effort this summer to put China out of the war so that their west flank will be secure and they can concentrate on the defense of coastal areas. It may also be within their capabilities to do this; only strenuous effort on our part will thwart their plans. Increased air tonnage will probably be the crux in determining our success or failure. It is my responsibility that such tonnages are not frittered away as they were in the past.

As you know, I have carefully analyzed operations in this Theater covering the past four years. The Chinese and American effort was dissipated over vast areas and throughout a tremendous number of ground forces so that today I find no effective combat units and a very ineffective S.O.S. There are 327 Chinese divisions. I have been urging the past few months a drastic reduction so that we can concentrate on an appropriate number and create, by combining Chinese and American effort, a real fighting force. The RASHNESS plan is in consonance with such ideas, and I am trying my utmost to resist diversions that will militate against that plan. I accept that enemy action or other conditions over which we have no control may prevent us from implementing fully RASHNESS, but at least it is a fine sound goal to which we should all work.

I have recently sent a strategic resume to Marshall for the Joint Chiefs of Staff, giving them information that will enable them to follow developments here. These are indeed critical months for China Theater. I do not wish to sound pessimistic, for if we give our best efforts at all times, at least we will have our own respect, even in defeat. Everyone is working hard, and the malcontents are few and far between. I will be glad when you are near me for I value your judgment and professional attainments highly.

Sincerely,

A.C. WEDEMEYER
Lieutenant General, U.S. Army
Commanding

PERSONAL

A.P.O. 879
May 1, 1945

Major General R. B. McClure
Headquarters, Chinese Combat Command
A.P.O. 627

Dear Bob:

Your fine letter of the 25th of April is most heartening. You may be certain that I will tighten reins and give increasingly strong direction as time goes on. Thrown into a maelstrom as I was some months ago, with only limited competent personnel upon whom I could rely, I had to tread carefully. No commander in any theater of war has the resources that he deems adequate or appropriate to accomplish his assigned mission. Of course, in the China area it is immediately accepted that we must continue to operate on unacceptably small resources until at least we establish sea communications. The splendid efforts being made to supplement our existing air and ground communications will provide only a restricted quantity. The allocation of personnel and materiel over the present lines of communication is one of my most difficult and immediate problems. I am trying to favor our S.O.S. and the CCC [Chinese Combat Command] in this regard . . .

In providing support for [the] Chinese both in personnel and materiel, I am sure you will agree we must strongly resist [the] dissipation which has been so rife in the past. Actually, we are trading time and space with the enemy in preparing for RASHNESS.

Your notes concerning the reduction of the Chinese forces are pertinent. For some months I have been urging the Generalissimo and the Minister of War to reduce the Chinese army, which consists of approximately 327 divisions. Actually, they have more officers in that army than enlisted men. Trying to maintain such a tremendous force in this impoverished country the past several years has resulted in deplorably ineffective ground forces. Our piddling contribution was also scattered about and did not produce the results that might have been attained if we had concentrated American personnel and materiel in ten divisions. However, we now have a program which is simple and sound. Strict adherence should be our watchword. I accept that enemy action and acts of God may cause changes in the plan, but in our approach we should all do our utmost to resist dispersal of means.

The suggestion you made concerning strikes along China coast by Pacific forces is fine. I spoke to MacArthur and Nimitz about this when I was en route home and we completed plans for their employment. On my return to the Theater, I initiated request to MacArthur that his planes strike targets in the interior of China within their effective range. This should also contribute.

You recall that we found no organization or proper staff procedure in Theater Headquarters when we arrived here. Experienced personnel was limited; consequently, you and I and a few others who knew how and were willing to carry on performed the duties of the General Staff. Now we are beginning to acquire a modicum of proper staff procedure. I am still not happy about the split of Theater Headquarters. If the Generalissimo would only agree to my location in the Kunming area, my problem would be solved. He will not do so; therefore I am now studying ways and means and inclined to the following views: Appoint a deputy theater commander and give him appropriate staff, all of whom would be located in the Kunming area. The deputy commander of the theater would be responsible for the coordination of CCC, air forces, and S.O.S. His staff would draw up the plans and thus insure complete and authorative integration by those three activities. Stilwell had a similar organization in India–Burma. His Theater Headquarters remained at Delhi. However, he established a headquarters at Myitkyina with his deputy commander, Sultan [Major General Daniel I. Sultan], who had a staff appropriately constituted to conduct coordination between air and ground combat units as well as the S.O.S. . . .

Your loyalty and selfless attitude in the solution of complex problems in this Theater I shall never forget . . .

Sincere good wishes.

As ever,

A. C. WEDEMEYER
Lieutenant General, U.S. Army
Commanding

A.P.O. 879
May 2, 1945

Major General J. E. Hull
Chief, Operations Division
War Department General Staff
Pentagon Building
Washington, D.C.

Dear Ed:

You have been most helpful and typically understanding of problems presented. I want to express my sincere appreciation. I should like nothing better than to carry on quietly and effectively the duties connected with my present post and refrain from bothering you and the War Department generally. I am fully cognizant of the demands made upon your time and assistance by others, and am an earnest advocate of the policy that one should resort to every expedient to accomplish assigned tasks with available means and resist the tendency to call for outside assistance . . .

Analysis of the enemy capabilities the next few months suggests the following (this has been somewhat confirmed in the past few days by Japanese documents captured in Paoching): The Japanese High Command has probably written off, and is prepared to sacrifice, those forces withdrawing from Burma and [the] Netherland East Indies. They are being concentrated in French Indo-China. We have had many reports confirming the fact that [the] Japanese have stockpiled considerable equipment in Hanoi and Haiphong. Their troops concentrating in French Indo-China could therefore be re-equipped. The Japanese High Command realizes that if they strike hard and fast with those forces, they might be able to take Kunming which would, to all intents and purposes, put China out of the war and would effectively neutralize the Allied effort, air and ground, from southwest China. They must recognize that this Allied effort is becoming increasingly a threat to their position in Asia. At present the Japanese are advancing in the Yellow River area, and also from Paoching on Kweiyang. We are trying to dispose forces to retard or stop such advances. Concurrently, we are striving to create effective ground forces, both combat and S.O.S., to sustain offensive effort late this fall by combined air and ground forces in consonance with RASHNESS plan . . .

I have sent messages to Washington indicating all of the above, and suggested that consideration be given for lodgment on the coast of China. The many advantages accruing to the overall Allied effort are at once apparent to you and your planners in Washington. Also, the disadvantages [of] broad strategic plans for continued advance in the Pacific are better known to you than to China Theater. I am confident, however, that our overall position against the Japanese would be much more greatly enhanced if we made a lodgment on the China coast instead of continuing operations in areas south of the Philippine archipelago.

The question of moving present U.S. Air Forces in India-Burma to China Theater has been carefully studied. General Arnold [General Henry H. "Hap" Arnold, Chief of Staff, U.S. Air Force] admonished me to do my utmost to create conditions in China Theater so that we could employ effectively maximum air forces. Everyone with whom I talked in Washington supported this premise. The increased tonnages coming over the hump for projected targets will definitely make this possible. I feel certain that I can fully employ the combined Fourteenth and Tenth Air Forces with approximately 40,000 tons monthly. I can also meet the requirements of my ground forces with the remaining tonnages that become available. The Tenth Air Force would not be closed in China areas until July 1 earliest . . .

I suppose that by the time this letter reaches you General Eisenhower will have announced that organized resistance in Europe has been liquidated, and at long last VE Day will be a reality. I hesitate to predict dates of such moment, for as a planner in the War Department, I predicted in strategic studies . . . that Russia would be rendered militarily impotent by July 1, 1943. This was at a time when I was urging so strongly a cross-channel operation in the late spring of that year, and I felt that we should take advantage of the Russian-German struggle which required the bulk of the latter's forces and would not be able therefore to stop our BOLERO plan.

Give my very best to mutual friends.

Sincerely,

A.C. WEDEMEYER
Lieutenant General, U.S. Army
Commanding

A.P.O. 879
May 14, 1945

Brigadier General George A. Lincoln
Chief, Strategy & Policy Section
Operations Division, W.D.G.S.
Pentagon Building
Washington, D.C.

Dear Abe:

.   .   .   .   .

We were terribly disappointed when the War Department found it necessary to reduce our hump tonnage approximately 25,000 tons a month. However, War Department decisions will be implemented loyally here and we are striving to exploit to the fullest every bit of support that you people back home can give us. You may rest assured that China Theater is preparing to justify the stupendous effort made by the Allies the past few years for the express purpose of implementing the Chinese effectively against the Jap.

The overall Jap plan probably envisages the withdrawal of troops from the Netherland East Indies, Malay, Burma and Thailand to the north. They probably will leave forces in Indo-China and Hainan to secure the coast for obvious reasons and then scatter forces north along the coast on up to Korea for [the] same purpose. It is imperative to them that the corridor which they now hold—extending generally from Hankow to Indo-China—be broadened so that they have available a route of egress and can readily redispose their forces. The operations that they are now undertaking in the Yellow River area and west of Paoching are undoubtedly for such purpose. They desire to capture the airfields in those areas from which we have been operating very effectively against their lines of communications. Whether or not I have the capability of stopping this remains to be seen. The Chinese with American supervision have been doing outstandingly well, fighting in a most creditable manner to preclude the advance of the Jap.

My overall plan envisages Active Defense. Concurrently I am striving to build up approximately 20 divisions on the standard of the five CAI divisions. I am creating an S.O.S. that will be well-organized and equipped to provide logistical support both to the ground and air forces. I hope to create an air-ground team by late this summer or early fall, and then revert from active defense to the RASHNESS plan which, as you know, envisages the first large-scale offensive action ever undertaken in China Theater.

The local successes that we have been enjoying in the Paoching area recently have greatly heartened both Americans and Chinese. The Japs suffered approximately 11,000 casualties. Spirit was so high that the Supreme Field Commander, General Ho Ying-chin, his American opposite, Major General McClure, and the Chinese commanders at the front, all wanted to undertake an offensive drive eastward to sever enemy lines of communications. It is excellent spirit and I appreciate the temptation to follow up their successes. However, my analyses of China Theater operations the past four years indicate unmistakeably that the greatest deterrents to their success have been premature and/or piecemeal commitments. Therefore I have ordered a continuation of active defense and have forbidden large-scale offensive action until I am certain that I have ground forces that are well equipped, well fed, and trained; until I have air-ground teams with each forward ground unit; until I have an S.O.S. that has surplus equipment in forward areas to insure logistical support for a concerted and continued drive eastward . . .

One can never tell how the situation will develop in China Theater. However, should we have success in our RASHNESS plan this fall, and should we reach our objectives, Nanning and Liuchow, I would appreciate very much consideration by your planners to the following two important points:

> *a.* Air supply flown in from Philippine bases to Nanning and Liuchow where we have fine air strips. This would greatly enhance our capability of exploiting further to the east. It is apparent to you and your planners that the lines of communications leading east from Kunming are very difficult, and if we could get tonnage flown in to the Liuchow-Nanning area, after we have established ourselves there, it would be a tremendous help.

> *b.* Assuming that we have reached our first objectives, Liuchow and Nanning, and are able to build up sufficient logistical support to permit continued advance to the coast, we would appreciate some help from the Pacific side in establishing a port. An amphibious operation involving only one division or possibly two timed with our approach to the coast would turn the trick and we would at last have our port . . .

Admiral Mountbatten and I are still not in complete accord concerning French Indo-China. I think it was most unfortunate that the directive sent to me . . . requires me to exchange complete information concerning my plans in Indo-China. My premise all the way through has been that no one should operate in the China Theater without prior authority of the Generalissimo, who is the recognized Supreme Allied Commander. Generalissimo considers that China, French Indo-China, and Thailand are in his theater. As his Chief of Staff, he holds me responsible for the coordination of all operations in that theater. The British have been operating in French Indo-China without notifying the Generalissimo, although the latter explicitly requires, in his so-called Gentlemen's Agreement with Mountbatten, that he be notified in advance. It really is not [a] straightforward approach, Abe, that Mountbatten is making, and of course it is entirely political.

Last winter and this spring when I was so urgently in need of airplanes, the British were using them for clandestine or unorthodox operations in great numbers within French Indo-China. Representations were made by Mountbatten to the British Chiefs of Staff that if one airplane were removed from India-Burma by me that his operations against Rangoon would be jeopardized, although he was using, as I stated, planes for unorthodox operations, and I was striving to obtain them to support orthodox operations in China. It just does not make sense to me, and I hope that you will clarify this with General Marshall and General Hull. The Prime Minister and the British Chiefs of Staff told Hurley when he was in London that I, without any regard for the security or success of the operations in Burma, would denude Mountbatten in order to accomplish the illusory support of China. I carefully and objectively evaluated Mountbatten's requirements in his operations. I was qualified to do this because I planned those very operations and was fully acquainted with his requirements. When the Japanese were driving westward last winter against Kweiyang, we have definite evidence of the fact that Kunming was their objective. They had the capability of driving on, and the Generalissimo—in fact, even Mountbatten's representative here, Lieutenant General Carton de Wiart—urged me to withdraw all five CAI divisions from Burma. I took more than a calculated risk and withdrew only two, which I carefully interposed to block the Jap advance. I took only two because I did not want to militate against the continued drive of Sultan's [Major General Daniel I. Sultan, Commander, Burma-India Theater] forces in Burma. I point these out merely to indicate the objectivity with which China Theater has made requests upon U.S. resources in India-Burma.

The above matters may appear trivial to you, however, they indicate the overall pattern of British plans in the Southeast Asia area . . . My own plans are phased carefully and are dependent upon so many imponderables, continued British interference will set the whole thing out of balance here. I would appreciate your help and request that you have a conference with your planners, giving them the background. I assure you that we Americans in China will justify your confidence and assistance. Actually we are making progress, and it is my conviction that we can and will make a realistic contribution against the Japanese if we are permitted to implement our present plans. Sultan has been absolutely wonderful in his support. He recently visited the Theater and was most enthusiastic about everything that he saw. He realizes the many difficulties inherent in Chinese organization but I have a setup now that is beginning to permeate the entire China war effort so that there should be a more practicable and sound approach to our problems.

I appreciate how very busy you are on a multitude of problems that do not pertain to China Theater. However, now that the Germans are liquidated, I feel justified in asking you and your cohorts to focus your attention and support on China Theater. We have experienced so many frustrations here, yet we all are of good heart and will not let you down.

Sincerely,

A.C. WEDEMEYER
Lieutenant General, U.S. Army
Commanding

12

The Problem of Two Chinas

1945

The internal revolution that had convulsed China throughout the twentieth century had not run its course when the Japanese struck in 1937. The Nationalist government of Chiang Kai-shek, heir to Sun Yat-sen's revolution of 1911, continued to face serious domestic opposition, especially the armed insurgency of the Communists. Although external aggression had brought the various factions together in uneasy truce, the Nationalists and Communists remained irreconcilable contenders for China's future.

While working closely with the recognized Nationalist government, the United States had sought throughout the war to maintain formal neutrality with respect to China's internal politics. American officials had made sustained efforts on both diplomatic and military levels to promote cooperation among the Chinese factions in the common interest of fighting the Japanese.

As the Pacific War moved into its closing phases, however, the long-smoldering fires of civil strife again burst into flame. Frequent armed clashes erupted as both Nationalists and Communists maneuvered for advantage in anticipation of Japanese collapse. In efforts to contain this strife until final victory was won, Wedemeyer in the summer of 1945 offered to monitor the field activities of both factions. His communications with the Generalissimo and Chairman Mao Tse-tung are presented herewith, along with his long personal letter to Marshall on the unfolding situation.

HEADQUARTERS
UNITED STATES FORCES
CHINA THEATER

Chungking, China
29 July 1945

No. 669-7
MEMORANDUM TO HIS EXCELLENCY,
THE GENERALISSIMO

From: A. C. WEDEMEYER
Lieutenant General, U.S. Army
United States Chief of Staff to the Generalissimo

Date: July 29, 1945

Attached herewith letter which I propose to send to the Communist Chairman, Mr. Mao Tse-tung. This letter embodies the ideas that you and I discussed on Friday afternoon, July 27th. If I can succeed in obtaining agreement from Mao Tse-tung to assignment of American representatives with Communist Divisions, I feel certain that factual and objective report can be made to the American public. Your early concurrence will be appreciated inasmuch as I would like to send this letter by Colonel Ivan Yeaton who will be head of the American Observer Group in Yenan, effective Tuesday, July 31st.

HEADQUARTERS
UNITED STATES FORCES
CHINA THEATER

Chungking, China
July 29, 1945

Mr. Mao Tse-tung
Chairman, Central Executive Committee
Chinese Communist Party
Yenan, China

My Dear Mister Chairman:

Having been notified that you enthusiastically received the information concerning the appointment of Colonel Ivan Yeaton, General Staff

Corps, as my representative, and as head of the American Observers Group in Yenan, I desire to express appreciation and also my confidence that contacts, both official and personal, will be satisfactory and pleasant between Colonel Yeaton and yourself.

Official information has reached me to the effect that General Chu Teh and General Peng Teh Hui, Commander and Deputy Commander respectively of the 18th Route Army, have issued radio appeal to the Generalissimo concerning recent armed clashes between elements of the Communist 18th Route Army and troops of the National government of the Republic of China. Especially, according to reports from units of the Communists' army in the Shen-Kansu border region, during the last week there has been anti-Communist activity. The report continues that serious fighting has gone on for three days with no sign of ceasing, and suggests that with a serious Japanese enemy still facing the Chinese, the destiny of China and her people depends upon the unity of the Kuomintang and the Communist Party.

As you know, I have very carefully refrained from participation since my arrival in the political affairs of this great country. My one purpose has been to help the Chinese help themselves in their struggle against the common enemy, the Japanese.

Today I do not propose to become involved in the Kuomintang-Communist political controversies. However, as Commanding General of U.S. forces in China, and as the Generalissimo's Chief of Staff, I am vitally interested in the employment of all Allied military forces operating throughout China Theater. I feel it is my duty to insure that all available resources, both materiel and personnel, continue to be employed against the common enemy, the Japanese. The report referred to above, therefore, from General Chu Teh and General Peng Teh Hui, has rendered mandatory immediate steps to insure that Chinese military forces are employed against the Japanese. Accordingly I made the following recommendations to the Generalissimo.

> *a*. That I assign at least two American officers and five American enlisted men with radio equipment [to] each Central Government division in contact with or in close proximity to the Communist forces. That these American representatives be instructed to keep me informed relative to the military employment of the Chinese Central Government divisions to which they are assigned.
>
> *b*. That I assign at least two American officers and five American enlisted men with radio equipment [to] each Communist Division in contact with or in close proximity to the Central Government forces. That these American representatives be instructed to

keep me informed through Colonel Yeaton relative to the military employment of the Chinese Communist divisions to which they are assigned.

c. That the commanders of the Central Government Divisions, to which I assign American officers and men, be directed by the Generalissimo to provide daily information and opportunity to the American representatives to observe the locations, movements, and employment of every element down to and including companies of the Central Government divisions concerned.

d. That the commanders of the Communist divisions, to which I assign American officers and men, be directed by you to provide daily information and opportunity to the American representatives to observe the locations, movements, and employment of every element down to and including companies of the Communist division concerned.

e. That I provide the Generalissimo promptly with a written summary of the reports received from American representatives with Central Government divisions.

f. That Colonel Yeaton provide you promptly with a written summary of the reports received from American representatives with the Communist units and concurrently dispatch similar report to me at Chungking.

g. That I inform the U.S. government relative to the facts obtained in the manner stipulated above.

There have been so many recriminations, misinterpretations, and misrepresentations concerning the employment of both Central Government and Communist military forces, I feel certain that the above realistic measures would enable me to obtain a true, objective, and nonpartisan report on the employment of military forces in China, and thus report factual data to my government.

Last winter when I first arrived in China, General Chou En-lai visited me in Chungking on two or three occasions. I had full opportunity to hear his discussions concerning the Communist viewpoint, including the avowed purpose of fighting the Japanese. I know that you and the Generalissimo share my feeling that the people of this war-torn and impoverished country yearn for peace, and that it would be most unfortunate if, after the Japanese are defeated, China is subjected to continued warfare with attendant chaos, suffering, and destruction.

I would appreciate it very much if you would discuss with Colonel Yeaton the above suggestions and notify me at your earliest convenience concerning your views in the premises. As indicated previously, I have discussed the above plans with the Generalissimo and he wholeheartedly approved. If approved by you, I will expedite American representatives to Yenan with their communications equipment for appropriate distribution to Communist divisions and concurrently to divisions of the Central Government forces.

Faithfully yours,

A. C. WEDEMEYER
Lieutenant General, U.S. Army
Commanding

A.P.O. 879
August 1, 1945

General of the Army George C. Marshall
Chief of Staff
United States Army
War Department
Washington, D.C.

Dear General:

When in the States last March you suggested that I write an occasional personal note to keep you informed of events transpiring in China. I have not done very well in this regard due to many interruptions and frequent absence from Chungking on a series of inspection trips in the field. I am sure that the China Theater staff, which is steadily improving, is keeping the War Department satisfactorily informed concerning the situation, and you therefore do learn indirectly of plans and the military situation in general.

The Generalissimo was grateful for your suggestion that a few outstanding European generals might be made available to China Theater. I have never seen him more cordial to anyone than he has been to General Simpson [Lieutenant General William H. Simpson, late commander of Ninth U.S. Army in European Theater]. In fact, the latter made a favorable impression everywhere we went on a recent trip along the front. As indicated in my radio to you . . . I feel that there is an important role in China for Simpson and am grateful for your [message] approving his assignment to the Theater. It is important that Simpson and his staff report as early as practicable to China. Our activities are rapidly accelerating with a view to an August or September offensive. I suggested to

Simpson that he return to the States via the Philippines and Guam in order to bring to you reports of conferences between my representatives and Nimitz's staff. Also, I have asked him to give you and key officials of War Department a comprehensive review of our undertakings. In addition to Simpson, I feel certain that Truscott [Lieutenant General Lucian K. Truscott, Jr., late commander of Third U.S. Army in European Theater] would make a contribution as commander of a Chinese Combat Command north of the Yangtze. I would retain McClure [Major General Robert B. McClure] as commander of Chinese Combat Command south of the Yangtze. Incidentally I feel that McClure is eminently qualified for promotion to Lieutenant General. He has done outstanding work and is virtually in command of approximately forty Chinese divisions.

The past few months the Generalissimo has been increasingly and embarrassingly friendly as well as many other Chinese leaders here. I have followed a course of action that I think you would follow under similar circumstances. In other words, I am carefully avoiding intimate contacts with any of the Chinese and am adhering to a straightforward, friendly demeanor with all of them. The Generalissimo often asks advice concerning political matters involving other countries and China's internal affairs. I have emphasized tactfully to him that advice under such circumstances is given with no official cognizance . . . I believe that he likes and enjoys Hurley [U.S. Ambassador Patrick J. Hurley] but realizes his proclivities—principally of talking constantly and often indiscreetly. Therefore the Generalissimo appears reluctant to confide freely in our ambassador. On one occasion he started to discuss Hurley's handling of the Communist problem. I quickly changed the subject. He sensed at once that I was not inclined to discuss fellow countrymen with him. He has never again attempted to discuss the relative merits of any American with me. Hurley's "freedom of speech," however, is a little embarrassing, and I wish that I might state to him straight from the shoulder, "Pat, you talk too much." Pat is the image of the finest man I ever knew, my father, and I have a genuine feeling of affection for him.

When informed by Hurley concerning the Potsdam Conference, the Generalissimo suggested that you and the President might visit China. I conveyed this information [by] radio . . . He may have been harboring in his mind since last fall the thought that your feeling for him might have been adversely affected by Stilwell's relief . . . Several days after mentioning the invitation to visit China, he returned to that subject and suggested that he would personally send you an invitation but was rather reluctant to do so because, on the occasion of President Roosevelt's death, he had sent condolences to you but received no reply. There was a veiled hint that you might be vexed with him because of General Stilwell's removal. I immediately assured him that you would never under any circumstances fail to reply to his note of condolences. I was certain you had replied. I emphasized that during my contact of several years with you in the War Department that you were always punctilious in acknowledging every courtesy and that I was positive in this instance we would discover that you had replied to the Generalissimo's note. Upon returning to my Headquarters I discovered in the records of my adjutant's office that a courier letter was delivered to the Generalissimo on April 26th . . . The Generalissimo is disappointed that your plans preclude a visit but fully understands that you will be very busy subsequent to the important Potsdam Conference. I too was disappointed, for all of us are proud of a few accomplishments and we do have some good spirit, all of which we wanted you to experience firsthand.

The Communist situation continues to be disturbing. I earnestly hope that we can prevent an increase in the scale and tempo of clashes currently reported between Central Government and Communist troops. My recent tours of inspection were conducted with a view to determining the military strength both in resources and in formed units that China as a whole could make available for employment against the Japanese. I found a large number of divisions fairly well equipped and trained that certainly should be required to exert maximum pressure against the enemy—phased with our planned operation CARBONADO [China Theater plan for a major fall offensive]. However, considerable military strength might very easily be absorbed in fratricidal war centering around the Communist-Kuomintang controversies. We recognize the seriousness of the situation and we are doing utmost to prevent smoldering fires from breaking out into wide-spread conflagration. As I indicated in my radio sent immediately prior to Potsdam Conference . . . , the only sure method of avoiding a civil war between the Communist and Central Government forces, with all of its potentially explosive consequences throughout the Far East, is to apply strong "outside pressure" from the United States and Russia. It is generally accepted that a unified, democratic China is necessary for world order. A civil war in China would reduce the advantages gained by military victory over Japan and destroy economic and political equilibrium in the Far East, the important objective for which we are fighting. Such an unfortunate sequel would certainly not be to the best interests of either Russia or America. I therefore strongly urge that realistic pressure be brought to bear against both factions, the Communists and the Central Government, by President Truman and Generalissimo Stalin.

It is difficult to obtain the truth concerning responsibility for current clashes between the military forces of the Communists and Central Government. I suggested recently to the Generalissimo that we place a small American cadre with each of his divisions in contact with or in close proximity to Communist forces so that we might obtain objective reports concerning locations, movements, and employment of those divisions. I suggested that we do likewise with the Communist divisions. The Generalissimo readily agreed to the arrangement. I am presenting [a] similar proposal to Mao Tse-tung, the Communist leader . . . There have been recriminations and misrepresentations on both sides; however, I feel that the presence of American representatives as indicated above will definitely act as a deterrent to surreptitious maneuver and continued Machiavellian gestures on the part of either side. Further, we Americans should be able to obtain a factual picture of the situation for presentation to Washington.

Lines of Communication

The Stilwell Road unfortunately has been closed a considerable part of the past month due to slides and inundations. Also, the pipelines upon which we counted so heavily for POL [petroleum, oil, and lubricants] tonnage have been out of order. The 6″ pipeline leading to Myitkyina was damaged by slides and the 4″ pipeline leading to Kunming was sabotaged. Remedial action has been taken in all instances, however, predicted tonnages have been greatly reduced, with corresponding effect on our intensified activity at the front, both air and ground. We have considerable difficulty in obtaining sufficient truck drivers and maintenance personnel for the vehicles arriving in the Theater. Although we had anticipated requirement of such personnel and had taken appropriate steps in organizing training schools, the dearth of American instructors, lack of equipment, and the difficulties of language militated strongly against the effectiveness of our program.

Other transportation problems have been injected by unfortunate attributes of the Chinese themselves. For example, a truck driving from A to B will be loaded under American supervision with appropriate 3 1/2 ton load. Along the route the Chinese driver will exercise every opportunity to "squeeze" by carrying an additional ton or so of freight or passengers. The latter will be debarked prior to arrival at B and it is therefore difficult to control. This abuse of transport results in broken springs and axles and attendant delays. These are only a few of the many problems presented in China. We continue to seek solutions and philosophically accept the Chinese. The Americans will retain their sense of humor, patience, and determination to get on with the job.

Student Divisions

When I arrived in China the Generalissimo explained a program that envisaged 100,000 student volunteers for military service to be formed into ten divisions. After three months training these divisions were to be made available for combat. Last March, all of the divisions had been organized, and now the three months training has been consummated. I have urged strongly that these divisions be broken up and increments of from two to three thousand student volunteers be placed in each of our so-called Alpha Divisions (U.S. sponsored). This would absorb approximately 80,000 of the 100,000, and the remainder could be profitably placed in increments with signal, artillery, [and] engineer battalions as well as with various Headquarters echelons. I have pointed out to the Generalissimo that these student volunteers, who are the sons of rich Chinese or of privileged classes and whose educational rating is generally high, should be distributed throughout the army. They should, I have told him, endure the same hardships and dangers as do the poor man's son. At present the student divisions receive much better food and equipment. I am repeatedly told by old China hands that they will never be employed in combat, but merely be retained as a corps elite . . . I am going to continue my efforts to utilize those young men in a practical way. Some of them are truly patriotic and may be willing to fight . . .

Inspection Trips

In June I had a most profitable trip covering several thousand miles north of the Yangtze along the corridor extending to Shanpa. In July, accompanied by General Simpson, I completed another long inspection trip along the front south of the Yangtze. General Simpson will describe our experiences. There have been frequent short trips to nearby bases in the Theater. A short jaunt here, however, would encompass all of Europe, for distances are so great. Personally, General, I am optimistic about the future. The splendid cooperation prevailing between American and Chinese in the field is very heartening. There are many logistical problems as yet unsolved but Aurand [Major General Henry S. Aurand, Commander, Services of Supply, China Theater] is working hard to surmount what often appears to be insurmountable obstacles. In this connection I think he should be given every support in experienced personnel. There must be some fine active officers with S.O.S. experience in European Theater who would gladly volunteer to help out in China. Instead of waiting for appeals for help, I believe ASF [Army

Service Forces] should report to Aurand availability of certain qualified officers. Generals Handy [General Thomas T. Handy, Deputy Chief of Staff, U.S. Army] and Hull [Major General John E. Hall, Chief of OPD] have repeatedly helped me in that manner. Aurand has the most difficult task in China Theater.

Military Situation in China

Enemy. The Japanese strategy continues to be defensive, and there are many indications confirming previous estimates that sacrificial forces, of various strengths and compositions, will be left by the enemy in Singapore, Saigon, Bangkok, Haiphong-Hanoi, Canton, Shanghai, [and] Hankow. It appears that they will select the Yangtze River line as their forward bastion on the continent to protect the "industrial crescent," Korea-Manchuria-Shantung. They probably would under strong Allied pressure fall back to the Yellow River line as the next defensive position. There has been confirmation the Japs are moving forces south from Indo-China, undoubtedly to strengthen defenses against projected SEAC operations in Malay Peninsula. They realize that it would have been very costly to attempt evacuation of their forces to Manchuria or the homeland because of Allied operations against their lines of communication. They therefore probably have elected to write them off and employ them in sacrificial roles with a view to denying as long as possible to the Allies the Straits of Malacca and the rubber, tin, and oil resources in that area.

Our Own. Currently throughout the Theater we are adhering to an active defense, continuing pressure wherever and whenever feasible but scrupulously avoiding the creation of a vacuum that might interfere with preparations for CARBONADO. Instructions have been issued to follow up and press enemy withdrawals but to avoid large-scale commitment, air or ground. In the meantime, we are feverishly deploying troops and supplies in preparation for CARBONADO. The fact that we already have attained the original *initial* CARBONADO objectives, Nanning-Liuchow-Kweilin, has greatly heartened everyone. We now look forward confidently toward a successful drive to the coast. We want very much to establish sea communications; however, we agree that it would be unsound to accept the tremendous cost in lives and resources as well as time to capture Canton-Hongkong area, should the Japanese elect to make a suicide "Manila" defense there. If the enemy stubbornly resists with strong forces in that area, we will invest the area and establish seaports elsewhere, for example, possibly at Swatow,

Foochow, Wenchow, Fort Bayard, and/or Amoy. There should be approximately twenty Chinese divisions equipped and trained to conduct a creditable offensive in September. These divisions will probably not be as well trained or as effective as the CAI [Chinese Army in India] divisions because of limited time available. However, the soldiers will be fed properly and there will be flow of ammunition and equipment as well as proper evacuation of wounded. These factors strongly influence the fighting spirit of any man but particularly the Chinese soldier who has been so pitifully and shamefully neglected in the past.

Everyone who comes to China, military or civilian, tries to analyze the situation and invariably speaks volubly and authoritatively upon return to the States. Still far from an authority with only nine months experience in the area, nevertheless I have had unusual opportunities to absorb information and to reach conclusions which may help you and the President in your considerations and decisions concerning China.

On the political side, one finds an embryonic nation, a great political entity about to be born. Previously, China consisted of a group of feudal dynasties which, through the years, resorted forcibly or voluntarily to varied degrees of political amalgamation or cohesion. Only a few decades ago the corrupt and arbitrary rule of warlords was overthrown. The leaders of the revolution established as their political tenets the three principles of Doctor Sun Yat-sen which, in reality, epitomize America's basic principles of democracy. During the course of this political transition or rebirth, Japan invaded and seized all of the most important sections of China, making more difficult and remote the realization of the three principles.

From the military viewpoint, the Chinese have been fighting an aggressive, infinitely superior enemy since 1937. One hears and reads many complaints and dire criticisms concerning the Chinese war effort. In my opinion, this is indicative of the reluctance of some observers to face facts. Actually, China at war does not mean large-scale modern organized fighting such as the European struggle just concluded, but means a stoic, amorphous mass resistance interspersed by isolated guerrilla activity. Further, we find lack of unity between the Kuomintang and the Communists, as well as on [the] part of some warlords or provincial groups. They all appear to be united on one point only, and that is continued resistance to the Japanese. This may be a facade; however, the record is clear that attractive surrender terms have been refused on several occasions the past few years. This, I think, has been most fortunate for us. If the Chinese had capitulated a few years ago, the military situation in the Pacific would have been a great deal different today. Today in China, effective military units are being created, equipped, and trained. However, guerrilla action will remain important, and if we can evolve a plan which will cause concerted and coordinated employment of all the available forces in China against the Japanese, I think we can strike decisive blows.

In this connection, you may not recall that you suggested to me over a year ago, when I was still a member of Mountbatten's staff, that the Chinese should create Commandos for employment more or less as guerrillas. Upon my return to India, I recommended this to Stilwell in keeping with your suggestion. Upon assuming command here, I retained the idea and immediately laid plans for the organization of twenty Commando units. These are being trained by the OSS [Office of Strategic Services] and they are doing a splendid job. Parachute work, night fighting, infiltration, sabotage, and similar work is in progress. We have already used some of these commandos very effectively in day and night actions against enemy installations and communications. We are now causing the enemy round-the-clock concern. It is he who is looking over his shoulder in dark shadows for fear of steel in his spleen. This will be increasingly true as the war goes on . . .

.   .   .   .   .

We are striving to prepare for any eventuality reference Japanese capitulation—early and sudden peace, fighting for the next few months, and even an extended period of war. Frankly, if peace should come within the next few weeks we will be woefully unprepared in China. On the American side we could handle our own unilateral personnel and property interests, but many of our activities are inextricably tied in with the Chinese and, if peace comes suddenly, it is reasonable to expect widespread confusion and disorder. The Chinese have no plan for rehabilitation, prevention of epidemics, restoration of utilities, establishment of balanced economy, and redisposition of millions of refugees. On the China Theater staff we have one U.S. military government officer, a Lieutenant Colonel Dobson, who at present is conducting a school in Chungking teaching selected Chinese civilian officials the functions of civil affairs. This school has been established one week. I have emphasized to the Generalissimo the necessity for advanced planning in connection with these problems, and he has issued instructions to his ministries. However, I am not optimistic about the results to be attained, if my experience with the military officials can be taken as a criterion. When in Washington last February I was informed that the United States would not become involved in the operation of civil affairs in China subsequent to Japanese surrender. We may unavoidably be drawn in as advisers to Chinese officials in a status analogous to that of Americans at present in Chinese military forces. I am sure that you will agree that we should assist the Chinese in that manner to re-establish a modicum of order and normalcy . . .

I still hope that circumstances will permit you to visit China Theater in the not too distant future. In the meantime sincere good wishes for your continued good health and every happiness.

Faithfully yours,

A. C. WEDEMEYER
Lieutenant General, U.S. Army
Commanding

13

Victory and Disillusion in China

1945

Events moved rapidly in the anxiety-filled summer and autumn of 1945. The city of Hiroshima was leveled by an atomic blast on August 6. The second A-bomb fell on Nagasaki on August 9, and that same day the Soviet Union entered the Pacific War with a large-scale invasion of Manchuria and Korea. On August 14 the Japanese government accepted the Allies' proffered terms of surrender.

The long-dreaded invasion of the Japanese home islands thus proved unnecessary, and Wedemeyer's carefully drawn plans for offensives in China were laid aside. To the American public, the surrender of the third and last Axis power meant that peace at last had returned. A clamor went up to "bring the boys home," and the far-flung forces of the United States began at once to dissolve.

Unfortunately, Japan's surrender failed to inaugurate the hoped-for era of universal peace. The war had shattered preexisting structures of Western power in the Orient as surely as it had denied Japan its "Greater East Asia Co-Prosperity Sphere." The future of the region was thus up for grabs. As the inevitability of Japan's doom became apparent, Nationalist and Communist forces on the mainland raced to exploit the anticipated collapse, and China slipped ever deeper into domestic violence.

Wedemeyer soon found himself torn by painful dilemmas. He was charged, on the one hand, with the major tasks of disarming and repatriating the Japanese on the Asiatic mainland even as his own forces—land, sea, and air—were being withdrawn. On the other hand, pursuing those goals or helping the government of China pursue them almost certainly risked armed conflict with the increasingly aggressive Communists. Such conflict was the last thing U.S. policymakers wanted, not only because the time had come to "bring the boys home," but because intervention in Chinese internal affairs was considered fundamentally unacceptable in principle.

From his post in the midst of the storm, Wedemeyer sought (with little success) to alert Washington to the rapid shift of focus in Asia from the war with Japan to the struggle for China's future. Finding his own instructions contradictory and inadequate, he repeatedly asked his superiors for more positive and consistent guidance.

The following documents recall some of the tense drama of these fateful months. They reflect Wedemeyer's early but short-lived hopes that the Great Powers, including the Soviet Union, would cooperate in building the postwar peace. They also reflect his growing conviction that the U.S. stance of neutrality in China was untenable, and that Chiang Kai-shek represented China's best hope and America's best ally on the mainland of Asia.

URGENT

No. CFB 4082
MEMORANDUM TO WARCOS [CHIEF OF STAFF,
WAR DEPARTMENT] (EYES ALONE)
From: COMGENCHINA [Commanding General, China Theater]
Date: August 9, 1945

Request information and guidance concerning U.S. policy in China when capitulation of Japan occurs.

Present directive is crystal clear that U.S. personnel and materiel will not be employed in activities of fratricidal and internecine character within China. The difficulty existing among Kuomintang and Communist parties and certain recalcitrant warlords introduces possibilities which require careful handling and complete understanding on [the] part of Americans and Chinese alike. Responsible American commanders and appropriate Chinese officials have been definitely informed that American forces and materiel will not . . . be employed against Chinese except to protect American lives and property. The tentative plan that certain seaports with adjacent air installations may be occupied by American units . . . may introduce intricate situations. For example, assume that U.S. Marines occupy Shanghai area. There is irrefutable evidence that the Communists are striving to gain control of that area. Their capabilities at present do not . . . appear formidable; however, the Generalissimo has asked me to insure that the American commander of the forces in the Shanghai area be instructed to relinquish control only repeat only to the Chinese Commander and forces designated by Central Government . . . He has agreed that he would move appropriate forces to the ports initially occupied and controlled by Americans as promptly as transportation facilities would permit.

It has been difficult to obtain firm commitments from Chinese concerning occupational troops they would make available for Manchuria, Japan, Formosa, or Korea. Have any agreements been made with Russia as to what parts of Manchuria, if any, Russian forces will occupy? It is apparent that Chinese are concerned about their ability to cope with situation presented by Communists and certain warlords . . . Although tacitly admitting uncertainty concerning their internal affairs, the Chinese are still interested in Thailand and French Indo-China. It is evident that they desire to participate in Allied action, military or political, in those areas. The degree and nature of U.S. participation in civil affairs, also the subject of lend-lease supplies for Central Government, are two other important subjects requiring urgently War Department advice and/or instructions. I posed many questions in my CFB 2320, answers to which would be most helpful.

TOP SECRET

URGENT

No. CFB 4317

MEMORANDUM TO MARSHALL (PERSONAL)

From: Wedemeyer

Date: August 11, 1945

In conference with Generalissimo this date, he raised following very important points, early answers to which will greatly facilitate our preparations for capitulation and postwar planning:

When will American units actually arrive on the Asiatic mainland as mentioned in WAR 40831 for immediate occupation of critical points? In this connection, we are striving to make appropriate plans and preparations to preclude outbreak of widespread disorders, possibly civil war. The Generalissimo requests two American divisions in Taku area, one of which to be advanced inland as far as Tientsin and Peking, [and] two divisions in Shanghai area, one of which to be advanced inland as far as Nanking and one division in Canton area. He expressed concern about security of railroads from Taku to Peking and from Shanghai to Nanking. He stated that he would move appropriate Chinese forces as rapidly as possible to areas occupied by Americans and thus effect early relief of latter. He emphasized that there are approximately two million enemy troops in China and suggested that their demobilization, disarmament, and deportation imposes stupendous difficulties. He added that he felt certain that you would agree that America should continue to assist China during this trying postwar period of rehabilitation—at least until Japan has complied with the Potsdam proclamation in its application not only to the Japanese Archipelago but to all of China . . .

.   .   .   .   .

Summarizing above, I request urgently first, guidance and instructions concerning the arrival of American units at key points in China, to include strength and approximate date, and second, the policy of the United States with regard to equipping Chinese military forces . . .

TOP SECRET

No. CFBX 4352
MEMORANDUM TO MARSHALL (EYES ALONE)
From: Wedemeyer
Info: MacArthur and Nimitz (Eyes Alone)
Date: August 12, 1945

Deeply concerned am I relative possible lack of appreciation in Washington of explosive and portentous possibilities in China when Japan surrenders. Instructions emanating from Washington . . . indicate that I have failed to impress the implications of Chinese Communist movement and effect upon realization of U.S. objectives in this area.

It is my considered opinion that the American contingents contemplated in occupational plans . . . must arrive as promptly as possible in China. WARX 47945 places Japanese archipelago in first priority, Korea in second, and China in third or last priority. As I view overall situation in Far East upon surrender of Japanese, the [Japanese] archipelago will present no immediate problems relative to control, repatriation, disarmament, or disturbances of revolutionary character; whereas, on the Asiatic mainland we are confronted with two serious possibilities requiring prompt action on part of Allies. First, Chinese Communist forces may precipitate civil war in China; second, the Japanese army remaining on the mainland, approximately two million strong, may continue to fight either in force or in isolated areas, requiring continued employment of air and land forces. The area of China is so vast and communications so limited, the problems posed by the above two conditions obviously require timely and appropriate disposition of Allied forces, American and Chinese. Definitely, China Theater's minimum requirements for American occupational forces should be given first priority.

The Chinese Communist leader today issued a radio proclamation to Japanese and Chinese puppets admonishing them to surrender to nearest anti-Japanese troops. Ambassador Hurley has provided State Department with copy of proclamation. The primary object of Chinese

Communists is to obtain Japanese arms and equipment and thus further strengthen their capabilities. It is not unreasonable to expect Japanese cooperation in this regard. The geographical objectives of the Chinese Communists have been and continue to be the very same, repeat, the very same key and strategic points and areas recognized as vital by the U.S. Joint Chiefs of Staff, who selected the majority of such points and areas for projected American occupation, including Shanghai, Nanking, Taku, Tientsin, Pekin[g], Tsingtao, and Canton. We will do utmost to redispose and employ Chinese forces in strength to preclude widespread uprising and disorder and to localize Chinese Communist efforts . . .

In my personal letter to you [dated August 1], and in subsequent radios, I have tried to portray the problems presented in China, particularly pertaining to the total lack of organization and planning. We Americans can and do make plans embodying sound recommendations, but their implementation in this land of confusion, intrigue, and indecision remains problematical. I am sure that you appreciate my position and earnest desire to comply with instructions from Washington. Throughout my service here I have tried earnestly and objectively to provide you and the Joint Chiefs of Staff with factual data and considered judgment relative to the application of instructions to the realistic conditions prevailing in China . . .

In view of above, [I recommend that] following forces be dispatched in first priority: (a) two divisions to Shanghai area; (b) two divisions to Taku area; and (c) one division to Canton area.

If above is impracticable, I consider it imperative that, as absolute minimum, two divisions be dispatched to Shanghai area, one division to Taku area, and one regiment to Canton area immediately . . .

TOP SECRET

No. CFB 4461
MEMORANDUM TO MARSHALL (PERSONAL)
From: Wedemeyer
Date: August 13, 1945

•   •   •   •   •

Immediately following enemy capitulation it will be necessary to place either U.S. or Chinese occupational forces in adequate strength in critical areas, particularly those areas in which enemy troops in large numbers are concentrated, and in the vicinity of which Chinese Communist military forces are also located. Chinese Communist forces have already made announcements indicating intention to undertake disarmament of enemy troops. If Chinese Communist forces are thus able to improve their capabilities, the implications are serious for peace in the Far East. In addition, there is to be considered possible consequences of approximately 2,000,000 Japanese armed forces on the Asiatic mainland, of which over 1,000,000 are in China proper and 600,000 are in Manchuria. Unless occupational forces in adequate strength can be made available in areas of enemy concentration within a reasonable time, Japanese commanders may be unable to restrain their troops from acts of violence. Current urgent examination indicates that transport aircraft now available in India–Burma and China Theaters will be inadequate to meet requirements for continued movement of essential supplies to China, and concurrently provide timely air lift of Chinese troops and equipment to critical occupational areas which is urgently desirable for reasons above indicated . . .

For reasons above stated, China theater is not repeat not in position to release C-54 aircraft prior to the opening of one or more ports and the establishment of an adequate flow of supplies to and through such port or ports. It is considered that hump operations must continue with only such limited reduction as will release aircraft for essential use in China for a minimum period of thirty days . . .

TOP SECRET
URGENT

No. CFBX 4580
MEMORANDUM TO WARCOS FOR JOINT CHIEFS OF STAFF
(EYES ALONE)
From: Wedemeyer
Info: MacArthur and Nimitz (Eyes Alone)
Date: August 14, 1945

.　　.　　.　　.　　.

I am sure that you recognize that Manchuria may properly be termed the critical area in connection with current and projected activities of

Chinese Communists and possibly Soviet Communists. If the General Order No. 1 to be issued by Japanese Headquarters [MacArthur's Headquarters as Supreme Commander, Allied Powers (SCAP)] provides for the surrender of Japanese commander and of forces within China to the Generalissimo, but excludes . . . Manchuria insofar as the Generalissimo is concerned, following implications should be noted.

The attitude of Soviet Russia toward the Chinese Communists has never been determined accurately, nor have Soviet intentions in China been formalized to a degree that Americans can view the situation with equanimity. However, it is not . . . unreasonable to expect penetration of Soviet Communist ideologies in Manchuria with cooperation of Chinese Communists. If the General Order above referred to excludes Manchuria as now contemplated, there is extreme danger that Japanese equipment will become available surreptitiously or openly to the Chinese Communists in Manchuria. Further, the Chinese Communist overall plans will be facilitated. If, on the other hand, the General Order clearly stipulates that Japanese Forces would surrender only . . . to Soviet Russian Forces and/or the Generalissimo's forces, the above dangers would be minimized, perhaps obviated.

The ideas embodied in this message, and in messages I have sent to you the past several days, might suggest partisan leaning on my part. This is not . . . the case. However, the U.S. policy has been and continues to be full support of the Generalissimo who heads the only officially and universally recognized constituted government in China. The Generalissimo is conceded at present to be the strongest Chinese leader and the only one capable of possibly accomplishing a modicum of stability during this period of uncertainty. It would therefore appear sound to create conditions by continued U.S. political, economic, and military support (short of involvement in fratricidal war) which would strengthen the existing Central Government's position. This support should include ironclad stipulations designed to insure surrender of Japanese forces and equipment to the Generalissimo throughout China including Manchuria, except in the immediate combat areas of the Russians.

I view Asia as an enormous pot, seething and boiling, the fumes of which may readily snuff out the advantages gained by Allied sacrifices [in] the past several years and may also definitely preclude realization of the objectives of the Atlantic Charter and the Teheran, Yalta, and Potsdam agreements . . .

I am so remote from international negotiations, it is with some misgivings that I submit following two alternate suggestions:

a. Schedule a conference with representatives from Soviet Russia, United States, Great Britain, [and] China in Delhi, India, as early as possible to investigate and recommend appropriate steps necessary to preclude civil war in China; or

b. Three Big Powers [United States, Britain, and the USSR] issue agreed proclamation to Chinese Communists and Chinese Central Government that civil war will not repeat not be tolerated in China in any form or degree; that Big Three are determined to take appropriate steps and employ necessary force in premises; that political and internal affairs must be settled without employment of force; that Big Three recognize China sovereignty and right to determination by Chinese of form of government; [and] that employment of force by factions in China has serious implications with regard to peace in the Far East and world order in general.

[The preceding paragraphs were substituted on second thought for the following, which apparently seemed improperly critical of U.S. political leadership]:

I view Asia as an enormous pot, seething and boiling, the fumes of which may readily snuff out the advantages gained by Allied sacrifices [in] the past several years and may also definitely preclude realization of the objectives of the Atlantic Charter and the Teheran, Yalta, and Potsdam agreements. America has unwittingly contributed to the trend of events in Europe which facilitate the substitution of Communism for Nazism, yet it is accepted that both forms of "-ism" are equally abhorrent to Americans and diametrically opposed to the ideologies of democracy; both forms of -ism abrogate the very principles for which we have made unstinted, astronomical sacrifices in lives and resources. The situation in Europe is a fait accompli; however we may still provide a framework for realization of ideas and ideals for which I feel we are fighting. In my CFB 526, July 9, . . . pertinent ideas and suggestions are expressed that have stronger and immediate application today.

TOP SECRET
URGENT

No. CFBX 4740
MEMORANDUM TO WARCOS
From: Wedemeyer
Info: COMINCH   [Commander in Chief, U.S. Fleet]
      CINCAFPAC [Commander in Chief, U.S. Army Forces
                 Pacific]
      CINCPAC   [Commander in Chief, Pacific Fleet]
      COMGENIB   [Commanding General, India–Burma Theater]
Date: August 15, 1945

In view of final decision that immediate *requirements of China Theater for U.S. troops to occupy key positions cannot be furnished,* determined measures must be taken to retain control of the situation here . . .

First, it is urgently requested that *no aircraft be removed* from the India–China Wing, ATC [Air Transport Command] . . . The present instructions issued General Tunner [Major General William H. Tunner, Commander, India–Burma Division, ATC] in personal ATC message from Washington have caused him to take the measure of alerting 50 C-54's, the removal of which from the hump is costing China Theater twelve thousand tons per month, and this loss, in the absence of immediate U.S. occupation forces on the China coast, is jeopardizing the new mission of China Theater . . . Chinese troops are being alerted for move to secure the most critical areas; however, their arrival will be a matter of weeks or months if airlift is not employed. Adequate forces to insure security of these key areas cannot be moved in time unless all presently assigned aircraft are available to lift the troops and to bring fuel into China.

·   ·   ·   ·   ·

The urgency and importance of the above must not be underestimated. There are reports that fighting is already in progress between Central Government and Communist troops in the Tsingtao area and elsewhere, with the Communists attempting to seize all key towns and air fields in northeast China. Each day's delay in placing a major force in the critical areas increases the probability of widespread civil conflict and jeopardizes our first task of securing the key areas within China . . .

TOP SECRET
URGENT

No. CFB 4880
MEMORANDUM TO WARCOS (PERSONAL)
From: COMGENCHINA
Date: August 17, 1945

Immediately following this message I am dispatching a confidential message that I received from Chinese Communists for transmittal to United States. This Communist message epitomizes attitude and intentions of Communist elements and reaffirms my concern that widespread disorder may occur soon in China. Unquestionably the Chinese people have many grievances concerning their treatment by warlords and unscrupulous, incompetent officials. However a satisfactory solution to [the] China problem or world order will never be accomplished by civil war in this area. Based on limited knowledge, neither [the] Chinese Communist Party nor the Kuomintang is democratic in spirit or intentions. China is not . . . prepared for a democratic form of Government with 95 percent of her people illiterate and for many other cogent reasons. The inarticulate masses of China desire peace and are not particularly interested in or aware of the various ideologies represented. An opportunity to work, to obtain food and clothing for their families, and a happy peaceful environment are their primary concern[s]. Conditions here could best be handled by a benevolent despot or a military dictator, whether such dictator be a Communist or a Kuomintang matters very little. From my observation, practically all Chinese officials are interested in their selfish aggrandizement. I retain . . . the impression that the Generalissimo's leadership offers best opportunity at this time for stabilization in the area, political and economic.

Recommendation

I still feel that a realistic approach to this problem, which is definitely a responsibility of world powers, is embodied in my CFB 4580 [see document above].

TOP SECRET
URGENT

No. CFBX 15120
MEMORANDUM TO WARCOS
From: COMGENCHINA
Info: SCAP, CINCPAC, COM 7th FLEET, COMGEN 3rd PHIB [amphibious] Corps, AND COMGENCHUNGKING Liaison Group
Date: November 20, 1945

Part One

Evaluation of overall situation in China was intentionally withheld until sources of information could be contacted and the implications of events transpiring in China Theater could be carefully and objectively analyzed. I have visited the Peking area and discussed the situation with the Marine Corps Commander (Major General [Keller E.] Rockey) and a Marine Division Commander (Major General [Lemuel C.] Shepherd) presently located in Tsingtao. Also many nationals including British, French, Dutch, and Chinese leaders were most anxious to talk, particularly about current and future conditions in the Northern provinces. In Shanghai I have talked to many nationals, including Chinese leaders, and have reviewed the situation with members of U.S. China Theater staff located there. Five days in Chungking, where I had several conferences with the Generalissimo, Doctor T. V. Soong, the Minister of War, the Minister of Finance, General Ho Ying-chin, American Minister [Walter S.] Robertson, the British Ambassador, the French Ambassador, and U.S. officers who are performing liaison duty with Chinese government. With that background, I submit herewith information, analyses, and recommendations which may be helpful in formulating continued policies and reaching decisions with regard to U.S. forces in China Theater.

I believe that Generalissimo Chiang Kai-shek is sincere in his desire to bring about stability within the country, to initiate democratic procedures, to unify China, and to implement wide-sweeping social reforms. Considering his background, training, and experience as warlord [and] politician, and his oriental philosophy, his approach to problems presented would probably be inefficient, incomprehensible, and unethical by American standards. The task is beyond the capabilities of one man. He lacks not only the organization, but also competent advisers and assistants. The Generalissimo is selfless in his approach to the problems presented; however, he is surrounded by unscrupulous men who are interested primarily in their self aggrandizement. The Generalissimo is extremely loyal to those warlords and officials who have supported him in the past. Consequently, even though they are unscrupulous and/or incompetent, he appoints them to responsible positions in the government. They exploit the opportunities presented. Further, they appoint worthless subordinates in lesser positions. Many are members of [the] same families or have connived in chicanery in the past.

To clarify further, the integrity of Chinese political leaders and business men might appropriately be contrasted with that of Americans in similar positions. The Chinese businessman has, and usually conforms to, an exemplary code of ethics, whereas the Chinese politician operates with the object of enriching himself through chicanery and machination. In fact, it is commonly recognized in China that governmental positions are normal lucrative means by which one can amass great fortune. In America, businessmen are accepted as a class that might amass great wealth. Their methods would not always, however, bear close scrutiny. In governmental positions, Americans, on the other hand, uniformly follow an ethical course and only in isolated instances acquire great wealth through unscrupulous political manipulation or through dishonest government processes.

I am confronted daily with problems created by the above type of officials who deal constantly in intrigue and machinations. For example, a senior Chinese general has been dealing surreptitiously and unilaterally with the Japanese General Okamura in the use of Japanese shipping available in Chinese waters. It had been carefully explained to the Chinese general that such shipping must be pooled in the Allied effort to accomplish rehabilitation and repatriation in the Far East. This is only one of numerous instances where high officials operate unilaterally, surreptitiously, or corruptly, rendering coordination and effective accomplishments difficult if not impossible. I report such circumstances to the Generalissimo, but there are so many of a similar nature, it is readily apparent and understandable that he is bewildered and impotent in evolving a solution.

The Generalissimo appointed uniformly Southern Chinese to key posts—governors, mayors, etc.—in the Northern provinces. Apparently he does not have confidence in Northern Chinese. These appointments have embittered the people of the North and thus further retard military, political, and economic stabilization in the area.

There is some evidence that the Chinese are determined to exclude and/or restrict foreigners, particularly British, French, Russians, and

Dutch, in a commercial sense. Prewar, most of the utilities, lines of communication, and industrial establishments were financed and operated by foreigners. There are not available sufficient Chinese executives or technicians to take over the operation of these facilities. Industrial effort is presently stultified and economic stabilization is impracticable, even in those areas where Central Government forces have undisputed control. Appropriate measures for recovery will be impossible unless foreigners are permitted to function with a reasonable amount of initiative and authority.

I have pointed out all of the above observations very frankly and clearly to the Generalissimo. I strongly urged that foreigners be retained to assist in economic recovery, indicating that this appeared essential, at least until the Chinese produced from among their own nationals sufficient trained executives and technicians capable of assuming the inherent responsibilities. Also I recommended that Northern Chinese be appointed governors and mayors in Northern provinces, and that the people be permitted to elect district magistrates. Further I suggested that civilians should be considered for these important posts, hoping thereby to eliminate the military hierarchy presently and disastrously entrenched.

The Chinese Central Government appears to have a modicum of control in the area including the Yangtze Valley and south therefrom, commonly referred to as South China. With foreign assistance as above depicted, economic stability could probably be accomplished promptly, particularly if small industries were created and operated efficiently.

In most of the area north of Yangtze Valley extending to the Great Wall, referred to as North China, Central Government control is strongly and at present effectively disputed by the Chinese Communists. I believe that the average Chinese in North China are in an understandable quandary relative to the political implications of Central Government vis-a-vis Chinese Communist control. They have been strongly propagandized by the Communists, who have emphasized the corruption and inefficiency of Central Government officials. Those who tend to support the Generalissimo are subjected to intimidation by the Communists.

I have advised the Generalissimo to concentrate his effort upon establishing control of North China and to execute promptly social and political reforms designed to remove prohibitive taxes and the practice of corruption by officials. I again suggested that the assistance of foreign executives and technicians who had been operating in the area prior to Japanese occupation should be retained, at least during the period [of] China's political and economic adolescence.

With reference to Manchuria, a complex situation has developed.

The importance of Manchuria both economically and psychologically to China is recognized by the Generalissimo as well as by the Communists, both Chinese and Soviet. Russian military forces quickly overran that area in August and are reported to have indulged in loot, rape, and pilferage. Their program, according to reports, included the destruction of property that they did not desire or that could not be removed. Further, the Generalissimo informs me that the Russians surreptitiously, often openly, collaborate with the Chinese Communists in making Japanese arms and equipment available and in placing definite obstacles in the way of Chinese Central Government troops when attempts are made to move them by sea and/or air to Manchuria. The Chinese do not have sufficient or appropriate resources to recover North China and concurrently to launch a successful military and political campaign for the recovery of Manchuria under existing circumstances. Further definite demands will be made upon Central Government resources to maintain order and to facilitate economic recovery in South China.

Actually I do not feel that the Central Government has sufficient forces to gain and retain control of North China, at least for many months, possibly years. The area is vast, communications limited, and loyalty of population doubtful. Communist guerrillas and saboteurs can and probably will, if present activities are criteria, harass and restrict movements of Central Government forces to such a degree that an extended, costly campaign will result.

The Generalissimo planned and urged me recently to provide U.S. air transport to move two armies from the Tientsin-Peking area to Manchuria. Logistical support for these forces and measures for their security in the heart of Manchuria had not been fully appreciated by the Generalissimo or his Chinese staff. Consideration of these factors, and the lack of appropriate forces as well as transport, caused me to advise the Generalissimo that he concentrate his efforts on the recovery of North China and consolidate his military and political positions there prior to attempting to occupy Manchuria. I received the impression that he agrees with this concept.

I pointed out that the Americans had assisted the Central Government in moving sufficient Chinese armies into North China, north FIC [French Indo-China], and Formosa for the explicit purpose of disarming and facilitating the deportation of the Japanese. With reference to Manchuria, sufficient armies were moved to occupy that area but entrance therein was prevented by Chinese Communists and Soviets. I also indicated that I am not authorized to employ American forces and resources to move additional Chinese Central Government troops and/or equipment under existing directive because, irrefutably, such action would provide direct assistance to the Central Government forces in their operations against Chinese Communists.

Related to the above is the position that developments in China have created in connection with my duties as the Generalissimo's Chief of Staff and concurrently as American Commander. The Generalissimo rightfully expects me to advise him in formulation of plans and in the procurement of assistance in the solution of his internal . . . problems, which are at present essentially full-scale operations against the Chinese Communists. When the President authorized designation of an American as the Generalissimo's Chief of Staff, I feel certain that he did not visualize that I, or any officer on active duty in the Army, should serve as the Generalissimo's adviser in matters pertaining to political and internal affairs—and, more important, to fratricidal or internecine warfare. When in Washington recently I suggested for this reason that the officer appointed as Chief of the Military Advisory Group should not be permitted to serve in any capacity on the Generalissimo's staff or in the Chinese government. Pertinent example: Only recently the French Consul General in Shanghai requested my assistance in connection with several hundred Frenchmen who were disarmed in [the] Shanghai area by the Japanese. The Chinese have now recovered the French equipment; however, they refuse to return it to the French. I explained to the French Consul General that this matter should be taken up direct with the Chinese government. He replied that he submitted his appeal to me as the Generalissimo's Chief of Staff. Another example: The Generalissimo asked me to contact the British in Chungking in order to secure shipping for the movement of additional forces to the North. I did this, and the British were most sympathetic; however, they recounted the many British grievances, including what they termed discriminatory acts and restrictions against British subjects who have heavy investments and important commercial interests in China and who desire to resume their various activities. The British strongly urged me to prevail upon the Generalissimo to take remedial action. I am asked to scratch the back of the British Lion to insure that the British Ambassador will do some scratching along the tortuous spine of the Chinese Dragon.

In North China the Generalissimo is determined to retain the [U.S.] Marines in their present areas. In fact, he would like to have them extend their occupational areas to include long lines of communications. His plans envisage using the Marines as a base of maneuver. Instead of repatriating Japanese, his plans and efforts are now concentrated upon conducting a campaign against the Chinese Communists. As indicated above, such campaign may last for several months or years. In the meantime, the Marine forces are subject to unavoidable incidents which may involve the United States in very serious difficulties and commitments. The implications of removing the American forces, including the Marines in China, have been carefully considered in suggesting that we withdraw all of our men from the area. Under the present circumstances it is impossible to avoid involvement in fratricidal warfare or political strife; yet I am admonished by my directive to do so. As I view it, the presence of American troops in the Far East is for the expressed purpose of accomplishing world order and insuring continued peace. However, I doubt that the American people are prepared to accept the role inherent in world leadership under the United Nations Charter. In removing our men we can be justly accused of deserting an ally in a critical period. We now recognize that China is incapable of repatriating the millions of enemy troops and civilians within her borders and also solving her political and economic problems.

Conclusions

a. The Generalissimo will be able to stabilize the situation in South China provided he accepts the assistance of foreign administrators and technicians and inaugurates economic, political, and social reforms through honest, competent civilian officials.

b. He will not be able to stabilize the situation in North China for several months, perhaps years, unless a satisfactory settlement with the Chinese Communists is accomplished, followed up realistically by action in subparagraph *a* above.

c. He will not be able to recover Manchuria for many years unless, again, satisfactory agreements are reached with the Chinese Communists and Soviet government.

d. A satisfactory understanding between the Chinese Central Government and the Chinese Communists appears remote.

e. The Soviet government is in effect creating favorable conditions for the realization of Chinese Communist and possibly their own plans in North China and Manchuria, this in contravention to recent Sino-Soviet agreements.

f. The continuation of American forces in China Theater, particularly in the North, will inevitably lead to serious involvement in fratricidal warfare and possibly in a tense and dangerous situation with Soviet government.

g. The dual capacities of American Commander and Chief of Staff to the Generalissimo are no . . . longer tenable.

h. The Americans have given appropriate and full assistance in consonance with existing Theater directive by moving with American air and sea transport Chinese Central Government forces to disarm and facilitate the deportation of the Japanese in North China. However, these Chinese forces are now being largely diverted and employed against Chinese Communists and/or dissident groups.

Recommendations

U.S. government [should] notify the Chinese government:

a. That the American Commander can be immediately relieved as the Generalissimo's Chief of Staff in that this appointment was approved during the war with a view to coordinating Sino-American combat activities against the common enemy, the Japanese.

b. That my decision to remove, as early as practicable, all American forces in China Theater, including Marines, be confirmed; or, my existing directives be changed to justify under U.S. policies their retention and employment in the area.

c. That plans and arrangements for the implementation of the projected American Military Advisory Group be continued; however, actual consummation [to] be withheld until the United States is satisfied that appropriate political and military stabilization in China has been accomplished.

Part Two

The following considerations cover the broader aspects and the strategic implications of the situation depicted in Part I. The policy of China to attain the goal frequently stressed by the Generalissimo, namely, the establishment of a strong, unified, democratic China will be definitely influenced if not actually determined by the policies of and the amount and form of assistance given by foreign nations including the United States, the British Commonwealth, France, Holland, and Soviet Russia, particularly the last named country.

It is my considered opinion that China is not yet capable of implementing, nor is she psychologically prepared for, democratic procedures in government. China is experiencing the difficulties that history accurately records in Western Europe when countries in that area passed from an amorphous mass of feudalistic dynasties to more homogeneous monarchies and republics. It is in the interest of world Peace and Advancement that China should be able to transcend from the medieval state to a democratic form of government by processes of evolution as opposed to bloody, chaotic revolution.

Based on the premise that China's resurgence will be determined by the assistance and policies of the world powers, it is fitting that we first examine Soviet Russia's possible policies, because China and Russia are in close juxtaposition geographically with several thousand miles of common border, and further, there exist in China certain facilities which are of paramount interest to Russia both commercially and militarily. It appears that Soviet Russia may pursue one of the following two courses of action.

> *a.* She may become intensely nationalistic and continue the policy epitomized the past few years by Stalin in the program of building a strong internal structure, industrially and politically. Concurrently she may establish on her frontier a buffer of areas in which she maintains the initiative. This is a fait accompli in Western Europe, for in the Baltic States, Eastern Poland, and throughout the Balkans she maintains [a] paramount sphere of influence. It is reasonable to assume that she will also establish such buffer areas in the Middle and Far East. At present there are indications of strong Russian military forces in the Caucasus with a view to intimidating Turkey, Iran, and Iraq. Her actions in Korea, Manchuria, Outer Mongolia, Inner Mongolia, Jehol, Chahar, and Sinkiang provinces suggest the pattern for the Far East where she may create conditions similar to those now existing on her western frontiers in Europe.

> *b.* Russia may have adopted the policies described in subparagraph *a* above as an expedient to cope with the situation created by the war and thereby permitted international revolutionary features of Communism to remain q[u]iescent. She may now adopt an aggressive policy and utilize the buffer areas above referred to as springboards for ideological penetration and territorial expansion by employment of military force. Her intention to implement such a policy may be indicated by worldwide invidious propaganda, establishment of Communist cells in South America, Afghanistan, and through Arabic areas, overt activities in Manchuria, Korea, and North China, and more than normal interest in MacArthur's stabilization program for Japan.

It is my considered opinion that Russia is not prepared to implement successfully the policy covered in subparagraph *b* above. Thousands of her cities, towns, and villages must be rehabilitated. Her industries even prewar were not effectively operating, although strongly permeated by American, British, and German technicians. Large numbers of Russian soldiers have come in contact with the armed forces of Allies and have received information concerning democratic procedures and the standards of living outside of Russia that strongly refute the disparaging propaganda to the contrary. There is increasing evidence also that bureaucratic procedures are being followed in Soviet Russia, and in numerous ways the basic communistic tenets of Karl Marx and Lenin are being abrogated. It probably will be many years before Russia would be sufficiently strong to undertake successfully an international program as depicted in subparagraph *b* above. For many years prior to June 22, 1941, the press and radio of most countries in the world bitterly assailed Communism with its associated atheism, pogroms, regimentation, stultification of free enterprise, and restriction of human liberties. After the Germans attacked Russia there was a complete about-face, and justifications were found in the Allied press to ameliorate public opinion and to justify military alliance. It is only natural that the Russians are suspicious of our motives today and are preparing bulwarks against possible interference with whatever program they adopt. Coupled with these facts, when one considers that the vast majority of the Russian people are not true Communists but are actually being controlled by a small group whose powers equal or may even surpass those of the Czarist rulers, it is logical to assume that Soviet Russia's policies today will conform to those defensive stratagems depicted in subparagraph *a*.

There is one other important consideration: Should Communism spread unabated and effectively throughout the Far East, that may influence the future policy of the United States and other powers interested in democratic or capitalistic forms of government. There are approximately 450 million people in China, 390 million in India, 100 million in Japan and Korea, and 100 million through the Philippine archipelago, the Melanesian and Micronesian Islands, Netherland East Indies, Malay, Burma and Indo-China, totaling about one billion 40 million persons, over half the population of the world, who might embrace Communism in various forms. If we were to add to this number approximately 190 million in Soviet Russia and the several million scattered through Western Europe and in other parts of the world, it will readily be apparent that strategically the position of democratic and capitalistic countries would be seriously jeopardized or rendered impotent.

American policy has always supported the aspirations of China to attain unity and a democratic form of government. The present situation, however, might indicate that several million Chinese are opposed to the attainment of that goal. Interference in the internal affairs of China would not only be repugnant to U.S. foreign policy recently enunciated in the President's Navy Day speech wherein the principle of self determination was reaffirmed, but also might involve the U.S. in serious dispute or possibly war with Soviet Russia.

Traditionally, our policy has insisted upon the territorial integrity of China and has always opposed the domination of China by any one power. We have not attempted colonization in the Far East but have encouraged Western economic, cultural, religious and political influences.

China represents a bridge between East and West. Today, as the result of the emergence of a powerful Soviet Russia, China is also a political and economic arena of the world's two greatest powers, Soviet Russia and America. If China were to become a puppet of the Soviet, which is exactly what a Chinese Communist victory would mean, then Soviet Russia would practically control the continents of Europe and Asia. Domination of so great an expanse, particularly by a totalitarian power, would jeopardize world peace. We were determined to prevent Japan from making China a puppet power. It is believed even more important, if we are to realize our policies with reference to China, that Russia not be permitted to do so.

The question may properly be asked: Are we backing the wrong horse, or is there realistic justification for the hope that China may emerge from her difficulties? When the Japanese attacked China, the Generalissimo was undertaking an industrial and political revolution to achieve self-government and unity, to provide barriers against foreign economic domination and to effect social changes including the emancipation of the coolies and peasants. He was making splendid progress, and this is often alluded to as the real cause of the Japanese attack in 1937. The militarists felt it necessary to strike before China became unified and strong—a realistic threat to Japan's program of aggression in the Far East.

The proof of the progress made, and of the unity achieved, includes the fact that China survived the loss of all her newly developed industries, her ports, and communication with the outside world. Although almost denuded of weapons and industrial support, China, as a totally blockaded nation, waged war for nearly eight years and performed this miracle under the Generalissimo and under the present government. It appears logical to retain confidence in China's ability to solve her problems. In consonance with present U.S. policy of noninterference with internal matters, we should continue to provide encouragement and material aid to the recognized government of China. However, we should not . . . participate militarily during the process of evolution or revolution within the Chinese government unless world peace is definitely jeopardized thereby.

It would appear sound, therefore, to withdraw all U.S. military forces from China proper and thus remove any chance of involvement in the internal affairs of China. Concurrently, we could provide arms and equipment as well as raw materials for newly created and revitalized small industries, and also we could import processed goods.

The United States, Great Britain, and Soviet Russia recognize China's legal and ethnological rights to Manchuria. Should we not repeat not invoke their combined aid to protect those rights? This seems to be a logical step, from the U.S. viewpoint, to preclude that area from becoming a Russian satellite or puppet government. The United States could invite Great Britain, China, [and] Russia to join in an immediate trusteeship over Manchuria and Korea until China as a government is sufficiently strong and stabilized to assume the responsibilities of full control in that area. Korea's autonomy could be determined after her people give satisfactory evidence of their capability to govern themselves.

Recommendations

a. Withdraw as early as practicable all U.S. military personnel from China Theater and concurrently provide continued and increased economic assistance to the existing recognized Chinese government; or announce a U.S. policy indicating determination to continue military and economic support to the Chinese Central Government until the Japanese troops and civilians in the area have been repatriated to their homeland and until China has evolved sufficient internal strength to assume her rightful role in the family of nations. (This latter course would entail a change in my directive.)

b. Establish immediately trusteeship under United States, Russia, Great Britain, and China over Manchuria and Korea. Duration of this trusteeship to last until these four nations agree that China is prepared to assume the responsibilities for control of Manchuria, and that the Koreans themselves are prepared for complete autonomy.

14

The Marshall Mission to China

1946

By the end of 1945, Wedemeyer was convinced that the U.S. China policy had reached a dead end. In November he outlined two major alternatives for the Washington policymakers: either promptly withdraw all U.S. military forces from the area to avoid inevitable entanglements, or introduce sufficient force to insure the orderly accomplishment of such war tasks as Japanese repatriation. In either case, he suggested the continuation of U.S. economic support to the Central Government. He also recommended United Nations trusteeships for Manchuria and Korea as a means both of testing and developing the potential of that new international organization and of forestalling unilateral communist advances in those areas.

However, none of these suggestions was favorably received. Washington opted instead for a long shot: a major U.S. effort to transcend China's divisions and build peace on liberal foundations by bringing the warring factions together in a coalition government. The chosen instrument of this undertaking was a *deus ex machina* in the person of Wedemeyer's old boss, the recently retired Army Chief of Staff, General George C. Marshall.

Wedemeyer received this news in Shanghai with mixed feelings. Although he was confident that his esteemed chief would succeed if anyone could, he doubted the basic feasibility of the enterprise. In the first instance, chances that the Communists would share power in a liberal state in good faith seemed almost nil; that the Nationalists would voluntarily relinquish power to their mortal enemies seemed equally unlikely. Moreover, unilateral U.S. initiatives of this sort ignored the fact that China's future depended, for better or worse, on the behavior of several other powers, including most ominously the Soviet Union.

Marshall arrived in China in mid-December 1945 to begin his historic mission of peacebuilding. Within weeks he had succeeded in obtaining a cease-fire between the warring Nationalist and Communist forces. He proceeded next with plans to integrate the armies of both sides into a single national force.

Wedemeyer in the meantime continued to command the rapidly diminishing U.S. military garrison in China and to serve as Chief of Staff to the Generalissimo. In March 1946 he relayed his views of the situation to the new Army Chief of Staff in Washington, General Dwight D. Eisenhower. While praising General Marshall's accomplishments, Wedemeyer felt obliged to register his opinion that the permanence of those achievements rested, unfortunately, on Marshall's personal presence in China.

A.P.O. 971
March 11, 1946

General of the Army Dwight D. Eisenhower
Chief of Staff
United States Army
War Department
Washington, D.C.

Dear General:

There are several subjects, some personal, but essentially concerning China Theater which I would like to discuss . . .

The establishment of Executive Headquarters under General Marshall with the disposition of field teams in far-flung places has introduced personnel problems that would of course influence our plans for inactivation of the Theater. General Marshall informs me that the Executive Headquarters with field teams will unquestionably be in existence throughout this calendar year. Today General Marshall's setup involves approximately 200 but may expand to 300 or even more in order to accomplish the necessary supervision and to insure the implementation of agreements reached by Marshall with Communists and [the] National Government. Both General Marshall and I will be careful to hold [these] to [a] minimum.

General Marshall feels that the inactivation of China Theater at an early date will greatly strengthen the Generalissimo's pressure for the removal of Russian forces from Manchuria. I concur in this idea, and we have been striving to evolve a *modus operandi* in order to submit appropriate suggestions to you and the Joint Chiefs of Staff. Since V-J Day, the Chinese Communists (with the support of Soviet Communists and fellow travelers in America) have been urging the removal of all Americans from China. The Generalissimo desires to retain U.S. forces, but agrees that their removal—that is, combat elements—might help his position vis-a-vis Russia. The present strength of our forces, air and ground, would preclude [an] effective fight against a determined Soviet Russian effort; however, the presence of the Marine Corps reinforced by an Air Wing has undoubtedly served as a deterrent to more aggressive steps by the Chinese Communists and even possibly the Soviet Communists. General Marshall feels that the presence of the Marines, in fact any American combat units in the area, is really an irritant and, inasmuch as we do not have sufficient strength to cope successfully with a serious Russian effort, he concludes that it would be better to remove the irritant.

We plan tentatively to remove the Marines as follows: By April 1, 1946, initiate reduction of Marines so that by June 1, 1946, there would be one regiment in Tientsin-Peking area and one regiment [would] remain in Tsingtao area. By July 1 the regiment at Tsingtao would be removed, and there would only remain one Marine regiment in North China based in Tientsin with administrative and supply detachments at Chinwangtao and Tangku.

With reference to [U.S.] Army personnel, China Theater as such would be inactivated May 1, and certain unfinished business or residual responsibilities would be assumed by the Navy, the Military Advisory Group, Shanghai Station Command, and Executive Headquarters. These residual functions should be terminating rapidly (for example the repatriation of Japanese and the movement of Chinese armies) so that it would not be very long before the normal functions of the Military Advisory Group would be assumed by personnel assigned to that group, and the Executive Headquarters personnel would carry on to full accomplishment of their mission in connection with the stabilization of the military and political situation within China. General Marshall desires to retain minimum U.S. personnel in China to include these officers and men with the Military Advisory Group and with required administrative, transport, and supply activities, as well as the Executive Headquarters in Peking.

The above factors have posed many problems. We have the bodies but they are not always equipped to accomplish the particular functions in the Theater. The personnel sent to Marshall's Executive Headquarters, and especially to his field teams, where tact, good judgment, and character are of utmost importance, must be carefully selected, and I have pared to the bone already to insure that he obtained the best we had available. In connection with the plans for the amalgamation or integration of the Chinese Communist and National Government armies, Marshall will require additional officer and enlisted personnel. We are doing everything possible to help him in this regard, but it is simply a question of having qualified men for the job. He will discuss this with you personally.

.   .   .   .   .

When home last September I was asked about succeeding Hurley as the Ambassador in China, and I discussed this with General Marshall who was then Chief of Staff. He advised against my leaving the Army and I was very much in accord. Only recently here in China, however, he suggested that I accept the post upon his relief. He indicated that he hoped to leave China late this summer or early fall, and that he wanted to recommend me as his replacement to the President. I am not particularly keen about leaving the military service to which I owe so much, but I told General Marshall that if he felt that I could help out here in this difficult situation, I would accept the post. Frankly, General, I do not want to become a professional diplomat or a politician. I am a soldier and have no untoward ambitions. No doubt General Marshall will also discuss this subject with you. I believe he has already proposed to the President that I be designated as his relief, perhaps sometime in the summer or early fall.

.   .   .   .   .

Up to the end of December 1945 only 36,000 Japanese military and civilian [personnel] were repatriated from this area. This may be attributed partially to the lack of available shipping, but essentially to the fact that the Chinese were not putting forth much effort. Of course they were involved in hostilities with the Communists, and also they are wholly lacking in organizational ability. After the President announced his new Far Eastern Policy, and other pronouncements from Washington confirmed U.S. interest and acceptance of increased responsibility for the repatriation of Japanese throughout the Pacific and Asiatic areas, we took firmer grip and revamped the program and distributed personnel to insure the effective execution of the plans. To date we have repatriated over 650,000, and we expect to complete the job about the first of July in all areas except Manchuria. We have tried every possible way to ascertain the number of Japs, military and civil, in Manchuria, but so far without success. The Russians simply will not give us the information. Our best estimates indicate approximately 800,000 military and about a million civilian Japanese in Manchuria. General Marshall has agreed to approach the Russian Ambassador on an informal basis to obtain firm information concerning repatriation in Manchuria. It may develop that the Russians will agree to repatriate the Japanese themselves; in fact, we have ominous reports to the effect that the Russians have already dispatched thousands of Japanese soldiers to Siberia as slave labor. Our efforts to obtain information about the Japanese in Manchuria, and about communications and billeting areas that would be related to the problems of repatriating these Japanese, have always been viewed with suspicion by the Russians, for of course they feel that we are trying to obtain information concerning their political, economic, and psychological gyrations in the area.

.   .   .   .   .

Last September, when I went with Pat Hurley to the States to discuss Far Eastern situation, I was reasonably optimistic. The Japanese had been defeated and were amenable. The Chinese Communist leaders,

Mao Tse-tung and Chou En-lai, were in Chungking conferring with the Generalissimo and his representatives. Ambassador Pat Hurley assured me that these negotiations were developing most favorably. Finally, the 30-year Sino-Soviet agreement that was signed on August 14 gave every indication of Soviet support of the Central Government of China. However, two of the above three reasons for optimism were removed by events that transpired during October. Negotiations between the representatives of the Central Government and the Chinese Communists accomplished nothing, and hostilities were rampant in North China where the Chinese Communist guerrilla forces intercepted lines of communications and committed depredations on a large scale. Also, the Soviet government did not act in good faith with reference to the 30-year Sino-Soviet agreement. There was considerable evidence of Soviet assistance to and connivance with the Chinese Communists in the Northern provinces of China proper and in Manchuria. Further, the Soviets refused to permit the Chinese to use Dairen as a port of debarkation for Central Government soldiers scheduled to move into Manchuria.

Conditions in general were deteriorating rapidly and events pointed toward a real widespread civil war. I returned to the Theater earlier than I had planned and made a very hasty survey of the situation and then dispatched a long radio to Washington (CFBX 15120, dated November 20 [see chapter 13 of this volume]). Several months have passed, and we all have been watching the situation carefully. I believe that events that have transpired in the interim serve to reaffirm my conviction . . . to the effect that a practical solution to the Manchurian and Korean problems would be the establishment of trusteeships. If this step is not taken promptly, it is my belief that Russia would enjoy the same dominating position in Manchuria and Korea that was formerly held by Japan.

I suggested the trusteeship in Manchuria to the Generalissimo last September before I went to the States. However, he was not concerned with Russian motives at that time and seemed to take great comfort in the favorable aspects of the 30-year Sino-Soviet agreement. He did, however, look with favor upon a trusteeship for Korea. Again in November I recommended Manchurian trusteeship to him. He stated categorically at this time that such an arrangement would have undoubtedly prevented the unilateral and arbitrary action on the part of the Soviets in Manchuria, but he felt that it was now too late. He stated that in his opinion the Soviet Russians would not accept trusteeship in either Korea or Manchuria. Furthermore, his own political position within China was precarious, and he could not afford to give evidence of weakness or suggest his inability to cope with internal problems of the country, including Manchuria. Within the past few days the Generalissimo discussed Manchuria, and he reiterated his November statement to the effect that a trusteeship would have denied the Russians their present favored position . . .

Of course you will discuss the current situation with General Marshall. However, I should like to contribute this observation which I am sure would not be forthcoming from him. He has done a fine job, quickly winning the respect and admiration of all with whom he came in contact. His approach to the problems presented has been logical, first accomplishing [a] cessation of hostilities, and now he is well on the way toward the successful implementation of a plan that will integrate military forces of the Central Government and the Communists. All of this has been accomplished in the background of intrigue, mistrust, selfish personalities and oriental cunning. Really a stupendous accomplishment, and I doubt seriously whether any other person in the world could have done as much in so short a time. The permanence of his accomplishments, however, is in my mind contingent upon his physical presence. If he were to be eliminated from the picture for the next several months, I feel that the opposing factions would soon be at each others' throats and the situation that existed last October would again prevail. General Marshall's international prestige and the very stature of the man have dominated the field and brought about conciliatory action on the part of the Communists and Central Government representatives. It would take years to remove the bitterness, hatred, and suspicion existing in the hearts and minds of both parties. I do not want to appear pessimistic, but I have tried to depict the situation realistically as I view it . . .

With every good wish for your health and happiness in your difficult job.

Sincerely,

A. C. WEDEMEYER
Lieutenant General, U.S. Army
Commanding

Wedemeyer's doubts about the permanence of Marshall's achievements in China grew with the passing weeks. Indications that progress had slowed—or even reversed—appeared in April during Marshall's brief absence from China on a visit to Washington. Wedemeyer, too, flew home in April (for minor surgery), fully expecting to return to China within a few weeks and continue his work. At the Washington airport, Marshall revealed that the groundwork had been laid for Wedemeyer to return to China in the near future as the new special ambassador.

Wedemeyer was troubled by the quandary that this prospect entailed. While personally devoted to General Marshall and determined to support him fully, he felt ever more certain that America's China policy had taken a most ill-advised turn and that his old boss—the key instrument of that policy—was embarked on a fool's errand. The prospect of seeing him fail, or of succeeding him in a wrong-headed and failing enterprise, was profoundly unsettling.

In May, while awaiting the summons to return to the Far East, Wedemeyer expressed some of his concerns in a letter to Marshall in Nanking. He encouraged his old chief and reaffirmed his personal loyalty, but sought also discreetly to alert him to lurking dangers.

May 29, 1946

General of the Army
George C. Marshall
Nanking Headquarters Command
Nanking, China

Dear General:

There are several matters which have been brought to my attention the past few weeks and I have been trying to absorb information and ponder over same before writing to you.

With reference to my own status, I hope that you will not construe my previous radios on the subject as ill-considered or tempestuous. Believe me, it is only because of my desire to help you in [your] difficult task that I have repeatedly expressed my conviction that I should return to China as early as practicable. Physically I am fit. Only yesterday I had a very careful physical examination which reaffirms this statement. I have expressed to Tom Handy [General Thomas T. Handy, Deputy Chief of Staff] and Ed Hull [Major General John E. Hull, Chief, OPD] my desire to return to my job in order that I might make any contribution possible. They understand completely, for they share the same sense of loyalty to you, and appreciate my determination to assist in any way possible.

There have been rumblings and rumors around Washington to the effect that you have been taken in by the Chinese Communists, and there are suggestions carefully veiled to the effect that your decisions have placed the Generalissimo and the Central Government in an embarrassing position. I have been striving to obtain something tangible and pin down persons responsible. In one instance, I phoned a columnist whose statements might be interpreted against you. When confronted, he was most contrite and assured me that it was not his intention to harm you or militate against the success of your negotiations. He expressed highest regard for you as an individual and assured me that he would give full support to your every endeavor. Further, I talked to Congressman [Walter H.] Judd . . . He also expressed great admiration for you, but emphasized the fact that the American people should know that apparently U.S. policy as now implemented would accord recognition of the Communist elements in the Far East. His discussion included the well-known line that the Chinese were our Allies throughout the war, that Chiang refused favorable terms of surrender, and that China is at present confronted with an armed rebellion, instituted and supported by Soviet Russia. After a discussion lasting over an hour, I believe that he realized that his views were not entirely defensible, but more important, that he must continue full support of your plans to eliminate private armies in China and to minimize or remove the employment of force in the resolution of problems presented by opposing factions in the area. I did not hear his recent broadcast in which Congressman ——————— of communistic leanings and John Carter Vincent [Director, Office of Far Eastern Affairs, Department of State] of milkweed tendencies discussed the China situation. I am told that the entire affair was innocuous. However, I feel that a State Department representative with moral courage and a modicum of intelligence could clarify the points raised by men like Judd and ———————. Instead of this realistic approach, I am informed that John Carter Vincent took a middle course. The fact that he is a State Department official connotes official cognizance, and he therefore was in a position to clarify our government's position.

On each occasion that I return to the United States for visits similar to the present one, I come in contact with two categories of people:

> *a.* There are those who criticize the President, Congress, and various departments and officials of the government. They offer nothing constructive.
> *b.* There is a group who smugly sit back and say "I told you so." They offer nothing affirmative.

The above conditions are created by lack of moral courage in our leaders. Apparently we have few men in positions of responsibility who will think a problem through to logical conclusion and then adhere to same. Instead, there appears to be the tendency to put out feelers and determine public reaction before making commitments. I sense also the growing conviction that we may have to resort to the employment of force in accomplishing our worldwide objectives, particularly in our relations with Soviet Russia. Recently I was invited to dinner in New York with the following group: [ex-President Herbert] Hoover, [Bernard M.] Baruch, Alfred Sloan, DeWitt Wallace, Dick Berlin (Hearst Papers), John D. Rockefeller, Jr., Roy Howard, and Henry J. Taylor. The consensus of this group called for stronger leadership in the solution of national and international problems. All of these gentlemen were most sincere and vociferous in their support of your past and present accomplishments . . .

The Bureau of Press Relations has asked me several times to hold a press conference. I have refused on the grounds that anything that I might say should have the single purpose of assisting you and U.S. policy in China, and there is nothing that I could contribute of press interest at this time. Tom Handy agreed with my attitude and I have avoided contact with the press individually or collectively. The Bureau of Press Relations only yesterday asked me to consider holding a press conference prior to my departure, indicating that pressure from several newspapers continued.

Doctor Wang of the Chinese Supply Mission has visited me on several occasions. He is concerned about the restrictions on the $500,000,000 loan. Also, he indicated that he has experienced great difficulty obtaining firm commitments on the four items which were covered by the $33,000,000 loan. He points out that he recognizes the necessity for certain safeguards on the part of Exim bank [Export-Import Bank] and is only desirous of obtaining the loans mentioned at least on terms similar to loans extended to France and Belgium. He emphasized that firm commitments are necessary now in order to facilitate definite plans for economic rehabilitation in China, and added that it is impossible to initiate steps necessary to obtain equipment, to allocate certain sums for various projects, and to organize and procure labor . . .

At present, Mrs. Wedemeyer is preparing to travel to China by water transportation leaving Washington sometime in July . . . My boy is graduating from West Point at the age of 20. My younger son is graduating from high school, from a private boys school in New England, and will enter the university if he is not drafted. Both he and I agree that teenagers should be drafted and he is prepared to do his duty. I have tried to instill in both of them the idea that too much emphasis is placed upon the "rights" of individuals as opposed to their responsibilities to their country. Colonel Carter [Colonel Marshall S. Carter, General Marshall's Special Representative in Washington] is doing a splendid job at this end and has won the confidence of those in the State Department with whom he comes in contact. Shepley [James R. Shepley, journalist (*Time, Life, Fortune*) and sometime assistant to General Marshall] drops in to see me occasionally and his loyalty is indeed an inspiration.

I hope that you and Mrs. Marshall are enjoying the best of health and that you will take advantage of the Generalissimo's offer of a mountain retreat during the hot weather.

Sincerely,

A. C. WEDEMEYER
Lieutenant General, USA
Commanding

Wedemeyer's expected summons to return to China never came. General Marshall sensed by the first of July that his mission was far from completed and realized that the Communists would never accept Wedemeyer in the role of arbiter; Marshall thus resigned himself to a longer stay in China. To handle normal diplomatic relations with the Central Government while his own work as special ambassador continued, he recommended the appointment of Dr. J. Leighton Stuart, an American educator in China, to the post of U.S. ambassador.

Wedemeyer recorded his reactions to these developments in a series of letters. One went to a one-time aide and interpreter, Captain Horace Eng. Another—a long letter of explanation and advice—was dispatched to the Generalissimo. A third was addressed to one of Wedemeyer's closest younger friends and former lieutenants, an officer serving on General Marshall's own staff in Peking—Colonel Claire E. Hutchin. This letter to "Hutch" is a poignant testament to its author's beliefs and hopes. It reveals Wedemeyer as an analyst who, more consistently than most of his contemporaries, insisted on grounding his thought (and strategy) on humane liberal values. It reveals him at the same time as an early and principled anti-communist.

Washington, D.C.
July 10, 1946

Mr. Horace Eng
539 Bush Street
San Francisco, California

Dear Horace:

An atomic bomb along diplomatic lines was dropped in my lap yesterday, and the only radiation noticeable includes smiles and heartfelt thanks within the Wedemeyer household. Marshall communicated with the State Department to the effect that it would not be desirable to appoint me as Ambassador to China and recommended Doctor Leighton Stuart, whom you know, a very able man with extended China background. Marshall did not go into details but suggested that my appointment would militate against the delicate negotiations between the Central Government and the Communists. Of course I have felt all along that the Communists could not possibly accept me in the role of mediator, for naturally they looked upon me as a partisan who had supported continuously Chiang Kai-shek and the Central Government. I indicated this to Marshall last February, if you recall, when the subject concerning my appointment as Ambassador was first brought up.

I am happy in this sense about the whole thing, Horace, because I do not feel that the approach to the problem has been sound. If I had been given the task with full powers last September—that is, immediately after V-J Day—I honestly believe that I might have evolved a solution that would have been acceptable, at least to those nations in the world who fought recently to put down totalitarianism.

Everyone recognizes that the Central Government is corrupt. But we must not forget that this same government, cut off from the rest of the world and offered increasingly favorable peace terms by the enemy, has kept on fighting to the limit of its ability to insure success against forces of aggression. It is my conviction that the Generalissimo is a sincere, selfless man who wants more than anything else in the world to create a higher standard of living for his people and to improve opportunities for all in an atmosphere of peace. He cannot do this without competent and scrupulous assistants, nor can he do that without a modicum of peace, and finally, he requires the outside aid, financial and psychological, of the United States.

Actually, I feel that we have made a wrong approach in trying to coerce a solution to the problem between the Kuomintang and the Communists. I would have given all-out help to the recognized Central Government of China and I would pay no attention whatsoever to internal troubles of that country but would continue my help until I had evidence that she was unworthy of same. I would insure that Americans carefully supervised every important activity to preclude manipulation and to provide safeguards for our investment. I think with American assistance a sound economy could be created, at least in the area south of the Great Wall, and I still advocate a trusteeship of the Five Powers over Manchuria and Korea along the line that I have discussed with you before.

One thing concerns me very deeply, and perhaps you can assist me. Before I left China I assured the Generalissimo that I would return. You are thoroughly familiar with all of the background concerning the Generalissimo's desire to have me take charge of the Military Advisory Group. You recall further that I indicated definitely to him that I did not wish to do so, but that if I were ordered by my government I would give my best effort. As the situation developed about February or March, General Marshall decided that I was the person who could best satisfy the interests of the U.S. government [in] China. General Marshall put this on a sense of duty basis and I told him I would accept and do my very best . . .

At this writing I do not know exactly what occurred, but the Under Secretary of State informed me that Marshall now feels that I should not come to China. The thing that disturbs me most is the fact that the Generalissimo does not have all of this background, and that he cannot help but think that I contributed in some way because he will recall that I told him very honestly last September that I wanted to return to the States and that I did not want to remain permanently in China. Just prior to my return to the States in April, I told the Generalissimo and the Madame, as well as other Chinese friends, that I would return to China, and now they will read in the papers or learn in other ways that this is not the case. All of the foregoing is a cumbersome way of explaining that I now have been placed in a position of breaking faith, or of not being straightforward. This position is untenable and, as you well know, undeserved. I am therefore going to ask you to insure through your various contacts to clarify the situation as it really developed. I may never see any of these people again, but the fact remains I was always straightforward with them and I want them to retain that picture and the feeling of respect that I have experienced the past two years. It means a lot to me personally, and also it means a great deal to our country. I have no idea just how this situation can be straightened out, but trust your excellent judgment and I know you will evolve a good solution . . .

. . . Affectionate regards to you and Elsie.

Sincerely,

A. C. WEDEMEYER
Lieutenant General, U.S. Army
Commanding

Washington, D.C.
August 2, 1946

His Excellency
Generalissimo Chiang Kai-shek
President of the Republic of China
Nanking, China
Dear Generalissimo:

Your fine letter of May 18 is deeply appreciated. I have completely recovered from my operation which I am sure has alleviated the sinus condition that caused me some discomfort the past several years. I received your letter about the first week in June, but I did not reply because I felt that my return to China was imminent, and I therefore could thank you personally for your good wishes and also discuss many of the ideas you presented.

President Truman has sent you a radio to the effect that he feels that I should be relieved as your Chief of Staff. Also, I sent a radio to you indicating that my assignment to China was apparently terminated and expressing my heartfelt appreciation of the unfailing courtesies and hospitality, as well as the splendid cooperation, that we Americans received in China the past two years. I should like to emphasize that I had every intention of returning to China when I left last April. I stated to you, and to many other Chinese officials there, that I expected to return shortly after my operation. Circumstances over which I definitely had no control have caused the President to appoint Doctor Leighton Stuart as Ambassador. I know Doctor Stuart fairly well and believe him to be an honest, able man, sincerely interested in the welfare of China. His knowledge of the Far East, the respect that the Chinese people have for him, and finally, the fact that he is acceptable to the Chinese Communists, should eminently qualify him for the role of Ambassador.

As long as the present U.S. policy maintains, it would be most difficult for me to serve as Ambassador because I would be placed in the position of executing a policy that I believe unsound. For example, after the past two years' experience in China, and also carefully analyzing international affairs in other parts of the world, I have concluded that the only way to deal with Communists is to be firm, requiring strict adherence to agreements, and resorting to employment of force if necessary. They (Communists) have not been acting in good faith, and we are naive if we expect them to honor their agreements. The Soviet Communists, under whose tutelage the Chinese Communists are operating, have broken agreements and dodged commitments indiscriminately the past several years.

My interest in the future of China will continue and from time to time, if you so desire, I will convey ideas or suggestions direct to you or to Madame Chiang. I do not pretend to be an expert on Far Eastern Affairs, but I have always had a great interest in history and economics. The past several months I have more or less confined my reading and studying to the economic and political history and current conditions in China and Russia. My objective, of course, was to prepare myself to make sound analyses of the many problems presented in the Far East.

I mentioned the fact above that I feel that the immediate solution to your difficulties with the Communists involves the actual employment or at least the intimidation of force. The Chinese Central Government air and ground forces should be disposed so that they can quickly and effectively suppress or annihilate Communist agitators and their armed forces. This is, however, not the permanent solution to the Communist problem. The best antidote to the spread of communistic ideologies is the establishment of good government, sound economy, and the uniform recognition of the individual rights of human beings. If these conditions could be created among your people in an area, for example, in South and Central China, we would have an important part of China absolutely immune to communism. Only in areas of unrest, chaos, and oppression are the Communists successful in spreading their invidious propaganda. They make all sorts of extravagant promises to the people, who, if they are oppressed and unhappy, are willing to try communism in the hope of relief.

After V-J Day you undoubtedly will recall that I recommended the immediate establishment of a Five Power trusteeship over Manchuria and Korea so that you could concentrate the bulk of your resources and effort on the stabilization and rehabilitation of China generally south of the Great Wall. I emphasized that our objective should be to establish [a] sound economy and good government in South and Central China. If we succeeded in stabilizing the situation in that area and brought about unification, prosperity, and happiness, we would thereby have available a nucleus or base area from which we could operate effectively to control and stabilize outlying areas including Manchuria. China is so vast we must accept that it is practically impossible at this time to bind all provinces together by an appropriate communications system. We can only accomplish a certain amount of construction and rehabilitation in a stipulated length of time. Therefore, we should not dissipate our efforts all over China and Manchuria, but we should concentrate on the establishment of the above-mentioned base area where we could build roads, railroads, and improve internal waterways as well as air lines; where we could inaugurate democratic procedures in government [and] social and tax reforms; and where we could facilitate existing and expand industries. Nothing that we might do would be more effective against the spread of communism in China than the successful execution of the above program. I feel certain that the vast majority of Chinese do not believe in, nor do they accept, communistic ideologies. At present many are bewildered. It is difficult for them to choose, particularly if their local government is corrupt, or living conditions are terrible. If the Central Government, on the other hand, can prove to the Chinese people and to the world both their *sincerity* and the *capability* in establishing honest government, social reform, and economic stability, enthusiastic support will be given to you and your government by the Chinese people and also by foreign powers interested in the democratic way of life . . .

I hope and pray for success in your inspiring and tireless effort to overcome the difficulties of rehabilitation and stabilization in war-torn China. My confidence in your ability, selflessness, and earnest desire to help your people has never faltered. Mrs. Wedemeyer joins me in heartfelt good wishes to you and Madame Chiang for health and happiness.

Sincerely,

A. C. WEDEMEYER
Lieutenant General
U.S. Army

Washington, D.C.
September 2, 1946

Colonel C. E. Hutchin
Office of General Marshall
APO 909, c/o P. M.
San Francisco, California

Dear Hutch:

There are many things which I should like to tell you . . . I had always felt that General Marshall would be returning this fall or early winter and I presumed that you . . . would return with him. Maybe this feeling was occasioned by the hope that he would not have to experience a winter out there, particularly under such frustrating circumstances . . .

Present indications are that General Marshall's mission may continue on into the winter, and in my opinion it would be wrong for . . . you to leave him. I am convinced that you have become [an] invaluable staff member in connection with his difficult task. Further, I know that he would release you if a favorable assignment were offered, for he is the type of commander who would not permit an organization that would result in any individual being indispensable. Also, I witnessed his continued release of key members on his staff during the critical war period when he unselfishly permitted them to go to accept increased rank and responsibility, although by so doing constantly broke up his team. The privilege and pleasure of serving so closely with him will assist . . . you throughout your military service, for you are assimilating his selfless approach to problems, the benefit of his keen analytical mind, and unquestionable courage. You see, Hutch, I had the opportunity to observe the Chief in many of the world conferences when he really carried the load for the Joint Chiefs of Staff. As a negotiator he was without peer, and I saw him confronted by some of the best, including Portal [Air Chief Marshal Sir Charles Portal] of the British Joint Chiefs of Staff and old Winston Churchill himself.

There is one observation that I should like to give you—sitting on the perimeter of official Washington. I have had contact, of course, with most of the War Department chiefs, some of the Navy and State Department, a few selected members of the press, some members of Congress, and for the most part I have been on the receiving end. I do not know whether I am entirely correct in stating that my contacts should equip me to provide a consensus of American opinion with regard to national and international affairs, but I have been compelled to draw a few conclusions.

Prior to the summer of 1941 our press and radio, in fact the propaganda media of England and certain other countries, were prone to criti-

cize unequivocally and continuously communism as epitomized by Soviet Russia. After June 22, 1941, when Germany attacked the Soviet, one
noted a complete reversal, and even responsible leaders of the government, both in the United States and England, sought justifiable reasons to
ameliorate the Communist program that included totalitarianism, atheism, stultification of free enterprise, and so forth and so forth. This change
in attitude toward Soviet Russia by the Allied press was not repugnant to,
in fact was probably hardly noticed by, the general public. There were
other great events transpiring in the world that attracted attention, including the Japanese attack on Pearl Harbor. This served to unify our country
in the combined effort with the Allies to crush militarily Germany, Italy,
and Japan. The fact that we were making superhuman efforts in assisting
one totalitarian power (Soviet Russia) to crush another was immaterial.
The conditions that would be created in Europe and in the Far East as the
result of defeating the Germans, Italians, and Japanese were not taken into
consideration by our policymaking agencies, with the result [that] we
achieved victory militarily but countenanced defeat politically, economically, and psychologically. The picture of the world viewed objectively
today reveals that we have substituted one totalitarian power or group of
powers for another, and both were and continue to be equally abhorrent
and unacceptable to the American people. Further, if one makes a comparative analysis of international events occurring during the period 1934
to 1939 with the frictions, suspicions, arrogance, [and] unilateral and
belligerent actions that have marked the past several months, there is
definite similarity injected into the international structure. In addition we
now have atomic and ultra destructive weapons which are suspended
ominously over mankind.

The world has been compartmented into two ideological camps,
Soviet Russia with her satellites, and the United States with her Allies.
Both sides are thinking in terms of employment of force and are jockey-
ing about to condition the minds of their followers in preparation for
any contingency. At present, two weapons appear to be available to
those opposing sides, the atomic bomb on the one hand, the Fifth Column on the other. Soviet Russia recognizes the great war-making potential of the United States and her Allies, and accordingly is doing her
utmost to preclude concerted and effective action by fomenting strikes,
impugning the motives of our military and political leaders and by
creating a security zone around the Soviet Russian citadel. Soviet Russia
understands that this security zone must be deep in order to minimize
the effect of guided missiles and heavy bombers whose radii of operation
have been greatly increased by science.

It is commonly accepted that the people who fight the wars and who suffer the aftermath abhor the thought of another armed conflict. However, within the Soviet Russia political structure, we find leaders who would abrogate agreements and whose program envisages the employment of force or intimidation. In fact, certain observers feel that the strength of these leaders (as in the pre-war Nazi regime) is directly dependent upon continued threat of violence and the injection of fear. Exactly following Hitler's pattern, the Soviets have impressed their people with the so-called program of extermination by encircling capitalistic powers. In Stalin's Red Army Day speech he stated clearly that continued conflict was inevitable and emphasized that the international revolution of the proletariat must be continued. We also have a book (*Lenin,* by Stalin) that clearly depicts the blueprint of such revolutionary activities not unlike Hitler's *Mein Kampf.*

Again, Hutch, from my position on the fringe of all the above manifestations, it is apparent to me that immediate and realistic action on the part of the United States and those nations desiring the attainment of these objectives established in the Atlantic Charter [is mandatory]. We cannot vacillate, for our task will be increasingly harder. Further, appropriate moves on our part today may minimize the scope of the conflict, or may even eliminate the necessity to employ force, including the ultra destructive weapons presently available to us.

The most portentous area remains in the Balkans, specifically Trieste. However, Asia is directly involved and very well could be the principal arena of the next conflict. The Central Government of China, with all its incompetence and corruption, at least is opposed to the expansion of Soviet influence in the Far East. Under our existing policy we are, as I understand it, attempting to bring about a coalition that would introduce Communist representatives and thus enhance their position to undermine Central Government resistance that one day we may so sorely need. I am not suggesting that the ultimate objective of China should not be a truly representative government. However, conditions in the world, as well as those prevailing within the confines of China, would indicate that the time is not propitious for such coalition, at least if the United States is to realize the objectives established in the Atlantic Charter. We advocate multiparty government for China, yet I have the conviction that, as Communist strength increases in that country, the possibility of multiparty government will become more remote. In no area under Communist influence in the world do we find representative government. Significantly, a one-party government controls the destinies of the people in such areas, and *the individual* is subordinated . . . to insure attainment ostensibly of the objectives of *the state.* However, when analyzed carefully, we find that the Soviet state has evolved into a bureaucracy and the sacrifices made by the individual operate essentially to increase the power, prestige, and well-being of a coterie of bureaucrats.

In discussing communism with Soviet friends, I have learned that they feel that our philosophy of life is a selfish one. We place a premium on the individual and stress individual liberties and rights, whereas they expound that their program contemplates sacrifice and extreme effort on the part of the individual for the well-being of the group or the state. I contend that the Soviet philosophy submerges the human being and eliminates any consideration of the soul and dignity of the human being. They place man in a harness to pull with the team, and feed and care for him as they would an animal. Free thinking and voluntary action that the Almighty gave to man are stultified, and predominantly his bestial qualities are emphasized. For thousands of years, according to our histories, man has struggled in order to exercise his God-given right to think freely and to act voluntarily. Under such aegis the developments, including decency in human relationships that we term civilization, have been made possible. It was through great sacrifices and superhuman efforts of our forebears, who believed in and struggled for liberty, that made possible our present enjoyment of freedom from want, freedom of thought, and freedom from fear.

As a natural aftermath of war, frictions are inevitable, tempers are short, and suspicions are everywhere present. Our immediate task is to alleviate these conditions without resorting to force. However, if one powerful member of the family of nations, such as Soviet Russia, refuses to recognize our sincerity and good purposes in connection with the solution of international problems, we must do everything within our power to restrict her policy of political and military expansion and concurrently continue our efforts to remove suspicion, to apprise the masses of Soviet Russia of our desire to live in peace, and to protect the rights of the individual man. Such a propaganda means that we must penetrate the so-called iron curtain either by peaceful means or through the employment of force or intimidation. We cannot tolerate existing conditions whereby Soviet Russia is consolidating her position from within, creating satellite or puppet governments in all of the areas about her perimeter, and universally undermining or distorting by Fifth Column activities the true purposes of the American people. I am told that we cannot penetrate the iron curtain in order to reach the approximately 198 million Russian people who are unaware of, and no doubt are entirely unsympathetic with, the belligerent war-mongering attitude of their leaders. Personally, I feel that we could in time penetrate this curtain. However, in the meantime, again I feel that realistic steps, political, economic, military and psychological, must be taken to preclude increased Russian strength vis-a–vis the United States.

More or less summarizing, Hutch, the following premises are indicated:

    a. The two ideologies, free enterprise and Marxism-Leninism, which seem to be compartmenting the world, are gradually creating—in fact may already have created—an international situation that is incapable of being reconciled or of affording solutions to conflicting or competing interests except by the employment of force or intimidation.

    b. Assuming that current negotiations fail, the United States must employ force or intimidation in the immediate future to provide practical international machinery to supervise development and safeguard against military employment of atomic or ultra destructive weapons. (This is an urgent *must.*)

    c. In negotiating with foreign powers, it should be recognized that international morality can never be depended upon as an exclusive means of control, and that collaboration with another power or group of powers will be effective so long as and to the degree that definite political, economic, and/or military advantages accrue to such powers. (Stalin once stated, "Healthy suspicion is the best basis for collaboration.")

    d. The United States is in the fortunate position of having national interests that correspond to the true interests of the bulk of mankind, whereas Soviet interests are in direct conflict with those deep-rooted, basically human interests—personal liberty, justice and individual rights, [and] decency in human relationships—for which men have struggled thousands of years. U.S. interests should remain our primary consideration in international negotiations and agreements. Concessions should invariably be made only on the basis of a tangible return.

    e. A fearful and uncertain world looks to the United States for leadership toward universal security and peace; failure to assert this leadership will promote the success of a predatory Soviet leadership that will conquer the world for Marxism-Leninism.

    f. Current Soviet Russian unilateral and arbitrary action is made possible, even encouraged, by the obvious determination of the American government and people to avoid the use of force or intimidation in the solution of international problems.

    g. The *time factor* in announcing or in executing policies, in the evolution of strategic plans, and in the employment of force or intimidation remains a paramount consideration. In a constitutional form of government, considerable time would be required to obtain the approval of the people without which firm decisions and concrete action would be impossible, or at least weakened to a prohibitive degree. Whereas, in a totalitarian form of government the minds of the people are continuously conditioned to policies and acts of the leaders, permitting the latter to retain important strategic advantages of surprise, initiative, and concerted action.

From the strategic viewpoint, I view Russia's objectives and position as follows:

> *a.* Creation of a broad security zone extending around the perimeter of the USSR. In view of the increased radii of operation of guided missiles and airplanes, an attempt will be made to insure that this zone will be a thousand or more miles in depth. Translated to the globe, this would mean that the surface of the earth, including the land masses of Eurasia and the northern half of Africa, must be brought into the Soviet orbit. Countries lying therein will be established as puppet states or rendered militarily impotent through political subversion.
> *b.* The war-making potential of the United States, which represents the dynamo or arsenal of capitalistic-democratic nations, would be rendered impotent through dissemination of propaganda and instigation of strikes. (Press, radio, screen, and political activity to undermine American appreciation of world situation and to disparage and impugn motives of political and military leaders. Infiltration of organized labor to disrupt production, communications, and transportation.)

Years ago, when I was Chief of Strategy and Policy, almost every Sunday morning I inflicted ideas upon the Chief in the Pentagon. These were the early days of the war, and he encouraged me to express views concerning strategic developments at that time. Today I am inflicting ideas upon you—writing again from a temporary office in the Pentagon on a Sunday morning. Old Hart [Colonel John H. Caughey] as well as Paul Caraway [Colonel Paul W. Caraway] and others of my fine planning group were frequently my sounding boards. Their honest, intelligent reactions to my proposals provided the modicum of success that I may have enjoyed. Therefore if you . . . will critique the above views and jot down a few ideas in between your multifarious duties, I would be glad to receive them. You are in a much better position to observe developments upon which many of my premises are based. I have no official status or responsibilities at present, and do not voluntarily express views here in Washington. Occasionally I am asked by General Ike, Handy, and others, who, like yoursel[f], are seeking solutions in the interest of the United States and mankind in general, and then I fear I burst forth with vehemence.

It was not my intention to inflict you with an opus; however, once I launched forth on this subject I attempted to cover the waterfront.

Next week I am flying to my home state, Nebraska, where I have been asked to make a dedication address in connection with the opening of a municipal airport. General Eisenhower encouraged me to do this; however, he does not realize how sorely lacking I am in forensic ability. Further, my talk will be merely a mass of platitudes, for so long as I wear the uniform of an officer, I cannot exercise the right of an American citizen to express freely my views.

Give my best to the Chief. A day never passes that I do not think of him and his tremendous responsibilities. I hope that you, Hart [Colonel John H. Caughey], Mrs. Marshall, and the Chief will soon be able to return to the homeland with successful accomplishments behind you. Tom Handy just informed me that I have been released from possible employment in China, so General Ike will probably assign me to command the Second Army with Headquarters in Baltimore.

Sincerely,

A. C. WEDEMEYER
Lieutenant General
U.S. Army

15

Report on China and Korea

1947

As Wedemeyer had feared, General Marshall's prolonged efforts eventually proved vain. Frustrated in his quest for peace and unity in China, Marshall returned home at the beginning of 1947 to pronounce a plague on both the Communists and the Nationalists. Later in January he assumed the post of Secretary of State.

To a large extent, official Washington thereafter turned its back on the Orient as attention shifted to what seemed a nearer and more urgent threat: communist aggression in Europe and the Near East. In March, President Truman requested funds to assist the governments of Greece and Turkey in their efforts to resist externally supported subversion. In June, the Secretary of State unveiled the "Marshall Plan," a broad program of U.S. aid to rebuild and strengthen a war-torn and vulnerable Europe.

Enough interest in the Far East survived, however, to generate a modicum of continuing support for the hard-pressed government of China. Half-measures and equivocation nonetheless continued to mark U.S. China policy (which increasingly became the subject of domestic political controversy). With the ostensible purpose of reviewing that policy, President Truman and Marshall recalled Wedemeyer from Baltimore (where he had been assigned to command the Second U.S. Army) and dispatched him in July on an extraordinary "fact-finding" mission to China and Korea.

Wedemeyer and a staff of experts promptly departed for the

Far East on a rigorous schedule of travel, briefings, and study. In the two years that had elapsed since the end of World War II, the situation in China had grown progressively worse. Prospects for a noncommunist future certainly had dimmed, and the options for U.S. policy had narrowed. Still persuaded, however, that the interests of peace would best be served by a noncommunist China, and that Chiang Kai-shek remained the most promising figure for rallying noncommunist forces, Wedemeyer recommended unambiguous (although not unlimited or unmonitored) U.S. support to the Nationalist government. Again he recommended that Washington seek United Nations trusteeship (or guardianship) over Manchuria and Korea. While recognizing the meager likelihood of achieving effective U.N. action at this late date, he urged this step as the last hope for challenging the Soviet Union and its Chinese allies in their quest for dominance of these crucial areas.

What came to be known as the *Wedemeyer Report*—a long, thoughtful, and explicitly anti-communist document that would figure importantly in the foreign policy debates of subsequent years—went to the White House on September 19, 1947. Excerpts from that report follow.

———————————————————

September 19, 1947

MEMORANDUM FOR THE PRESIDENT

My dear Mr. President:

In compliance with your directive to me of July 9, 1947, the attached Report on China-Korea is respectfully submitted.

In consonance with your instructions, advisers from State, War, Navy, and Treasury Departments accompanied me on a two-month fact-finding mission in the Far East. The principal cities and some rural areas in China and Korea were visited. Successful efforts were made to reach all categories of people as measured by economic position, intellectual attainment, and divergent political viewpoints. Conferences were held with public officials and with private citizens in all walks of life. Approximately 1,200 memoranda from individuals and groups were received and considered.

The report includes pertinent data in appendices which may be of interest and assistance to appropriate government departments and agencies. The report presents against a global background my estimates of the situations, current and projected, in both China and Korea, and recommends what I deem to be sound courses of action for achievement of U.S. objectives in the Far East.

Respectfully yours,

A. C. WEDEMEYER
Lieutenant General, U.S. Army

Report to President on China and Korea
Part I: General Statement

China's history is replete with examples of encroachment, arbitrary action, special privilege, exploitation, and usurpation of territory on the part of foreign powers. Continued foreign infiltration, penetration, or efforts to obtain spheres of influence in China, including Manchuria and Taiwan (Formosa), could be interpreted only as a direct infringement and violation of China's sovereignty and a contravention of the principles of the Charter of the United Nations. It is mandatory that the United States and those other nations subscribing to the principles of the Charter of the United Nations should combine their efforts to insure the unimpeded march of all peoples toward goals that recognize the dignity of man and his civil rights and, further, definitely provide the opportunity to express freely how and by whom they will be governed.

These goals and the lofty aims of freedom-loving peoples are jeopardized today by forces as sinister as those that operated in Europe and Asia during the ten years leading to World War II. The pattern is familiar: employment of subversive agents; infiltration tactics; incitement of disorder and chaos to disrupt normal economy and thereby to undermine popular confidence in government and leaders; [and] seizure of authority without reference to the will of the people. [These are] all the techniques skillfully designed and ruthlessly implemented in order to create favorable conditions for the imposition of totalitarian ideologies. This pattern is present in the Far East, particularly in the areas contiguous to Siberia.

If the United Nations is to have real effect in establishing economic stability and in maintaining world peace, these developments merit high priority on the U.N. agenda for study and action. Events of the past two years demonstrate the futility of appeasement based on the hope that the strongly consolidated forces of the Soviet Union will adopt either a conciliatory or a compromising attitude, except as tactical expedients. Soviet practice in the countries already occupied or dominated completes the mosaic of aggressive expansion through ruthless secret police methods and through an increasing political and economic enslavement of peoples. Soviet literature, confirmed repeatedly by Communist leaders, reveals a definite plan for expansion far exceeding that of Nazism in its ambitious scope and dangerous implications. Therefore in attempting a solution to the problem presented in the Far East, as well as in other troubled areas of the world, every possible opportunity must be used to seize the initiative in order to create and maintain bulwarks of freedom.

Notwithstanding all the corruption and incompetence that one notes in China, it is a certainty that the bulk of the people are not disposed to a Communist political and economic structure. Some have become affiliated with communism in indignant protest against oppressive police measures, corrupt practices, and maladministration of National Government officials. Some have lost all hope for China under existing leadership and turn to the Communists in despair. Some accept a new leadership by mere inertia.

Indirectly, the United States facilitated the Soviet program in the Far East by agreeing at the Yalta Conference to Russian re-entry into Manchuria, and later by withholding aid from the National Government. There were justifiable reasons for these policies. In the one case we were concentrating maximum Allied strength against the Japanese in order to accelerate crushing defeat and thus save Allied lives. In the other, we were withholding unqualified support from a government within which corruption and incompetence were so prevalent that it was losing the support of its own people. Further, the United States had not yet realized that the Soviet Union would fail to cooperate in the accomplishment of worldwide plans for postwar rehabilitation. Our own participation in those plans has already afforded assistance to other nations and peoples, friends and former foes alike, to a degree unparalleled in humanitarian history.

Gradually it has become apparent that the World War II objectives for which we and others made tremendous sacrifices are not being fully attained, and that there remains in the world a force presenting even greater dangers to world peace than did the Nazi militarists and the Japanese jingoists. Consequently the United States made the decision in the spring of 1947 to assist Greece and Turkey with a view to protecting their sovereignties, which were threatened by the direct or inspired activities of the Soviet Union. Charges of unilateral action and circumvention of the United Nations were made by members of that organization. In the light of its purposes and principles such criticisms seemed plausible. The United States promptly declared its intention of referring the matter to the United Nations when that organization would be ready to assume responsibility.

It follows that the United Nations should be informed of contemplated action with regard to China. If the recommendations of this report are approved, the United States should suggest to China that she inform the United Nations officially of her request to the United States for material assistance in order to facilitate China's postwar rehabilitation and economic recovery. This will demonstrate that the United Nations is not being circumvented and that the United States is not infringing upon China's sovereignty, but contrary-wise is cooperating constructively in the interest of peace and stability in the Far East, concomitantly in the world.

The situation in Manchuria has deteriorated to such a degree that prompt action is necessary to prevent that area from becoming a Soviet satellite. The Chinese Communists may soon gain military control of Manchuria and announce the establishment of a government. Outer Mongolia, already a Soviet satellite, may then recognize Manchuria and conclude a "mutual support agreement" with a *de facto* Manchurian government of the Chinese Communists. In that event, the Soviet Union might accomplish a mutual support agreement with Communist-dominated Manchuria, because of her current similar agreement with Outer Mongolia. This would create a difficult situation for China, the

United States, and the United Nations. Ultimately it could lead to a Communist-dominated China.

The United Nations might take immediate action to bring about cessation of hostilities in Manchuria as a prelude to the establishment of guardianship or trusteeship. The guardianship might consist of China, Soviet Russia, the United States, Great Britain, and France. This should be attempted promptly and could be initiated only by China. Should one of the nations refuse to participate in Manchurian guardianship, China might then request the General Assembly of the United Nations to establish a trusteeship, under the provisions of the Charter.

Initially China might interpret guardianship or trusteeship as an infringement upon her sovereignty. But the urgency of the matter should encourage a realistic view of the situation. If these steps are not taken by China, Manchuria may be drawn into the Soviet orbit, despite U.S. aid, and lost, perhaps permanently, to China.

The economic deterioration and the incompetence and corruption in the political and military organizations in China should be considered against an all-inclusive background lest there be disproportionate emphasis upon defects. Comity requires that cognizance be taken of the following:

[a.] Unlike other powers, China has never, since V-J Day, been free to devote full attention to internal problems that were greatly confounded by eight years of war. The current civil war has imposed an overwhelming financial and economic burden at a time when resources and energies have been dissipated and when, in any event, they would have been strained to the utmost to meet the problems of recovery.

[b.] The National Government has consistently, since 1927, opposed communism. Today the same political leader and some civil and military officials are determined to prevent their country from becoming a Communist-dominated State or Soviet satellite.

[c.] Although the Japanese offered increasingly favorable surrender terms during the course of the war, China elected to remain steadfast with her Allies. If China had accepted surrender terms, approximately a million Japanese would have been released for employment against American forces in the Pacific.

I was assured by the Generalissimo that China would support to the limit of her ability an American program for the stabilization of the Far East. He stated categorically that, regardless of moral encouragement or material aid received from the United States, he is determined to oppose communism and to create a democratic form of government in consonance with Doctor Sun Yat-sen's principles. He stated further that he plans to make sweeping reforms in the government, including the removal of incompetent and corrupt officials. He stated that some progress has been made along these lines but, with spiraling inflation, economic distress, and civil war, it has been difficult to accomplish fully these objectives. He emphasized that, when the Communist problem is solved, he could drastically reduce the army and concentrate upon political and economic reforms. I retain the conviction that the Generalissimo is sincere in his desire to attain these objectives. I am not certain that he has today sufficient determination to do so if this requires absolute overruling of the political and military cliques surrounding him. Yet, if realistic U.S. aid is to prove effective in stabilizing the situation in China and in coping with dangerous expansion of communism, that determination must be established.

Adoption by the United States of a policy motivated solely toward stopping the expansion of communism without regard [for] the continued existence of an unpopular repressive government would render any aid ineffective. Further, U.S. prestige in the Far East would suffer heavily, and wavering elements might turn away from the existing government to communism.

In China and Korea, the political, economic, and psychological problems are inextricably mingled. All of them are complex and are becoming increasingly difficult of solution. Each has been studied assiduously in compliance with your directive. Each will be discussed in the course of this report. However, it is recognized that a continued global appraisal is mandatory in order to preclude disproportionate or untimely assistance to any specific area.

The following three postulates of U.S. foreign policy are pertinent to indicate the background of my investigations, analyses, and report:

[*a*.] The United States will continue support of the United Nations in the attainment of its lofty aims, accepting the possible development that the Soviet Union or other nations may not actively participate.

[*b*.] Moral support will be given to nations and peoples that have established political and economic structures compatible with our own, or that give convincing evidence of their desire to do so.

[*c*.] Material aid may be given to those same nations and peoples in order to accelerate postwar rehabilitation and to develop economic stability, provided: that there is continuing evidence that they are taking effective steps to help themselves, or are fully committed to do so; that such aid shall be used for the purposes intended; [and] that such aid shall not jeopardize American economy and shall conform to an integrated program that involves other international commitments and contributes to the attainment of political, economic, and psychological objectives of the United States.

Part II: China

Political

Although the Chinese people are unanimous in their desire for peace at almost any cost, there seems to be no possibility of its realization under existing circumstances. On one side is the Kuomintang, whose reactionary leadership, repression, and corruption have caused a loss of popular faith in the government. On the other side, bound ideologically to the Soviet Union, are the Chinese Communists, whose eventual aim is admittedly a communist state in China. Some reports indicate that Communist measures of land reform have gained for them the support of the majority of peasants in areas under their control, while others indicate that their ruthless tactics of land distribution and terrorism have alienated the majority of such peasants. They have, however, successfully organized many rural areas against the National Government. Moderate groups are caught between Kuomintang misrule and repression and ruthless Communist totalitarianism. Minority parties lack dynamic leadership and sizable following. Neither the moderates, many of whom are in the Kuomintang, nor the minority parties are able to make their influence felt because of National Government repression. Existing provincial opposition leading to possible separatist movements would probably crystalize only if collapse of the government were imminent.

Soviet actions, contrary to the letter and spirit of the Sino-Soviet Treaty of 1945 and its related documents, have strengthened the Chinese Communist position in Manchuria, with political, economic, and military repercussions on the National Government's position both in Manchuria and in China proper, and have made more difficult peace and stability in China. The present trend points toward a gradual disintegration of the National Government's control, with the ultimate possibility of a Communist-dominated China.

Steps taken by the Chinese government toward governmental reorganization in mid–April 1947 aroused hopes of improvement in the political situation. However, the reorganization resulted in little change. Reactionary influences continue to mold important policies even though the Generalissimo remains the principal determinative force in the government. Since the April reorganization, the most significant change has been the appointment of General Chen Cheng to head the civil and military administration in Manchuria. Projected steps include elections in the fall for the formation of a constitutional government, but, under present conditions, they are not expected to result in a government more representative than the present regime.

Economic

Under the impact of civil strife and inflation, the Chinese economy is disintegrating. The most probable outcome of present trends would be, not sudden collapse, but a continued and creeping paralysis and consequent decline in the authority and power of the National Government. The past ten years of war have caused serious deterioration of transportation and communication facilities, mines, utilities, and industries. Notwithstanding some commendable efforts and large amounts of economic aid, their overall capabilities are scarcely half those of the prewar period. With disruption of transportation facilities and the loss of much of North China and Manchuria, important resources of those rich areas are no longer available for the rehabilitation and support of China's economy.

Inflation in China has been diffused slowly through an enormous population without causing the immediate dislocation which would have occurred in a highly industrialized economy. The rural people, 80 percent of the total Chinese population of 450 million, barter foodstuffs for local handicraft products without suffering a drastic cut in living standards. Thus, local economies exist in many parts of China, largely insulated from the disruption of urban industry. Some local economies are under the control of Communists, and some are loosely under the control of provincial authorities.

The principal cause of the hyper-inflation is the long-continued deficit in the national budget. Present revenue collections, plus the profits of nationalized enterprises, cover only one-third of governmental expenditures, which are approximately 70 percent military, and an increasing proportion of the budget is financed by the issuance of new currency. In the first six months of 1947, note-issue was tripled but rice prices increased seven-fold. Thus prices and governmental expenditures spiral upwards, with price increases occurring faster than new currency can be printed. With further price increases, budget revisions will undoubtedly be necessary. The most urgent economic need of Nationalist China is a reduction of the military budget.

China's external official assets amounted to $327 million (U.S.) on July 30, 1947. Privately held foreign exchange assets are at least $600 million and may total $1500 million, but no serious attempt has been made to mobilize these private resources for rehabilitation purposes. Private Chinese assets located in China include probably $200 million in gold and about $75 million in U.S. currency notes. Although China has not exhausted her foreign official assets, and probably will not do so at the present rates of imports and exports until early 1949, the continuing deficit in her external balance of payments is a serious problem.

Disparity between the prices of export goods in China and in world markets at unrealistic official exchange rates has greatly penalized exports, as have disproportionate increases in wages and other costs. Despite rigorous trade and exchange controls, imports have greatly exceeded exports, and there consistently has been a heavy adverse trade balance.

China's food harvests this year are expected to be significantly larger than last year's fairly good returns. This moderately encouraging situation with regard to crops is among the few favorable factors which can be found in China's current economic situation.

Under inflationary conditions, long-term investment is unattractive for both Chinese and foreign capital. Private Chinese funds tend to go into short-term advances, hoarding of commodities, and capital flight. The entire psychology is speculative and inflationary, preventing ordinary business planning and handicapping industrial recovery.

Foreign business enterprises in China are adversely affected by the inefficient and corrupt administration of exchange and import controls, discriminatory application of tax laws, the increasing role of government trading agencies, and the trend toward state ownership of industries. The Chinese government has taken some steps toward improvement but generally has been apathetic in its efforts. Between 1944 and 1947, the anti-inflationary measure on which the Chinese government placed most reliance was the public sale of gold borrowed from the United States. The intention was to absorb paper currency and thus reduce the effective demand for goods. Under the circumstances of continued large deficits, however, the only effect of the gold sales program was to retard slightly the price inflation and dissipate dollar assets.

A program to stabilize the economic situation was undertaken in February 1947. The measures included a wage freeze, a system of limited rationing to essential workers in a few cities, and the sale of government bonds. The effect of this program has been slight, and the wage freeze has been abandoned. In August 1947, the unrealistic official rate of exchange was replaced, for proceeds of exports and remittances, by a free market in foreign exchange. This step is expected to stimulate exports, but it is too early to determine whether it will be effective.

The issuance of new silver currency has been proposed as a future measure to combat inflation. If the government continued to finance budgetary deficits by unbacked note issue, the silver would probably go into hoards and the price inflation would continue. The effect would be no more than that of the gold sales in 1944–1947, namely, a slight and temporary retardation of the inflationary spiral. The proposal could be carried out, moreover, only through a loan from the United States of at least $200 million in silver.

In the construction field, China has prepared expansive plans for reconstruction of communications, mines, and industries. Some progress has been made in implementing them, notably in the partial rehabilitation of certain railroads and in the textile industry. Constructive results have been handicapped by a lack of funds, equipment, and experienced management, supervisory, and technical personnel.

On August 1, 1947, the State Council approved a "Plan for Economic Reforms." This appears to be an omnibus of plans covering all phases of Chinese economic reconstruction but its effectiveness cannot yet be determined.

Social-Cultural

Public education has been one of the chief victims of war and social and economic disruption. Schoolhouses, textbooks, and other equipment have been destroyed, and the cost of replacing any considerable portion cannot now be met. Teachers, like other public servants, have seen the purchasing power of a month's salary shrink to the market value of a few days' rice ration. This applies to the entire educational system, from primary schools, which provide a medium to combat the nation's grievous illiteracy, to universities, from which must come the nation's professional men, technicians, and administrators. The universities have suffered in an additional and no less serious respect—traditional academic freedom. Students participating in protest demonstrations have been severely and at times brutally punished by National Government agents without pretense of trial or public evidence of the sedition charged. Faculty members have often been dismissed or refused employment with no evidence of professional unfitness, patently because they were politically objectionable to government officials. Somewhat similarly, periodicals have been closed down "for reasons of military security" without stated charges, and permitted to reopen only after new managements have been imposed. Resumption of educational and other public welfare activities on anything like the desired scale can be accomplished only by restraint of officialdom's abuses and when the nation's economy is stabilized sufficiently to defray the cost of such vital activities.

Military

The overall military position of the National Government has deteriorated in the past several months, and the current military situation favors Communist forces. The Generalissimo has never wavered in his contention that he is fighting for national independence against forces of an armed rebellion, nor has he been completely convinced that the Communist problem can be resolved except by force of arms. Although the Nationalist army has a preponderance of force, the tactical initiative rests with the Communists. Their hit-and-run tactics, adapted to their mission of destruction at points or in areas of their own selection, give them a decided advantage over Nationalists, who must defend many critical areas including connecting lines of communication. Obviously large numbers of Nationalist troops involved in such defensive roles are immobilized, whereas Communist tactics permit almost complete freedom of action. The Nationalists' position is precarious in Manchuria, where they occupy only a slender finger of territory. Their control is strongly disputed in Shantung and Hopei provinces, where the Communists make frequent dislocating attacks against isolated garrisons.

In order to improve materially the current military situation, the Nationalist forces must first stabilize the fronts and then regain the initiative. Further, since the government is supporting the civil war with approximately 70 percent of its national budget, it is evident that steps taken to alleviate the situation must point toward an improvement in the effectiveness of the armed forces with a concomitant program of social, political, and economic reforms, including a decrease in the size of the military establishment. Whereas some rather ineffective steps have been taken to reorganize and revitalize the command structure, and more sweeping reforms are projected, the effectiveness of the Nationalist Army requires a sound program of equipment and improved logistical support. The present industrial potential of China is inadequate to support military forces effectively. Chinese forces under present conditions cannot cope successfully with internal strife or fulfill China's obligations as a member of the family of nations. Hence outside aid, in the form of munitions (most urgently ammunition) and technical assistance, is essential before any plan of operations can be undertaken with a reasonable prospect of success. Military advice is now available to the Nationalists on a General Staff level through American military advisory groups.

The Generalissimo expressed to me repeatedly a strong desire to have this advice and supervision extended in scope to include field forces, training centers, and particularly logistical agencies.

Extension of military aid by the United States to the National Government might possibly be followed by similar aid from the Soviet Union to the Chinese Communists, either openly or covertly—the latter course seems more likely. An arena of conflicting ideologies might be created as in 1935 in Spain. There is always the possibility that such developments in this area, as in Europe and the Middle East, might precipitate a third world war.

Part III: Korea

Political

The major political problem in Korea is that of carrying out the Moscow Agreement of December 1945 for the formation of a provisional Korean government to be followed by a Four Power trusteeship over Korea. The U.S.-Soviet Joint Commission, established in accordance with that agreement, reached a deadlock in 1946 in an effort to implement the Moscow Agreement due to Soviet opposition to consultations with the Commission of all Korean democratic parties and social organizations, as provided for in that agreement. Soviet motives have been to eliminate the extreme rightist groups in the U.S. zone from consultations and subsequently from participation in the new government, thus ensuring a Communist-dominated government in Korea. Soviet objections to such consultations have been based on the rightist groups' openly expressed opposition to trusteeship, while the United States has taken the position that to disqualify these groups would deprive a large section of the Korean people of an opportunity to express views regarding their government.

A resumption of the Joint Commission meetings in May 1947, following an exchange of notes between Secretary Marshall and Foreign Minister Molotov, resulted in a further deadlock on the same issue, although these notes had established a formula which would have permitted participation in consultation by the rightist groups in question. After the Soviet government failed to reply to Secretary Marshall's note of August 12 requesting the submission by the commission of a joint status report or separate reports by each delegation, the U.S. Delegation on August 20 transmitted a unilateral report to Washington. An American proposal then made to China, the United Kingdom, and the Soviet

Union for a Four Power Conference to discuss Korea has been agreed to by China and the United Kingdom but has been rejected by the Soviet Union.

Internally, the Korean problem has been complicated by the Soviet establishment of a Communist regime in North Korea and by the machinations in South Korea of Communist groups, openly hostile to the United States. The terrorist activities of extreme rightists, who have strongly opposed trusteeship, have continually obstructed the efforts of U.S. authorities. The latter, in accordance with their directives, are endeavoring to turn over to Koreans as rapidly as possible full administrative responsibility in governmental departments. In consonance with this plan, they have organized an interim Korean legislative assembly and in general are striving to carry out a policy of "Koreanization" of government in South Korea.

Economic

South Korea, basically an agricultural area, does not have the overall economic resources to sustain its economy without external assistance. The soil is depleted, and imports of food as well as fertilizer are required. The latter has normally come from North Korea, as has most of the electric power, timber, anthracite coal, and other basic products.

The economic dependence of South Korea upon North Korea, and of Korea as a whole, in prewar years, upon trade with Japan and Manchuria, cannot be too strongly emphasized. Division of the country at the 38 degrees north parallel, and prevention of all except smuggling trade between North and South Korea, have reduced the Korean economy to its lowest level in many years. Prospects for developing sizable exports are slight. Food exports cannot be anticipated on any scale for several years, and then only with increased use of artificial fertilizer. South Korea's few manufacturing industries, which have been operating at possibly 20 percent of prewar production, are now reducing their output or closing down. In part this is a natural result of ten years of deferred maintenance and wartime abuse, but lack of raw materials and essential repair parts, and a gross deficiency of competent management and technical personnel, are the principal factors.

A runaway inflation has not yet occurred in South Korea, because the military government has restrained the issuance of currency by keeping governmental expenditures and local occupation costs at reasonable levels; because cannibalization and the use of Japanese stocks have kept some industries going; and because the forcible collection of rice at harvest time has brought in sufficient food to maintain—with imports provided by the U.S.—an adequate official ration in the cities. Highly inflationary factors, such as the exhaustion of raw material stocks, cumulative breakdowns in public services and transportation, and the cutting of power supply from the North, might occur simultaneously. The South Korean economic outlook is, therefore, most grave.

A five-year rehabilitation program starting in July 1948, and requiring U.S. financing at a cost of $647 million, has been proposed by the military government. A review of preliminary estimates indicates that the proposed annual rehabilitation cost would be substantially greater than the relief program of $137 million which was tentatively approved for fiscal 1948 but later reduced to $92.7 million. These preliminary estimates of costs and the merits of individual projects need careful review. It is not considered feasible to make South Korea self-sustaining. If the United States elects to remain in South Korea, support of that area should be on a relief basis.

Social-Cultural

Since the Japanese were expelled, the Korean people have vehemently and unceasingly pressed for restoration of their ancient culture. There is particular zeal for public education. Individual and collective efforts to reduce illiteracy have produced results meeting the praise of American military government officials. There will be materially better results when there are more school buildings, more trained teachers and advisers, and many more textbooks in the Korean language. Current American activities aim at adult visual education on a modest but reasonably effective scale. South Korea's health and public welfare work are at present fully as effective as under Japanese administration and considerably more so in the prevention of serious diseases. Even the Koreans' eagerness for improvement cannot immediately overcome the unquestionable need for large funds for social betterment.

Military

The military situation in Korea, stemming from political and economic disputes which in turn are accentuated by the artificial barrier along the 38 degrees north parallel, is potentially dangerous to U.S. strategic interests. Large-scale Communist-inspired or abetted riots and revolutionary activities in the South are a constant threat. However, American forces supplemented by quasi-military Korean units are adequate to cope with such trouble or disorder except in the currently improbable event of an outright Soviet-controlled invasion. Whereas

American and Soviet forces engaged in occupation duties in South Korea and North Korea respectively are approximately equal, each comprising less than 50,000 troops, the Soviet-equipped and trained north Korean People's (Communist) Army of approximately 125,000 is vastly superior to the U.S. organized Constabulary of 16,000 Koreans equipped with Japanese small arms. The North Korean People's Army constitutes a potential military threat to South Korea, since there is strong possibility that the Soviets will withdraw their occupation forces and thus induce our own withdrawal. This probably will take place just as soon as they can be sure that the North Korean puppet government and its armed forces, which they have created, are strong enough and sufficiently well indoctrinated to be relied upon to carry out Soviet objectives without the actual presence of Soviet troops.

It appears advisable that the United States organize, equip, and train a South Korean Scout Force, similar to the former Philippine Scouts. This force should be under the control of the U.S. military commander and, initially should be officered throughout by Americans, with a program for replacement by Korean officers. It should be of sufficient strength to cope with the threat from the North. It would counteract in large measure the North Korean People's Army when American and Soviet forces are withdrawn from Korea, possibly preclude the forcible establishment of a Communist government, and thus contribute toward a free and independent Korea.

Conclusions

The peaceful aims of freedom-loving peoples in the world are jeopardized today by developments as portentous as those leading to World War II.

The Soviet Union and her satellites give no evidence of a conciliatory or cooperative attitude in these developments. The United States is compelled, therefore, to initiate realistic lines of action in order to create and maintain bulwarks of freedom, and to protect U.S. strategic interests.

The bulk of the Chinese and Korean peoples are not disposed to communism, and they are not concerned with ideologies. They desire food, shelter, and the opportunity to live in peace.

China

The spreading internecine struggle within China threatens world peace. Repeated American efforts to mediate have proved unavailing. It is apparent that positive steps are required to end hostilities immediately. The most logical approach to this very complex and ominous situation would be to refer the matter to the United Nations.

A China dominated by Chinese Communists would be inimical to the interests of the United States, in view of their openly expressed hostility and active opposition to those principles which the United States regards as vital to the peace of the world.

The Communists have the tactical initiative in the overall military situation. The Nationalist position in Manchuria is precarious, and in Shantung and Hopei provinces strongly disputed. Continued deterioration of the situation may result in the early establishment of a Soviet satellite government in Manchuria and ultimately in the evolution of a Communist-dominated China.

China is suffering increasingly from disintegration. Her requirements for rehabilitation are large. Her most urgent needs include governmental reorganization and reforms, reduction of the military budget and external assistance.

A program of aid, if effectively employed, would bolster opposition to Communist expansion and would contribute to gradual development of stability in China.

Due to excesses and oppressions by government police agencies, basic freedoms of the people are being jeopardized. Maladministration and corruption cause a loss of confidence in the government. Until drastic political and economic reforms are undertaken, U.S. aid cannot accomplish its purpose.

Even so, criticism of results achieved by the National Government in efforts for improvement should be tempered by a recognition of the handicaps imposed on China by eight years of war, the burden of her opposition to communism, and her sacrifices for the Allied cause.

A U.S. program of assistance could best be implemented under the supervision of American advisers in specified economic and military fields. Such a program can be undertaken only if China requests advisory aid as well as material assistance.

Korea

The situation in Korea, in its political, economic and psychological aspects, is strongly and adversely influenced by the artificial barrier of the 38 degree north parallel separating agricultural South Korea from the more industrialized North Korea.

The South Korean economic position is grave. Agriculture is debilitated and there are few other resources.

The establishment of a self-sustaining economy in South Korea is not feasible. Accordingly, U.S. aid should include a minimum of capital investment and should consist chiefly of items required for support on a relief basis.

Korean Communist agents are creating unrest and fomenting disorder in South Korea. The terrorist and obstructive activities of extreme rightist groups are further aggravating this situation.

Since the U.S.-Soviet Joint Commission meetings have twice ended in deadlock and offer no real hope of success, the United Nations now seems to be the appropriate medium through which a provisional Korean government, functioning under a Four Power trusteeship, can be established.

The United States may be confronted with a situation requiring decision concerning continued occupation in South Korea should the Soviet Union withdraw her occupation forces. This could reasonably be expected to occur when the Soviet-created puppet government and its armed forces are sufficiently well established to carry out Communist objectives without the presence of Soviet troops.

The creation of an American-controlled and officered Korean Scout Force, sufficient in strength to cope with the threat from the North, is required to prevent the forcible establishment of a Communist government after the United States and Soviet Union withdraw their occupation forces.

·   ·   ·   ·   ·

Recommendations

It is recommended:

That the U.S. government provide as early as practicable moral, advisory, and material support to China and South Korea in order to contribute to the early establishment of peace in the world in consonance with the enunciated principles of the United Nations, and concomitantly to protect U.S. strategic interests against militant forces which now threaten them.

That U.S. policies and actions suggested in this report be thoroughly integrated by appropriate government agencies with other international commitments. It is recognized that any foreign assistance extended must avoid jeopardizing the American economy.

China

That China be advised that the United States is favorably disposed to continue aid designed to protect China's territorial integrity and to facilitate her recovery, under agreements to be negotiated by representatives of the two governments, with the following stipulations:

[*a.*] That China inform the United Nations promptly of her request to the United States for increased material and advisory assistance.

[*b.*] That China request the United Nations to take immediate action to bring about a cessation of hostilities in Manchuria and request that Manchuria be placed under a Five Power guardianship or, failing that, under a trusteeship in accordance with the United Nations Charter.

[*c.*] That China make effective use of her own resources in a program for economic reconstruction and initiate sound fiscal policies leading to reduction of budgetary deficits.

[*d.*] That China give continuing evidence that the urgently required political and military reforms are being implemented.

[*e.*] That China accept American advisers as responsible representatives of the U.S. government in specified military and economic fields to assist China in utilizing U.S. aid in the manner for which it is intended.

Korea

That the United States continue efforts for the early establishment of a provincial Korean government in consonance with the Moscow Agreement and meanwhile provide necessary support of the political, economic, and military position of South Korea.

16

The End of a Mission

1947

Confident in the belief that his *Report on China and Korea* was sound and that its recommendations were persuasive and urgent, Wedemeyer returned to Baltimore to await what he hoped would be a decisive shift in U.S. Far Eastern policy.

Again he waited in vain. No summons to further consultation was forthcoming; no change in policy occurred; the report was buried without explanation in the files of Washington officialdom. There it would remain until the long struggle in China ended with the decisive military triumph of the Communists in 1949. Throughout the final two years of the contest, U.S. policy drifted passively in a mood of "wait and see."

Wedemeyer's disappointment was profound. His disillusionment began, as the following letter to General Douglas MacArthur suggests, within a month after the report was submitted in September 1947.

PERSONAL-EYES ALONE

October 20, 1947

General of the Army Douglas MacArthur
Commanding General, Far East Command
APO 600, c/o Postmaster
San Francisco, California

My dear General:

I have delayed writing because I had hopes of relating clearly our projected policy in the Far East. Although I submitted my report on September 18 to the President and the Secretary of State, no action has been taken. Both of these gentlemen stated categorically that they agreed with my conclusions and recommendations. In fact they were complimentary about the work of the mission. I have misgivings because I tried to emphasize, in writing and orally, the urgency of action necessary to alleviate the seriously deteriorating situation in Manchuria and North China.

It would appear that our policy is presently one of piecemeal implementation. We are focusing our attention and efforts in Western Europe while dangerously destructive forces are moving successfully forward in the Far East. I pointed this out to Marshall and suggested that a global appraisal be made to determine the capabilities of the Soviet Union as well as our own in various areas in order that we could adopt and implement a global plan that would insure timely and proportionate effort in vital areas. We cannot stop the expansion of communism until we evolve and implement vigorously an orderly plan.

Increasing pressure has been exerted from every facet to compel the Secretary of State and the President to reveal the contents of my report, but [to] no avail. The President announced yesterday that General Marshall would soon publicly state to the country our projected U.S. policy in the Far East.

Bill Bullitt's article on China [*Life,* October 13, 1947] has had good effect. Harry Luce, whom I have known for many years, very kindly submitted the draft for comment. There were overstatements in the article, and I think this unfortunate for they detracted from the good premises that he established. As a whole it should be helpful, though, in arousing interest among the American people. I admire the Chinese people; however, I simply could not recommend all-out aid. It is my belief that aid given to any country should be subject to careful supervision to insure that it is used for the purposes for which intended. Without supervision in China, U.S. aid would surely make rich men richer and the Chinese Communists would march on successfully against the National Government.

In addition to talks with the President, Secretary of State, and the Under Secretary of State, I have talked to Admiral Leahy, Eisenhower, Forrestal, Averell Harriman, Ken Royall, Admiral Nimitz, Harry Luce, and many other people who are interested in our policies. I note a lamentable bewilderment in general concerning the direction or the orientation of our national and international policies. We seem to lack dynamic leadership and vision in the higher echelons. The President himself is really confused. Unfortunately he is said to be incapable of comprehending the problems presented. I would state that we have a fine honest *little* man in a *big* job . . .

The presidential boom for Eisenhower continues. Although he disclaims interest, it is my conviction that he would accept the nomination. In a recent Gallup Poll he was given a slight preponderance over President Truman in the event they are opposing candidates. It is very significant that in a more recent Gallup Poll involving you and Truman (although you have not been back in the States for several years), you were accorded an almost even chance with the President. I predict that, should you return early next spring, you will be acclaimed by a vast majority as the logical man to be president in this critical period of our history. I have heard so many men whose judgment I value highly, and whose integrity I respect, state emphatically that the American people would enthusiastically rally behind your leadership.

Regardless of your personal reaction, I believe that you should carefully weigh these developments from a sense of duty. I know Bob and Martha Taft quite well and I am quite certain that he would throw his support in your direction. Also ex-governor Martin, now senator from Pennsylvania, and speaker Joe Martin as well as ex-president Hoover are loyal and enthusiastic supporters. You enjoy the confidence of the American people and, although the task would be difficult, nevertheless if your health maintains, I hope that you will consider the post.

Subsequent to my arrival in the States, I have been required to visit Washington frequently. This provides opportunities to observe the operation of various planning agencies. I am very much discouraged. Everyone seems to be "behind the eight ball," and instead of creative thinking, or deliberate and intelligent action, we are resorting to ill-considered, hasty decisions of expediency in the political, economic, psychological and military fields. Organization and execution along sound lines are urgently needed; otherwise we will continue to be pushed around by nations interested only in their self-aggrandizement. There is a bottom to the American economic barrel, yet we are currently distributing monetary and material aid in an unintegrated and uncoordinated manner. I wish that I could report a more encouraging picture . . .

Sincere good wishes to you and Mrs. MacArthur for good health, happiness, and continued success.

Faithfully yours,

A. C. WEDEMEYER
Lieutenant General, U.S. Army
Commanding

17

The Maturing of the Strategist

1946–1949

Wedemeyer had come increasingly to view public policy as an integral whole, the foreign and military components of which are inseparable. He was accordingly troubled by the radical fragmentation of U.S. policymaking. Nothing was effectively tied together; the left hand often did not know what the right was doing, and vice versa. A solution seemed to lie in the adoption of a more comprehensive theory of strategy. Strategy, he began to argue, should be understood not merely as the business of generals—"the art and science of employing *military* means to achieve the ends of policy"—but the art and science of employing *all* the nation's resources in pursuit of those ends. He assigned by far the greater priority to the nonmilitary "instruments of policy" (political, economic, and what he called psycho-social) over the military, and he stressed the importance of better intelligence and more explicit objectives.

The earliest formal explications of this doctrine (which would be elaborated on many subsequent occasions) were presented at various military academic institutions beginning in 1946. The following version was delivered at the National War College in Washington, D.C., on January 27, 1948.

UNITED STATES POSTWAR STRATEGY
by Lieutenant General A. C. Wedemeyer

. . . In order that the term "strategy" may have the same connotation to all of us, at least during the course of this talk, I shall give you my definition. Strategy is the art and science of applying resources to accomplish national objectives. The resources may be military, political, economic, psychological, or, as is more usually the case, a combination of all of these.

According to this definition, broad strategic plans involve not only the essential military factors—time, space, munitions, communications, and terrain—but must also include the whole complex of measures involved in the implementation of national policies. Patently, military plans as well as political, economic, and psychological plans must be thoroughly integrated in the broad strategic plan in order to contribute as much as possible to the attainment of national objectives.

Before strategic plans can be composed effectively, there are two important conditions that must be fulfilled: First, national policy must be clearly defined; that is, the conditions to be created at home and abroad in order to preserve or obtain national objectives must be definitely stated. The determination of these policies devolves upon the President, and under him the principal responsibility falls upon the Secretary of State. The Congress, too, exercises a strong influence in this regard through its control of appropriations, and because the Senate must approve all treaties and foreign commitments.

Second, accurate and current intelligence concerning the capabilities of potential enemies, friendly nations, and neutrals must be provided. We must have knowledge and intelligent evaluation of all foreign influences that might facilitate or militate against the realization of our objectives. Domestic intelligence must also be available to provide information concerning the effectiveness of foreign propaganda, or of Fifth Column activities, and to evaluate accurately the temper of our own people.

Having clear-cut national policies, and assuming that accurate and timely strategic intelligence is available, the strategic planner studies the various possible combinations in the employment of national resources to determine appropriate methods of attaining national objectives. He notes the capabilities of other nations and makes a comparative appraisal of the potential strength of his own country. Economy in the use of resources, simplicity in implementation, and assurance that we do not jeopardize one national aim in the attainment of another, should all be carefully considered.

The attainment of national objectives does not always require the actual employment of military force. Political or economic pressure or outright intimidation may suffice. There are often many alternatives that may be successfully employed. These include preclusive buying of strategic materials, cleverly conducted propaganda, and economic pressures. When an international situation does develop requiring the employment of force, care must be taken to provide for the integration and effective employment of *all* available resources. Political, economic, and psychological warfare must continue and must be completely coordinated with military operations. Comprehensive strategic plans therefore recognize and provide for continued struggle in the international field regardless of whether that struggle employs primarily political, economic, psychological, or military means. In consonance with the foregoing, broad strategic plans must outline how, when, and where a nation's available resources will be employed to implement national policies.

It cannot be too strongly emphasized that modern war makes mandatory resolute plans to provide an effective [and] timely military effort. Any future war may reasonably be expected to develop into, or swiftly assume, the characteristics of a war of extermination. Strained relations may be so long drawn-out as to no longer constitute a warning. There may not be time or space available to prepare defenses and then to create the means required for the conduct of military operations. There may be no allies to hold off enemy thrusts while we prepare. New, ultra-destructive weapons may span swiftly the vast water areas that have served in the past as barriers between our homeland and enemy forces. It is imperative, therefore, even in peacetime, that the United States maintain completely integrated strategic plans and, in addition, have in being the requisite effective forces as well as the industrial capacity necessary to support prompt and continued operations against an enemy.

I mentioned the fact that the Department of State was primarily responsible for the determination of U.S. foreign policy. Deliberations and studies obviously must not be accomplished in a vacuum, that is, without the advice of other governmental agencies in pertinent fields, for example; legislative, economic, military, and scientific. It is especially important in this age of super-blitz war that officials of the Department of State confer continuously with military experts concerning existing and projected foreign commitments and policies. This would insure that such commitments are brought into proper balance with military power and resources. Under existing conditions, the United States should not adopt foreign policies that it cannot immediately and realistically back up.

There is a relatively new factor in the formulation of U.S. foreign policy which is of increasing importance. This is the requirement for consultation and collaboration with friendly governments in the accomplishment of mutual objectives. Formerly, such consultation and collaboration were the exception, and that is understandable. The United States enjoyed a position of geographic isolation and—even more important—was practically self-sufficient economically. However, as we advance technologically, we are increasingly dependent upon other parts of the world for certain important materials. Further, because science has shriveled the world, we no longer have *time* and *space* serving as guardians of our homeland. Everyone recognizes today that we must be alert to events transpiring in what were formerly remote areas. As the United States abandons the last vestiges of her isolationist policy and participates openly and realistically in world affairs, collaboration in the discharge of international responsibility becomes more and more essential. Actually, due to our strength and influence, we must take the initiative and assume the leadership in this collaboration.

In order to emphasize the necessity for overall strategic planning and to point up the disasters which follow the lack of proper planning, let us review our mistakes in the past two wars in terms of the two required conditions mentioned at the outset. Our announced national and international objectives at the time we entered World War I, couched in such alluring phrases as, "The war to end all wars" and "The war to make the world safe for Democracy," were neither realistic nor clear-cut. We neglected to achieve agreement with our allies, at any time, concerning the political, economic, and psychological conditions which we might have hoped to create in Europe after defeating Germany and her satellites. The military defeat of Germany was, at best, only an empty victory. Empty because of our failure to achieve the political, economic, and psychological objectives which might have established conditions for a permanent peace. Empty because a situation was permitted to develop in Europe that led to the acquisition of power by another German leader more aggressive and arrogant than the Kaiser.

During the period between World Wars I and II, U.S. foreign policy returned to isolationism. The American people were apathetic toward events transpiring abroad. We did not join the League of Nations, nor were we especially concerned in maintaining the political and economic stability of Central Europe in order to forestall dictatorships and aggression.

Gradually events indicated clearly the inevitability of American participation in World War II. When these events crystallized at Pearl Harbor, we found ourselves somewhat better prepared than at the time of our entry into World War I. There had been some preliminary military planning with British and Canadian staffs. Industry had stepped up its productive capacity progressively in order to supply the British and their allies. We had thus taken important initial steps toward converting from peace to a wartime economy. Finally, there were available more and better trained naval and air units, and there was the nucleus of a small army.

Except for the glittering generalities of the Atlantic Charter and occasional vague pronouncements by leaders of the Allied nations, neither we nor our allies, during World War II, enunciated detailed common objectives for rebuilding a sound world order. Our failure to declare our war aims in the political, economic, and cultural fields, with the widespread uncertainty and doubt engendered by that failure, is responsible for much of the world's suffering today. We must abandon, once and for all, the old habit of offering pious platitudes in the field of diplomacy. We must place before the bar of world opinion our objectives. We must explain clearly the principles for which we are prepared to make any sacrifice.

Again, as in World War I, there was a dearth of accurate and comprehensive intelligence, not only concerning our enemies but also with reference to friendly powers, particularly Russia. Even Germany underestimated Russian capabilities and paid a high price. The Russians exploited our lack of information to the fullest, repeatedly threatening to make a separate peace with Germany and constantly pressing the Allies with extravagant demands.

Practically everything concerning World War II strategic planning was based on the purely military consideration to bring about early, crushing military victory. In the absence of definitive Anglo-American postwar political and economic objectives, our planners had no alternative but to plan for the earliest possible military defeat of Germany followed by a similar defeat of Japan.

The Western Allies apparently failed to realize sufficiently early the extent to which chaotic conditions generated in Europe and the Far East by the defeat of our enemies would create vacuums into which would flow, irresistibly, such new ideologies as were most promptly available. Soviet Russia recognized this in 1944—perhaps even earlier—and quickly took advantage of her dominant position to extend her frontiers and to spread her influence throughout war-weary Europe and the Far East. Our government unquestionably lost hard-earned opportunities to supplant the Nazi-created system by one based on Western democratic ideas of constitutional government. A complete plan for rehabilitation and territorial adjustments should have been provided to insure political and economic developments throughout Europe in consonance with our national interests. This plan should have been proposed, and agreement with our allies reached, at the time of our entrance into the war or shortly thereafter, when we were lend-leasing billions of dollars worth of supplies to Soviet Russia and our other allies, and when we possessed the greatest military power, particularly in the air and on the sea.

It should have been recognized that it would be of great importance for political and postwar considerations to have Anglo-American forces on the continent, in France, Germany, Poland, and the Balkans, occupying and controlling as much of these areas as practicable at the war's end. The ideology of Soviet Russia with a totalitarian political structure, a regimented economy, and an abnegation of individual liberties were and are abhorrent to the American people. In retrospect, it is clear that our strategic planning should have been oriented toward denying to the Soviet Union the opportunities—which she embraced so promptly and effectively—to make the direct contacts with defeated peoples susceptible to the Soviet ideology. There is some evidence that the political implications of developments in Europe were foreseen to some degree by certain Anglo-American leaders, but no appropriate action was taken.

Our strategy was ineffective because it was incomplete. We failed to relate or to integrate the military factor in strategy with political, economic, and psychological considerations. Military victory was achieved, but today we find that the national aims for which we fought were jeopardized by the very conditions of that victory. We liberated most of Europe from one totalitarian system only to let it fall under another.

From the foregoing, it becomes clear that in strategic planning there must be complete coordination and integration in the employment of all our resources in order to attain our objectives or to protect our interests. In accomplishing military plans, it is important that they be so developed and implemented as to insure that desired political and economic conditions are created in the country where we are employing our forces. A concomitant of this is the assurance that, in conducting military operations, we are alert to their impact upon our own political and economic structure. This statement could be broadened in its scope. One might appropriately state that our strategy—and the political, economic, psychological, and military operations being conducted in consonance with our strategy—should be tested to preclude the creation at home of the very conditions that we are striving to counter or eliminate elsewhere.

In the world today there are two divergent ideological groups creating situations which are apparently incapable of peaceful resolution. The Soviet Union and her satellites compose one group, and the so-called Western democracies the other. A state of moral belligerency exists. In a political, economic, and psychological sense we are already virtually at war with the Soviet Union. No other country has the war-making potential to threaten our security. In fact, there can be no major war involving the world for a long period of time unless the United States and the Soviet Union are involved and are opposed.

The Soviet Union has pursued certain objectives in various areas of the world under the guise of providing "security" for herself and satellites. Her immediate objective, already well along the way to attainment, is to establish a continuous belt of Soviet-dominated nations along the Soviet perimeter, particularly where a truly independent nation might constitute a danger. The Soviet Union's current strategic policy— a policy which, so far, does not require the employment of armed force excepting as a threat—will probably continue. When the allegedly "defensive" policy objectives have been reached in their entirety, or possibly even prior to their complete attainment, Soviet Russia may attempt to consolidate the entire Eurasian landmass *and dominate the strategic approaches thereto.* The next step might then be toward the attainment of the ultimate objective, so frequently expressed in the writings and pronouncements of Marx, Lenin, and Stalin, to dominate the world.

I would not state categorically that this ultimate global objective will remain unchanged. There are many factors which could radically affect the Soviet Union's present attitude and alter her overall objectives in the international field. These include the emergence of new leaders who might be more tolerant of the Western democracies and their ideals. A great spiritual resurgence of irresistible proportions among the Russian people is a distinct possibility. There may be drastic modifications in the political and economic structure of the Soviet government impelled by international pressures or by new influences not clearly discernible today.

We should, of course, attempt to promote developments of this nature by all means possible. It is our expressed desire that international differences be resolved without the employment of intimidation or force. The United Nations Organization epitomizes this effort. But until a realistic world organization with appropriate security forces becomes effective, we military men have an inescapable responsibility to assist in evolving plans and making appropriate preparations to forestall aggressions that threaten our way of life.

I believe that the Soviet Union will avoid a "shooting war" for several years. She is not prepared for a major war. It is reasonable to assume that the Soviets will continue the current political-economic-psychological "cold war," with the frequent changes of pace and the maximum employment of surprise which have become familiar to us.

I emphasized at the beginning of this talk that before effective strategic plans can be developed, two conditions are necessary. First, our national policies must be clearly defined, and, second, we must have accurate and timely intelligence.

Today these conditions are not fully realized, but we are infinitely better off than we have ever been in the past. We have learned that close coordination of all govenrment agencies is essential in the determination of national policy. The recently established National Security Council is an excellent example of our efforts to accomplish coordination and integration. Although this council has been in existence only a short period of time, it has already been able to establish firm policies with respect to a few recent critical situations. There is no single document which lists all of our national policies or specifically defines our national objectives. Recent pronouncements by the President and other responsible government officials provide some broad bases upon which to work. The charter of the United Nations Organization also provides the strategic planner with further policy guidance, for we remain strong supporters of that organization and its lofty international aims.

The most immediate and pressing problem is to stop further Soviet expansion. Admittedly this is a difficult task. The situation today must be vastly improved if peace is to become a reality. No isolationist policy or purely defensive strategy will accomplish this. Rather, it requires the dynamic coordinated employment of the political, economic, and psychological means at our disposal.

In the political and economic field, many of these steps have already been undertaken. These include such measures as the program of hemispheric solidarity, mutually beneficial trade agreements with friendly governments, the original Greek and Turkish aid programs, and, more recently, the Marshall Plan—now officially called the European Recovery Program. It is hoped that by these measures we will be able to prevent effectively further communist expansion and to assist in the rebuilding of free, stable, and friendly governments throughout the world.

Also, we are engaged in psychological operations, but so far on a pitifully inadequate scale. For many years the Soviets have been conducting an intensive and effective propaganda campaign directed primarily against the United States and employing coordinated psychological, political, and economic means designed to undermine noncommunist elements in all countries. Their objective is to weaken and divide world opinion to such a degree that effective opposition to the spread of the communist ideology is impossible. Our efforts to counter this propaganda campaign have so far been almost negligible. No strong, coordinated psychological measures have been employed to enable us to attain our objective. The extent, the true motive, and even the existence of our aid programs have often been unknown to the recipients of our generosity. Obviously, it is imperative that we develop, strengthen, coordinate, and implement all possible information means susceptible of influencing attitudes in foreign countries in a direction favorable to the attainment of our objectives. Without such a comprehensive program, our political and economic recovery measures can never achieve full effectiveness.

In addition to the measures noted above, the existence and proper deployment of armed forces play a definite part in the attainment of our objectives without having recourse to a "shooting war." Much of the effectiveness of political, economic, and psychological measures is lost if there is no suggestion whatsoever of force to back them up. Even the limited military occupation forces in Germany, Austria, and Korea present a deterrent to communist penetration. The effectiveness of these forces cannot be measured solely by their military strength, for they constitute a political, and particularly a psychological, power factor which is far in excess of their actual numbers. Their presence also limits Soviet freedom of action by restricting communist covert operations.

I indicated earlier that the Soviet Union and her satellites are implementing steps that confute, strongly militate against, and in some instances definitely block our attempts to accomplish current American foreign policies as I interpret them. I use the term "as I interpret them" advisedly, because I am not yet certain of the political, economic, and psychological objectives that our government wishes to attain . . .

Upon completion of your present course of instruction, you gentlemen will serve in key positions of the higher echelons of our national defense structure. You must strive individually and collectively to obtain the broad background and experience that will qualify you to assist in the formulation of our national and international objectives. We have fought in two recent wars to prevent free peoples from falling under the domination of tyrants. We have fought two world wars to crystallize the ideas of decency in human relationships. In both cases we won military victories but failed miserably to create conditions for a permanent peace.

18

Strategic Planning
in the Postwar Army

1947–1949

At the end of October 1947, Wedemeyer returned to the Pentagon as director of the Army's Plans and Operations Division. He remained in this post for two turbulent years while the Army sought once more to regain its bearings and maintain its effectiveness in a profoundly changed new world of atom bombs and cold war.

In these circumstances, Wedemeyer's chief objective was to foster sound strategic doctrine and practice throughout the U. S. government. That goal, unfortunately, proved elusive. To Wedemeyer's continuing frustration, his earnest proposals met with little more than polite approval, even within the defense establishment. For example, when he urged the Army Chief of Staff, General Omar N. Bradley, to seek needed policy guidance for the military in the form of specific international goals, Bradley reportedly demurred on the ground that initiative in such matters was the business of the State Department.

The persistent strategist outlined his views in an informal memorandum to the Chief of Staff on September 12, 1948.

MEMORANDUM FOR THE CHIEF OF STAFF
From: A. C. Wedemeyer
Subject: American Strategy
Date: September 12, 1948

Herewith a few personal views that I should like to pass on for your consideration and possible use. In order that the national military establishment may accomplish its role as contemplated in the Constitution and in the National Defense Act, certain high-level guidance and strategic intelligence are required. The high-level guidance should include national objectives in the political, economic, and psychological fields. The strategic intelligence should include information concerning the capabilities in the political, psychological, economic, and military fields of all nations in the world, including friendly powers and potential enemies.

In World War I and in World War II, the United States made strong contributions to military victories. However, we have found that our sacrifices in lives and in material things have been fruitless in each instance, because we did not create conditions that would insure the peaceful resolution of international problems. We can accurately state that our World War I victory was empty because twenty years later we were again at war. Similarly, we can state that World War II victory was empty [because] today, only a few years after cessation of hostilities, we are again confronted with the holocaust of war.

Obviously, with the ever-increasing destructiveness of weapons being made available to armed forces, not only our own but also all potential enemies, mankind must create conditions whereby international problems will be resolved without the employment of armed forces. The alternative is the destruction of civilization, or at least the retardation of civilization as we understand it for several hundred years.

Atomic weapons, bacteriological warfare, radiological warfare, and chemical warfare are today lethal Frankenstein monsters that may be unleashed almost indiscriminately against mankind. It would appear that the Joint Chiefs of Staff should submit a request upon the State Department for [a statement of] the political, economic and cultural objectives of the United States for the next five years in Western Europe, the Balkans, the Middle and Near East, the Scandinavian countries, the Far East, Southeast Asia, and the Latin-American countries.

The Joint Chiefs of Staff should submit requests on the CIA [Central Intelligence Agency], ONI [Office of Naval Intelligence], MID [Military Intelligence Division, Department of the Army], and AID [Agency for International Development] for . . . information concerning the capabilities of countries in the [same] regions of the world in the political, economic, cultural, and military fields.

Assuming that we have obtained the above information, our strategic planners in the national military establishment should then evolve military plans that would insure the attainment and protection of our national objectives through the employment or intimidation of military force.

It is absolutely mandatory that the strategic war plans that are so evolved should next be war-gamed, that is, submitted to a thorough test for feasibility, practicability and capability. In war-gaming the plans, it is essential that they be conducted under simulated war conditions as realistically as possible, and right on through until military victory is attained. Realistic assumptions should be injected to insure that the war-game is of maximum practical value, and every effort should be made on the part of the control group as well as all other participating officers to visualize or conjecture as accurately as possible the conditions that maintain, not only within their own country, but also in countries of friendly peoples and of our enemies. It is particularly important that we determine the conditions that will exist in the world, and specifically with reference to belligerent nations, at the time that hostilities are ended. We can then better ascertain whether or not our military operations will accomplish fully, or will militate against, the realization of our national objectives at home and abroad. In other words, simply stated, we can then assure ourselves that we have created the conditions whereby international problems can be resolved in the future without employment of force.

Considerable work has been done on strategic plans by various agencies within the national military establishment and also within the State Department. The above approach to our strategic problems would, in my opinion, greatly facilitate our preparation for war and, if the latter must come, our realization of worthwhile victory . . .

19

Farewell to China— and Washington

1949

On October 1, 1949, the "Central People's Government of the People's Republic of China" was proclaimed in Peking.

In the days immediately preceding this historic event, the State Department had laid plans to convene a group of knowledgeable Americans to consider the future of U.S.-China relations in the light of the oncoming crisis.

At precisely this time, Wedemeyer was motoring through the Midwest enroute to the Presidio of San Francisco and a new assignment (his last as an active duty army officer) as commanding general of the Sixth U.S. Army. In view of his recent association with Far Eastern affairs, he was invited to attend the State Department's conclave in Washington. He asked to be excused. With heavy heart he summarized in a telegram his thoughts on what, if anything, the U.S. could or should do about China at that moment of resounding tragedy.

TELEGRAM

From: Lieutenant General A. C. Wedemeyer
      enroute to Sixth Army
      Presidio, San Francisco, California

Action to: Under Secretary James Webb
      State Department
      Attention Francis Russell
      Washington, D.C.

Information to: General J. Lawton Collins
      Chief of Staff, U.S. Army
      Washington, D.C.

Date: September 26, 1949
      (Dispatched from Headquarters Fifth Army
      Chicago, Illinois)

Reference your kind invitation to attend meetings of twenty leading Americans for exchange of views on problems [of] U.S. policy in China, October 6, 7, and 8, respectfully request that I be excused. Mrs. Wedemeyer and I are motoring across the country in my private car in accordance with a prearranged schedule which enables me to obtain a long deferred vacation . . . Acceptance of invitation . . . might interfere with my timely arrival in Sixth Army. Further, I have stated my views pertaining to China to State Department and National Military Establishment officials and representatives both orally and in writing. Only recently I conferred with a special group of analysts, [including] Ambassador [Philip C.] Jessup . . . It would seem reasonable to assume that my personal views are sufficiently well-known by responsible individuals within the government as to render my attendance at the meetings unnecessary.

Herewith resume of views substantially as expressed in the manner and to the individuals referred to above:

The United States should not surrender the initiative in any field of international endeavor, in any area of the world. The timing, the scope, and the character of our efforts in one area (for example the Far East) should be carefully coordinated and integrated with our efforts in other areas of the world (for example, Western Europe, Central Europe, the Middle East, et cetera). To insure economy of means, and to make our efforts more purposeful to all nations, our efforts should be integrated and coordinated with those nations and peoples having objectives compatible with our own.

Specifically with reference to policies and objectives in China, the following ideas appear pertinent:

1. The pronounced and progressive deterioration of China's political and economic structures, also the impotence of government military forces, render it impractical at this time to provide large-scale material aid. The remaining Chinese noncommunist forces or elements, with or without the National Government's cognizance, are not organized or equipped to assimilate or to use effectively large-scale material aid.

2. The Chinese people, individually and collectively, would receive a tremendous uplift in morale, and would derive strength and hope for the future, if the United States (also Great Britain, France, and other friendly countries) publicly affirmed the determination to support anti-communists or noncommunist elements in China and throughout the Far East. Such a public pronouncement by the President or the Secretary of State would provide the moral support so urgently needed by bewildered millions not only in the Far East but in other important areas of the world.

3. Material aid . . . to Chinese leaders, communities, provinces or specific areas actively resisting or tangibly striving to generate realistic opposition to communism should be given by the United States on an evaluated scale—carefully supervised by United States representatives—[and] progressively increased in scope if developments warrant. In this connection, military equipment, propaganda media, medical equipment, food, and clothing might be distributed at times, in areas, and in quantities determined by careful evaluation of the existing and developing situation. Our initial objectives should be to restrict and harass the military and economic activities of the Communists and concomitantly to confute and refute the ideas, the ideals, and the ideologies of the Communist political and cultural forces.

4. Continued observation and evaluation of the results attained by the above unequivocal moral support, accompanied by evaluated material aid, might justify later greatly increased material aid . . . in certain localities or, for example, in support of indigenous movements that give tangible evidence of momentum and substance in their struggle against Communist domination.

If clarification or expansion of above ideas is desired, I would be glad to comply. My exact location is known at all times to the Chief of Staff, U.S. Army.

20

Reaping the
Whirlwind in Korea

1950

In his 1947 report on Korea, Wedemeyer had sketched a likely
scenario for an attack from the communist North against the
noncommunist South. Precisely such an attack came on June 25,
1950.

By that time, U.S. occupation forces had been withdrawn
from the peninsula, and Washington had signaled a lack of strategic
interest in the area. However, when the lightly armed South Korean constabulary fell back before the armies of the North, President Truman decided to resist the invaders by committing U.S.
forces drawn from occupation duty in Japan and elsewhere.

Wedemeyer at Sixth Army in San Francisco hastily readied
reinforcements and supplies to support this new campaign in the
Orient. The bitter irony of the situation—especially after the Chinese Communists entered the war in December—appalled him. A
scant five years earlier, U.S. armed might had stood victorious and
unchallenged throughout the Pacific region and indeed around the
globe. Now, hastily assembled and largely unprepared GI regiments were not only fighting for their lives, but fighting a *ground*
war on the *mainland* of Asia. The strategic folly of thus accepting
battle on the enemy's terms was exceeded only by the blindness
and irresolution of the postwar years that had set the stage for the
tragedy in the first place.

Wedemeyer viewed Korea as another costly episode in the

ultimately self-defeating drama of "containment." In its strategic essence, containment was a passive and losing game: the enemy was free to choose self-serving times, places, and modes of attack, and the defender was obliged to reply in kind or retreat. Moreover, as the policy had been applied in Greece and Turkey (under the so-called Truman Doctrine of unilateral U.S. aid to governments threatened by externally supported communist subversion), containment had meant a late and thus a primarily military response, and the assumption by Uncle Sam of a disproportionate share of the free world's defense costs.

When the political will to continue the fight in Korea ebbed, the see-saw war bogged down in the vicinity of the original boundary, the 38th parallel. The architects and practitioners of containment (including official Washington) thereupon proclaimed victory. Wedemeyer understood the need for the proclamation, but felt certain that the Communists were less defeated than disappointed by the outcome of Korea. He was sadly certain, in any event, that "victories" of the Korean kind would eventually sap the nation's substance.

As an officer on active duty, Wedemeyer was constrained from public criticism of U.S. war policy. However, in the great debate that followed the dismissal of General Douglas MacArthur from his post as Supreme Allied Commander in the Far East in 1951, a joint congressional committee pressed him for specific advice. Believing it irresponsible to prescribe on so fateful an issue in the absence of full knowledge [he had been away from Washington for two years], he declined to recommend the military reunification of Korea that MacArthur had advocated. As his brief introductory statement to the committee indicates, however, he preferred either that course or complete withdrawal to the prospect of a debilitating stalemate.

STATEMENT PRESENTED TO MEMBERS OF JOINT ARMED SERVICES–FOREIGN RELATIONS COMMITTEE, UNITED STATES SENATE

From: A. C. Wedemeyer

Date: June 12, 1951

Either we should fight in Korea with a view to decisive and victorious culmination or we should get out.

I would consider carefully military advice from experts in the Pentagon that we may require some time to prepare for the decisive action I refer to if we elect to remain there. However, I would not accept an interminable delay, for we would be expending our resources, human and material, to a prohibitive degree. This is exactly what the Soviets would have us do. The cost of such "containing" tactics would be wholly incommensurate, in my judgment, with the intangible gains that have been suggested to the members of this committee. Under conditions of indefinitely extended containment, we would be playing the game according to the rules of a scheming unscrupulous group in the Kremlin.

Either we should play this tragic game in Korea to win or, at the propitious time, [we should] take our fine team off the field—mobilize fully our spiritual and material resources in conjunction with friendly nations and set about the task of creating conditions that would enable free peoples to prescribe the rules and select the arenas of conflict in all fields of strategy. We, along with the free nations, must seize and maintain the initiative in this unfortunate but currently unavoidable international struggle which may so strongly influence the destiny of mankind.

21

China: Remembered
but not Revisited

1983

U.S. relations with the People's Republic of China remained profoundly embittered in the decades following the Korean conflict.
The case for reconciliation with Peking—to include recognition of
that regime's right to China's seat in the United Nations—
nonetheless continued to gain favor in the United States. Such
formal reconciliation finally took place in 1972 under the administration of President Richard M. Nixon.

This development represented a major diplomatic victory for
the People's Republic of China over its old enemy (the U.S.'s
wartime ally), the Republic of China on Taiwan. To consolidate
that victory, and to enhance the advantages of its new relationship
with the United States, Peking sought positively to woo all shades
of American opinion. Wedemeyer's reputation as an unreconstruc-
ted anti-communist and a perennial supporter of Taiwan occasioned an informal inquiry in 1983 concerning his willingness to
return to mainland China as an official visitor. In a brief reply to
the inquiring party, he explained his reasons for declining.

A. C. WEDEMEYER

February 1, 1983

My dear ——————:

I have received your letter in which you inquire whether Mrs. Wedemeyer and I would accept an official invitation to visit the People's Republic of China. Let me say that the thought of returning to mainland China—a land of which we have such fond memories, for which we hold such friendly hopes, and where we still have so many valued friends—is a tempting one for both of us.

It has always been my conviction that real peace, prosperity, and happiness are possible in a society only when basic human rights are respected, and when individual men and women are free to develop and express their natural talents and expectations in an atmosphere of substantial freedom. I have tried throughout the years, and especially during the period of my wartime and postwar service in the Far East, to encourage the people of China to seek their destiny in accordance with these principles.

The People's Republic of China—as available evidence overwhelmingly demonstrates—is founded precisely on the negation of these values. That regime came to power, and maintains itself in power, by the imposition of despotic social control and by the ruthless suppression of life and liberty. I find it impossible to believe that such a regime represents the true interests of the Chinese people or the inevitable pattern of their future.

These are matters, however, that ultimately must be decided by the Chinese people themselves. In the meantime, it seems to me that reconciliation among the Chinese, and between the Chinese and Americans, is something very much to be hoped for and worked for.

Genuine reconciliation must of course be based on a demonstrated relaxation of the Marxist-Leninist agenda on the part of the leaders of Communist China—not on promises, appearances, false hopes, or self-deceptions. If Mrs. Wedemeyer and I thought for a moment that our visiting the People's Republic would contribute to the cause of such reconciliation, we would accept an invitation at once. Although I am not so foolish as to suppose that our decision will make any difference, one way or another, in the historic scheme of things, I fear that any gains our trip might achieve would be more than offset by the losses. Journeying to mainland China, even for the purpose of visiting old friends, could not fail to be interpreted and exploited as approbation—or at least acquiescence—in the status quo in China.

It is thus with sadness that I advise you that we would feel obliged to decline such an invitation if it were extended at this time. We would welcome the tangible evidence of those changes in China which would make it possible for us to return once more during our lifetime—with good conscience—to that great land with its admirable people and "Good Earth."

Faithfully,

A. C. WEDEMEYER
General, U. S. Army (Ret.)

22

The Second Front
in Europe Revisited

1985

Debate over the conduct and outcome of World War II has continued unabated since 1945. In September 1985, John Colville, Prime Minister Churchill's private secretary during the war, published a thought-provoking article in *Commentary* entitled, "How the West Lost the Peace in 1945." In this article, Colville argued that, although a grand coalition of Britain, the Soviet Union, and the United States won the war, it was the Soviets who won the peace. He attributed the Soviet triumph largely to the "folly" of U.S. policy during the final critical months of the war in Europe.

Colville's argument ran as follows: From the time when a dying President Roosevelt lost his grip early in 1945 until President Truman applied his some time later, American political leadership experienced a "deadly hiatus" (Churchill's words). The burden of leadership consequently shifted by default onto the shoulders of two soldiers—Marshall in Washington and Eisenhower in Europe. Yet these men had been thoroughly schooled in the belief that their role was to make war and not play politics. As a result, they made "strictly military" decisions in Europe that lost for the Western Allies golden opportunities to seize Berlin, Prague, and perhaps Vienna ahead of the Red armies.

Wedemeyer read this article, and agreed with much of Colville's analysis, especially with the conclusion that the Soviets had won the peace. He was moved, however, to restate in a letter to the editor of *Commentary* his own theory of how the West "lost" the peace. The real mistakes were made, he argued, not in 1945 but in 1942 and 1943. Had the Western Allies pursued the American rather than the British strategy, and concentrated for an invasion of the continent a year earlier than they did, their armies probably could have beaten the Soviets to the ancient capitals of Central Europe.

To the Editor of *Commentary*:

John Colville's "How the West Lost the Peace in 1945" (*Commentary*, September 1985) stirred me deeply. Colville is fully justified, in my opinion, in emphasizing the awful ironies that marked the outcome of the Second World War. Although a grand coalition of Western powers and the Soviet Union won the war, it is hard to deny that the Soviets won the peace. The enormous efforts and sacrifices through which the democracies sought to defend freedom thus ended in historic gains for tyranny.

The question of how all this came about is surely one of fundamental and continuing importance. Mr. Colville, writing from the perspective of the summit in wartime Britain, provides some thought-provoking answers. "The Soviet triumph," he concludes, "was in large part due to the folly of American policy in the last, vital months of fighting; and that folly stemmed from what Winston Churchill called 'the deadly hiatus' between President Roosevelt's losing his grip and President Truman's imposing his. It occurred at precisely the most inopportune time." With German power crumbling under assault from East and West, issues of crucial military political significance arose that required prompt as well as shrewd and thoughtful attention. Such attention, alas, could not be given by "a dying President, a blind State Department, and generals who saw no reason to inject political considerations into strategic decisions."

Although I shortly am going to challenge this interpretation, let me say that there is more truth in Colville's analysis than I, as an American, am happy to admit. The President was indeed a dying man during the fateful months in question. I last saw him toward the end of March 1945, when I reported to the White House to brief him on the situation in China, where I was serving as commander of U.S. forces. As I breakfasted with the President off the edge of his desk, I was shocked by his pallor and obvious weakness. I found it necessary to repeat statements again and again, for his mind seemed to wander and he failed to grasp simple points. He would throw his head back and pause, mouth agape, as if to gather strength and breath. I remember clearly how he admonished me against aiding the French in Southeast Asia. He added—with as much force as he could muster—that he hoped to see the end of the European colonial empires in Asia.

There is sad truth, too, in Colville's characterization of the U.S. State Department as "blind." Our foreign policy establishment certainly was ill-equipped during this period to provide either dynamic policy leadership or wise advice. Moreover, prevailing sentiment in the Department (as at the White House) was almost uncritically dedicated to the myth that "Uncle Joe" Stalin was a good and potentially cooperative democrat as well as a great wartime ally.

Colville also is perceptive in observing what he calls the "cocoon" which shrouded the professional vision of the American military. All of us in uniform—certainly we of the Regular Army—had been conditioned throughout our careers to accept and observe the limits of "strictly military" concerns. We defined ourselves, and were defined by others, as *executors,* not *makers,* of public policy. We were expected rigorously to refrain from "politics"—a restraint that often was interpreted as discouraging even the exercise of the ballot, for voting meant choosing one set of candidates or policies over others. These practices certainly achieved their intended effect of insulating the Republic from militarism. They did little, however, to prepare military professionals to function imaginatively in those crucial but sensitive areas where strategy and policy necessarily overlap.

(The isolation of the military had more general consequences in the realm of ideas: it promoted the notion that military strategy and foreign policy, however related, are in fact distinct and separable in theory as well as practice. In the American system, the military Departments handled strategy, the State Department foreign policy. Hence, no one, with the exception of a single grossly overextended human individual, the President, was charged with the ultimate function of statesmanship—the endlessly challenging task of intelligently relating military power to political purpose. Some of the implications of this absurd state of affairs were brought to my attention during my three years as a strategic planner in War Plans Division of the War Department General Staff.)

Having said all of this, however, let me return to Colville's central thesis: that the follies of American policy during the "deadly hiatus" between effective presidencies in the spring of 1945 were largely responsible for the Soviet triumph. To illustrate this folly, Colville cites Eisenhower's allegedly naive decision to launch a final drive across central Germany with Bradley's 12th Army Group in lieu of the previously planned thrust by Montgomery's 21st Army Group in the direction of Berlin.

Perhaps this decision of Eisenhower's *did* cost the Western Allies a great opportunity to "beat the Russians to Berlin." Inasmuch as I was in China at the time, I am not in a position to offer a firsthand opinion on the issue. I *was* personally and deeply involved, however, from 1941 onward, with planning U.S. and Allied strategy for Europe as well as other theaters of war. That experience convinced me (and my subsequent reading in the postwar literature has only confirmed the view) that the decisions which opened the door for ultimate Soviet capture of Berlin were taken *not* in 1945 but in 1942 and 1943. It is indeed my belief that the Western Allies, in consequence of the course they actually followed in 1942 and 1943, forfeited opportunities to meet the Red Army at points *far to the east of Berlin.* Moreover, responsibility for these lost opportunities must be laid, in my opinion, not on the follies of the Americans (great though these doubtless were!), but on the tenaciously pursued strategy of our British ally.

The history of Allied disagreements on European strategy has been told many times. I shall not attempt, therefore, to retell it, except to note that the Anglo-American conflict centered on the question of the timing and nature of a second front. The American military staffs, supported wholeheartedly by Secretary of War Henry L. Stimson and (at times) by President Roosevelt, favored a rapid concentration of Allied air and ground strength in the British Isles (with rigid economies in all other theaters), a constantly intensified campaign of aerial attack and blockade of *Festung Europa,* a major amphibious assault on the northwest coast of France *in the early summer of 1943,* and a drive eastward with highly mobile forces toward the industrial heart of Germany. U.S. planners viewed this bold scenario as offering the best possible chances for early, decisive, and economical victory.

In contrast with this approach, British staffs (headed most effectively by the indomitable prime minister, Sir Winston Churchill) were resolutely dedicated to an indirect strategy of attrition in Europe. Their preferred road to victory lay in what we often called in Washington "periphery-pecking" operations: they would seize opportunities and exploit weaknesses on the fringes of the continent—in Scandinavia, the Mediterranean, the Balkans, [and] the Near East. By gradually "closing the ring" and exhausting the foe, they would hasten the day when the Western Allies could return to the continent at acceptable levels of risk to deliver a *coup de grace.*

Mr. Churchill's views prevailed to a decisive degree. The great "D-Day" invasion of Europe came not in 1943, as the American planners had urged, but an entire year later—in 1944. Instead of rallying for an early decisive blow, the Western Allies opted for major campaigns in the peripheral areas of North Africa, Sicily, and Italy. Departing from the sound resolve of earlier agreements to defeat Hitler first, they also accelerated operations in the far-flung war against Japan. By the time they got around to the Normandy landings, the Red armies already had been in Poland and the Balkans for several months. By the time Eisenhower's forces reached the Rhine, the Soviets indeed were well advanced on their road to Berlin.

It remains my contention that, had the Western Allies followed the U.S. plans, had they resisted the temptation to pour resources into costly but indecisive operations in the Mediterranean area and elsewhere, had they assigned timely and adequate industrial priority to the construction of landing craft, had they single-mindedly concentrated their strength in Britain for an assault on the continent in 1943—at a time when the mass of the German army was still irretrievably committed far to the East, when the relative strengths of the belligerents would probably have favored the Allies, and when the defenses of the Atlantic Wall had not yet been developed—Anglo-American forces might well have met the Red Army on the Vistula rather than the Elbe.

It will not do, as Mr. Colville attempts, to discredit the American planners by suggesting that they advocated—in the rash and premature style of military amateurs—an all-out assault of *Festung Europa* in *1942*. I had thought that that old canard had been laid to rest by historians on both sides of the Atlantic; yet it continues to be repeated, especially by British writers, as though mere repetition would make it true. The confusion on this point arose from the existence of contingency plans prepared in Washington which contemplated emergency operations to be undertaken in the event of a sudden collapse either of German or of Soviet power. (As most of your readers doubtless know, contingency plans are constantly being drafted by planning staffs who must try to anticipate any and all plausible eventualities.) I personally played a part in drafting those documents, along with the other more ambitious plans that looked toward the main event of 1943. I am sure it would greatly surprise my late chief, General Marshall, were he to be told that he advocated the cross-channel invasion under the conditions actually prevailing in 1942.

Several additional points deserve comment. In his discussion of Operation Anvil or Dragoon (the Allies' diversionary landing on the Mediterranean coast of France in August 1944), Colville restates the case for a movement into Europe by way of the "soft underbelly" of the Balkans. However attractive the thought of "threatening Vienna from the east" might have been, the attendant difficulty of forcing what would have been a fiercely contested passage of the Alps impresses me now, as it did then, as rendering such an operation utterly impractical. I simply cannot visualize major ground forces "marching through" the Ljubljana gap with the facility Mr. Colville suggests.

The question of Soviet-British-U.S. relationships during the war also requires comment. I share the view expressed by Mr. Colville that President Roosevelt's expectations respecting the Soviets were unwarranted and most unfortunate. The Prime Minister certainly took the measure of Stalin in a way the President never did. I share, too, the belief that the dogmatic anti-colonialism of U.S. policy in the generation of World War II was fraught with consequences quite unforeseen and dangerous. I do not believe it accurate or fair to suggest, however, as Mr. Colville does, that President Roosevelt or any other American official felt at war's end that the welfare of mankind *should* rest in the hands of the United States and the USSR. Americans, for all their new-found sense of global responsibility, were earnestly dedicated to the ideal of collective security; as I interpreted the mood, they had no ambition whatsoever to establish worldwide hegemony in cooperation with the Soviets. The increasing emphasis that U.S. policy seemed to place on its postwar relationship with the USSR reflected no more than a recognition that shifts in global power relationships actually were occurring. Certainly the U.S.-Soviet agreement at Teheran on the second front did not signal American abandonment of Britain. That incident represented little more than a continuation of the old tug-of-war between proponents of an early invasion, on the one hand, and further Mediterranean commitments on the other. Stalin, for his own reasons, sided with the Americans in favor of the second front.

One final comment on Anglo-American relations during the war: Mr. Colville speaks of an undercurrent of anti-British sentiment in America rooted in memories of George III, the Redcoats, Bunker Hill, etc. That factor was not, in my opinion, especially important. Of much greater significance was the second factor mentioned, namely, the feeling that the British were in fact "outsmarting" American policy-makers and manipulating American policy. My own concern, and I believe that of most of my military colleagues, arose from observation of the skill and energy with which our British allies pressed their interests and points of view at all levels of the U.S. government (including the presidency) and throughout American society. The openness of the American system, the divided structure of our government, and the particularly haphazard Administration of President Roosevelt all invited and contributed to the success of those efforts. One had only to attend combined staff meetings and the historic summit conferences, especially during the early years of the war (Casablanca comes forcefully to mind), to sense the superior state of preparation and effective policy coordination achieved by the British military and civilian staffs. The performance of the Americans, by way of contrast, often seemed bungling and ineffective.

I seldom observed among my American colleagues, military or civilian, any attitudes that could fairly be described as "anti-British." Most of us were unreserved in our admiration, even affection, for our British allies, and wholeheartedly dedicated to the Alliance. We felt it important to the integrity of that Alliance, however, and to the self-respect and mutual respect of the partners, to preserve, even in the midst of war, a healthy sense of our distinctive national goals and interests. Some American "Anglophiles" lost their balance in this respect and characterized those who did not as "anti-British." (Eisenhower, I hasten to add, was *not* such an Anglophile.) Fortunately, most of my British comrades-in-arms and friends understand where I stood on these matters, and I believe they respect me for taking the stands I did.

A. C. Wedemeyer
General, U. S. Army (Ret.)

23

The Perennial Quest

1983

The unfocused aimlessness of U.S. policy has long troubled
Wedemeyer. As in World War II, he continues to sound alarms and
urge more prudent foresight. Warning of needless waste and point-
less bloodshed, of dangers unheeded and opportunities foregone,
he foresees inevitable decline for a nation that reacts myopically in
the present with little vision beyond tomorrow.

The challenging question remains: What is to be done? One of
Wedemeyer's perennial prescriptions for introducing at least a modicum of sustained purpose into the councils of state has centered
on the idea of a properly constituted board or council. His first
recommendation along these lines was made in 1942. The most
recent—a more detailed proposal for a National Strategy
Council—was written in 1983 and circulated privately amongst
Wedemeyer's friends in and out of government.

MEMORANDUM ON A NATIONAL STRATEGY COUNCIL

From: A. C. Wedemeyer
　　　　General, U.S. Army (Ret.)

Date: July 9, 1983

　　　For forty years and more, I have been concerned about the adequacy of our national policymaking machinery to deal with the challenges of an increasingly turbulent and complex world.

　　　My first clear awakening in this regard occurred back in 1941 in the months before Pearl Harbor. I was a staff officer in the War Department charged with drafting a broad plan (later known as the "Victory Plan") for the mobilization and employment of U.S. resources in a possible global war with the Rome-Berlin-Tokyo Axis. The American public was sharply divided in its attitudes toward the conflicts raging in Europe and elsewhere. A babble of voices urging various degrees of involvement or noninvolvement arose on all sides. Torrents of foreign and domestic propaganda sought to sway opinion. The nation's fate and future unquestionably were at stake in a world drifting ever closer toward general war.

　　　It is perhaps not surprising that in this situation official Washington seemed as confused and divided as the nation itself. However, it was the task of the small group of strategic planners, of which I was a member, to chart and propose a specific course. Before long I rediscovered the obvious: a journey can be charted only with a destination in mind, and STRATEGY can be plotted only with goals or aims in mind. I accordingly set out to discover what the objectives of U.S. involvement might be—other than the physical destruction of the forces which might then be arrayed against us. What were our country's true interests? How could those interests best be protected and advanced? What kind of world did we wish to see emerge from the cataclysm of another terrible war?

　　　To my consternation, I could find few if any concrete answers to these vital questions. So far as I could discover, no systematic official attention had been given them. No mechanisms for considering them in an orderly and informed way existed within the government. Indeed, I found little awareness or acceptance of the notion that supreme issues of war and peace *required* thorough analysis in the top echelons of the national government. An uneasy feeling came over me that the ship of state was rudderless in the storm; or, if the rudder were still intact, there at least were no charts or orders on the bridge to guide the navigator.

　　　And so, when war came, we embarked on a great crusade to slay the dragons which then confronted us. Plunging emotionally into the conflict, we endured much bloodshed and suffering (and imposed even more on others), expended untold treasure, and helped wreak destruction on large portions of the earth's surface. When the smoke of battle lifted, we spent billions more to restore the damage that had been done. Then, to our sorrow, even the idealistic slogans (e.g., the "Four Freedoms") that had inspired and sustained the crusade were mocked by the rise of new tyrannies, new wars, and a flood of new problems that dwarfed the old ones. Instead of ridding the world of tyranny we found that, in destroying one set of tyrants, we had simply paved the way for the rise of other more dangerous ones.

After World War II, a few promising steps were taken in Washington to improve the mechanisms of interagency coordination. I am thinking here of the establishment of such agencies as the National Security Council and the Policy Planning Staff at the State Department. But it is my considered opinion that those steps have long since proven inadequate. In general we have continued to follow the previous patterns of expediency. New policies unfold from year to year and from administration to administration in response to external events or to the shifting requirements of domestic opinion and partisan opportunism. In foreign affairs we have observed since 1945 alternating patterns of *realpolitik* and fuzzy idealism, containment and detente, irresolute engagement and confused withdrawal. At home we have seen an endless patchwork of economic policies, fiscal policies, military policies, [and] social policies—and these too frequently have developed haphazardly, in response to particular pressures, with little concern for the harmony of the whole, the conservation of resources, the advancement of our national aims and objectives, or the good of the country.

Let me briefly illustrate the effects of this fateful state of affairs on foreign policy. In the years immediately following World War II, U.S. leaders awakened to the realization that the Soviet Union, far from being the cooperative postwar partner they had led themselves to expect, was in fact embarked on a relentless course of territorial and ideological self-aggrandizement. In response, they embraced the much-touted policy of "containment." Whereas this policy appeared at first to reflect a needed sharpening of Uncle Sam's eyesight and a stiffening of his spine, it soon degenerated (in the absence of strategic vision) into an excuse for unilateral intervention everywhere. It meant the almost automatic commitment of American resources wherever a "threat" appeared—in Western Europe, Greece, Turkey, Korea, Vietnam, Lebanon, or elsewhere. It meant the frequent shedding of American blood. It meant not only the early abandonment of our faith in collective security, but even of our insistence that others play a primary role in defending themselves. It thus meant the gradual shifting of many of the security burdens of the noncommunist world onto the shoulders of the United States. It meant the constant dissipation of American resources. The debacle of Vietnam provided an indescribably tragic climax to this process. The Kremlin, it will be noted, has quite consistently conserved its resources and retained its freedom to maneuver. The Soviet strategists are playing a patient game in which "the objective balance of forces" is shifting gradually in their favor. The scolding once administered to the ancient Athenians by one of their public men can thus be directed most appropriately at present-day Americans: "Shame on you Athenians," Demosthenes exclaimed,

> for not wishing to understand that in war one must not allow oneself to be at the command of events, but to forestall them. You Athenians are the strongest of all the Greeks, in ships, cavalry, infantry and revenue, and you do not make the best of them.
> You make war against Philip like a barbarian when he wrestles—if he suffers a blow, he immediately puts his hand to it. If he is struck again he puts his hand there too, but he has not the skill or does not think of parrying the blow aimed at him or of evading his antagonist. You, likewise, if you hear that Philip has attacked the Chaeronea, you send help there; if he is at Thermopylae, you run there, and if he turns aside you follow him, to right or left, as if you were acting on his orders. Never a fixed plan, never any precautions—you wait for bad news before you act.

I am not so naive as to believe that all of the ordeals America has experienced over the past 35 years could have been avoided or even alleviated. I have some appreciation of the complexity and intractability of historical forces. I have some appreciation of the difficulties of governing a free society, and I concede the necessity—indeed the high wisdom—of basing all public policy in America on the solid foundation of popular consent. I do believe, however, that with more effective means for guiding the development of coordinated national policies, and with more coherent strategies in pursuing those policies, the record could have been much brighter.

My present concern arises not only from the conviction that our governmental machinery and methods are little improved over those of the past, but also from the knowledge that today's world is a far more dangerous one than that of yesteryear. We could get by in World War II with what we had and with what we did. Our security and prosperity in the future, I am positive, will require more.

It is a commonplace to note that the relatively secure, isolated, inward-looking world of the Founding Fathers is long gone. Modern communications and transportation have shrunk the world to the dimensions of an eighteenth-century township. Events in the remotest corners of the globe now can, and often do, affect conditions everywhere. Improved nutrition and medicine have swollen the earth's populations, introducing an era of intensified struggle for space, power, and resources. Intense ideological conflicts divide nations and peoples. Traditional values and authority are everywhere besieged. The rise of ultra-destructive weapons (biological and chemical as well as nuclear) has jeopardized life. Access to these weapons by small, irresponsible states— or even terrorist groups—has introduced an incalculably destabilizing and dangerous element into human affairs.

To compete in this struggle and to meet successfully these challenging conditions, our government must introduce elements of foresight and forehandedness into the management of affairs that have not heretofore been compelling. As in 1941, the American people are sharply divided today on issues of defense and foreign policy. They are probably more divided than in 1941 on so-called social issues. The babble of voices arising from the media, institutions of learning, think tanks, countless private organizations, action groups, lobbies, etc., far surpasses in volume and variety the clamor during the months preceding World War II. This uninhibited expression—although seldom fully informed, often misinformed, and sometimes mischievous—is a sign of social and intellectual vitality; it must continue as the primary engine of our democratic system.

However, the clash of private views and interests (as expressed in the political process) is in itself no longer an adequate method for development of sound and foresighted national policies in this age of perpetual crisis. The efforts of the existing branches and departments of the government to develop and guide policy simply *must* be supplemented. In my opinion, we sorely need an official agency of the government to serve as a steadying gyroscope to the ship of state. We need what I would call a National Strategy Council—which I will hereafter briefly describe.

May I emphasize that I am not using the term "strategy" in its usual military connotation. In fact, I would subordinate the military connotation of strategy in a much broader and comprehensive interpretetion, emphasizing the political, economic, cultural, and psycho-social forces as instruments of national policy. Strategy I would define as the art and science of developing and employing all the political, economic, and psycho-social resources of a nation, together with its armed forces, in the ongoing struggle to insure the security and well-being of the people.

This comprehensive interpretation of strategy would give U.S. policy a measure of coherence and stability it has not had, and does not now possess, but which is utterly mandatory if our Republic is to meet the challenges of the future. It would encourage the integration of matters (for example, economic and military programs) which too often have been treated in isolation, and thus unrealistically or unwisely. It is my conviction that if all the instruments of national policy are employed imaginatively and in a timely and coordinated manner, the frequency of occasions requiring a resort to military force would dramatically decline. We would not find ourselves—as we so often have done in the past— "backing into" wars or being obliged to employ naked military force because opportunities to pursue peaceful options were either unperceived or neglected.

To return to the National Strategy Council: Although the idea of yet another agency of government may be viewed by some with skepticism, I unequivocally urge its favorable consideration, and soon. May I summarize my concept of the nature and functions of a National Strategy Council. I visualize a relatively small continuing council of perhaps eleven distinguished citizens who would devote their full time and talents to studying and formulating recommendations concerning national strategy in its broadest aspects. This body would possess advisory functions only. It would regularly provide advice for the enlightenment and guidance of the legislative and executive branches of the government— and indeed, when appropriate, for the American people. The council would have semi-autonomous status comparable to that of the Federal Reserve Board. The members would have access to all sources of official and unofficial information and strategic intelligence, and possess the experience, expertise, and time required to evaluate basic policy in the foreign and domestic fields. The Council would be in a position to judge the significance of international developments, especially the implications of such developments for U.S. interests, and to weigh the mutual effect of domestic policy proposals on each other and on foreign policy.

Members of the council, like Supreme Court Justices, would be appointed for long terms by the President with the advice and consent of the Senate. To the degree that such qualities could be identified, men and women of wisdom and vision would be sought. They would be chosen as individuals of unquestionable patriotism and mature judgment. They would be drawn from the practical as well as academic fields of politics, economics, history, law, business, and the military. A small secretariat would be provided to support the council. Further, a small professional staff would be provided for each member, as in the Supreme Court. Members would be free from the heavy administrative duties that burden department heads. I would hope that, in time, the council would so establish itself in the public mind as an objective, nonpartisan agency of such extraordinary competence that it would be accorded the prestige and authority (although not the formal power) now enjoyed by the U.S. Supreme Court. Indeed, I believe that this council would be in a position to contribute more to the future prosperity and well-being of this nation than any other single agency, arm, or organ of the government . . .

Although war in its narrower military aspects would continue to be studied by the armed services, the focus of the National Strategy [Council] would be on coordinated employment of all the instruments of national policy. Varying circumstances would suggest the application of one or another combination of such instruments in particular circumstances. At times, one combination would be indicated; at other times, another. Force and the use or threat of force would always play a role in national strategy. But force should be employed only in coordination with other instruments and only when those instruments, by themselves, are unable to achieve national aims and objectives.

In summary, let me again emphasize the following crucial points:

1. The contemporary world presents our nation with challenges that are truly unprecedented.
2. Our traditional patterns of national policymaking have become increasingly inadequate; they are dangerously inadequate today.
3. The crying need of the future is for strategic vision and for the instruments through which sound national strategy can be developed and directed.

Never in my career as soldier or civilian have I written in greater concern for the future of our country, or with greater conviction of the need for reforms of the sort I have herein tried to describe.

Index

Chennault, Major General Claire L., 68, 81, 87, 104–7 *passim;* Wedemeyer letter to, 108–10
Cheves, Major General Gilbert, 86
Chiang Kai-shek, viii, xiv, xv, xix, 67–72 *passim* 80–90 *passim,* 106, 113, 118–28 *passim,* 134, 135, 136, 140–53 *passim,* 160–68 *passim,* 180, 184, 185; Wedemeyer memoranda to, 91–100; Wedemeyer letters to, 121, 169–71.
Chiang Kai-shek, Madame, 168, 170, 171
Chicago Tribune, 12–13
China-Burma-India Theater (CBI), xv, 67, 81
China Theater, 81, 87; U.S. objectives in, 80–83; Wedemeyer's concept of his role in, 90; Wedemeyer efforts to revitalize, 87–88, 104–6, 113; post-VJ Day dilemmas, 133–42 *passim,* 147, 148–49, 150
Chinese Army in India (CAI), 96, 116, 118, 130
Chinese army rations: Wedemeyer initiatives concerning, 85–86, 98–99
Chinese army reorganization: Wedemeyer recommendations concerning, 94–96, 98–99, 111, 112, 128
Chinese Civil War, xix, 120–32; intensification of conflict at war's end, 133–46 *passim,* 151–52; communist triumph in, 214
Chinese communist army, 121–24
Chinese economic situation: Wedemeyer's 1947 estimate, 187–89
Chinese military situation: Wedemeyer's 1945 estimate, 130–31; 1947 estimate, 190–91
Chinese political situation: Wedemeyer's 1945 analysis, 130, 143, 144–54; 1947 analysis, 186–87
Chinese War Production, 96–98, 106

Chou En-lai, xiv, 123, 160
Chu Teh, General, 122
Churchill, Sir Winston S., xiii, 41–42, 43, 53, 54, 62, 63, 67–68, 71, 83, 118, 172, 223–29 *passim,*
Civil-military relations: Wedemeyer's views on, xvi, xxi, 204–7, 226
Clark, General Mark W., 48; Wedemeyer evaluation of, 66
Clausewitz, Karl von, vii, xvii, 1, 32
Collins, General J. Lawton, 215
Colville, John, 223–30
Command and General Staff School, U.S. Army, xv, 1, 3, 4
Commandos, China, 131
Commandos, SEAC, 62, 72
Communism: as threat to allied war aims, 140–41, 183; as threat to China, 143, 147, 149; as threat to democratic/capitalist countries, 152, 182; compared with Nazism, 174, 182, 183
Coningham, Air Vice Marshal Sir Arthur, 50
Conolly, Rear Admiral Richard L., 58, 66
Containment policy, 218, 219, 233
Corregidor, xiv, 31
COSSAC (Chief of Staff to Supreme Allied Commander), 61, 66
Creighton Preparatory School, xiv
CULVERIN Plan, 61
Cunningham, Admiral Andrew B., 54

Demosthenes, quoted, 234
Devers, Lieutenant General Jacob L., 61, 62; Wedemeyer evaluation of, 66
De Wiart, Lieutenant General Carton, 118
Dobson, Lieutenant Colonel Arthur, 131
Dorn, Brigadier General Frank, 105
DRAGOON Plan, 228

Truscott, Major General Lucian K., Jr., 48, 55, 58, 125; Wedemeyer evaluation of, 65

Trusteeship proposals for Manchuria and Korea, 154, 155, 168, 170, 180, 184, 196–97; Chiang's attitude toward, 160–61

Tunner, Major General William H., 142

Ultimate Requirements Plan, *see* Victory Plan

Union of Soviet Socialist Republics (USSR), 16, 18, 19; World War II military cooperation with, xviii, 32–45 *passim*, 52, 53, 54, 104, 115, 135; role in Far Eastern war, 133, 135, 140–41, 147, 149, 154, 182; postwar global behavior, 151–53, 159, 160, 175–77, 183–84, 186, 191, 193–94,196, 208–10; blindness of Western allies toward in World War II, xviii, 172–74, 206–7, 223–24, 233–34

United Nations, 208, 209; role in Far East urged, 181–84, 196–97

U.S. China policy, 80, 90, 198; post-VJ Day confusions, 135–38; question of U.S. occupation forces, 136–39, 142, 148–49, 150, 154, 157–58; Marshall Mission, 155–56, 162; Wedemeyer Mission and Report, 1947, 179–97; Wedemeyer recommendations, 1949, 214–16

U.S. Military Academy, xiv

U.S. Military Advisory Group to China, 158, 168

U.S.-Soviet Joint Commission for Korea, 191–92

Versailles, Treaty of, vii, 1

Victory Plan, viii, xv, xvii, 10–30 *passim,* 232

Vietnam War, xix, xxii, 234

Vincent, John Carter, 164

Wallace, DeWitt, 164

Wang, Shou-chin, 165

War Plans Division, War Department General Staff, xv, 10, 11, 27

Wavell, Field Marshal Sir Archibald P., 61, 62, 67, 68

Webb, James, 215

Wedemeyer, Albert Anthony, xiv

Wedemeyer, Elizabeth Dade Embick, xvi

Wedemeyer, Margaret Coady, xiv

Wedemeyer Mission to China and Korea, 1947, xv–xvi, 179–80; report on, 181–97

Wheeler, Burton K., 13

Wilson, Woodrow, xvi

Wingate, General Orde C., 62

World War I: Wedemeyer's view on, xvi–xvii, 205–6

World War II: Wedemeyer's views on U.S. involvement, xvii; on outcome, xvi, xix, 173, 206–7

Yalta Conference, 140, 141, 182

Yeaton, Colonel Ivan, 121, 122, 123

Yenan Observer Group, 121–24

Yunnan Force (U.S.-Chinese), 72

HOOVER ARCHIVAL DOCUMENTARIES
General editors: Milorad M. Drachkovitch (1976–83)
Robert Hessen (1983–   )

The documents reproduced in this series are drawn from the archives of the Hoover Institution on War, Revolution and Peace at Stanford University. The purpose of publishing them is to shed new light on some important events concerning the United States or the general history of the twentieth century.

Herbert Hoover and Poland: A Documentary History of a Friendship
George J. Lerski, compiler; foreword by Sen. Mark O. Hatfield

Negotiating While Fighting: The Diary of Admiral C. Turner Joy
at the Korean Armistice Conference
Allan E. Goodman, editor; foreword by Gen. Matthew B. Ridgway

Patriot or Traitor: The Case of General Mihailovich
David Martin, compiler; foreword by Hon. Frank J. Lausche

Behind Closed Doors: Secret Papers on the Failure
of Romanian-Soviet Negotiations, 1931–1932
Walter M. Bacon, Jr., translator and compiler

The Diplomacy of Frustration: The Manchurian Crisis of 1931–1933
As Revealed in the Papers of Stanley K. Hornbeck
Justus D. Doenecke, compiler

War Through Children's Eyes: The Soviet Occupation of Poland
and the Deportations, 1939–1941
Irena Grudzinska-Gross and Jan Tomasz Gross, editors and compilers; foreword by Bruno Bettelheim

Berlin Alert: The Memoirs and Reports of Truman Smith
Robert Hessen, editor; foreword by Gen. A. C. Wedemeyer

Lenin and the Twentieth Century: A Bertram D. Wolfe Retrospective
Lennard Gerson, compiler; foreword by Alain Besançon

A Question of Trust: The Origins of U.S.-Soviet Diplomatic Relations:
The Memoirs of Loy W. Henderson
George W. Baer, editor

Wedemeyer on War and Peace
Keith E. Eiler, editor; foreword by John Keegan